The Ultimate Book of Fun Things to Do in Retirement

Hundreds of ideas to spark your imagination for planning an exciting, active, happy, healthy, and mentally sharp life after work

Volume 1

S.C. Francis

Into The Unknown Publishing

Under no circumstances will any blame or legal responsibility be held against the publisher, or author, for any damages, reparation, or monetary loss due to the information contained within this book.

Please note the information contained within this document is for educational and entertainment purposes only. All effort has been executed to present accurate, up-to-date, and reliable, complete information. No warranties of any kind are declared or implied. Readers acknowledge that the author is not engaging in the rendering of legal, financial, medical, mental health, or professional advice. The content within this book has been derived from various sources. The author generated this text in part with GPT-3, OpenAI's large-scale language-generation model. Chapter art by A.I. The activities and information contained herein may not be suitable for your situation. You should consult a licensed professional before attempting any techniques outlined in this book. Each individual's health situation is unique; readers are urged to consult with their physicians or other medical professionals before attempting any activities outlined in this book.

By reading this document, the reader agrees that under no circumstances is the author responsible for any losses, direct or indirect, which are incurred as a result of the use of the information contained within this document, including, but not limited to, — errors, omissions, or inaccuracies.

The internet is always changing, and you may find that some of the links in this book no longer work. Visit www.funretirementbooks.com/v1-links to be updated as to any changes to the links in this book that have come to our attention since the last printing, or contact us at links@funretirementbooks.com to let us know about any problems you have had accessing any of the references in this book.

We hope you enjoy this book from Into The Unknown Publishing. Our goal is to provide high-quality, thought-provoking books that provide inspiration and confidence to step into life's new experiences. For more information on other books, please go to funretirementbooks.com. Thanks for reading!

ISBN: 979-8-9881451-0-3 (Paperback)

ISBN: 979-8-9881451-2-7 (Hardback)

ISBN: 979-8-9881451-1-0 (Ebook)

First Edition

For My Parents-

Thank you for always supporting and encouraging me to follow my dreams. I love you.

For My Family-

Watching you girls grow into brave adventurers has given me so much happiness. To my wife, I'm lucky to be living in the clouds with you. Whatever our next crazy idea is, I know you're "ALL IN." 🐾

Contents

Your Free Bonus

As an additional BONUS to thank you for your purchase, I'd like to give you a gift.

Travel Planning Simplified:

This 61-page PDF will show you how to use free Google Apps and Artificial Intelligence (AI) to plan vacation travel easier.

Get the free gift now here:

https://www.funretirementbooks.com/bonus

Alternatively, scan the QR code below:

If you have any issues, you can email me at
Francis@FunRetirementBooks.com

Start Planning Your Future Trip Today!

I'd like to ask for a favor before you start reading. If you find value in this book and Bonus Guide, it would mean the world to me if you'd leave a quick, simple review or rating on Amazon, Goodreads, or another site where you purchased it. It helps others find my books and motivates me to keep writing. Thanks for your support!

- S. C. Francis

Introduction

Beep! Beep! Beep! Beep!... Jamie excitedly wakes to the unpleasant sound of his annoying alarm clock for the last time. It's finally THE day he has dreamed of for so many years. The day flashes by in a blur of smiling faces. He's flooded with mixed emotions as longtime coworkers wish him well, and they share one final laugh together. Handing over his office keys and walking out to his car for the last time, the finality of it all comes rushing in at once. He's overwhelmed by feelings of excitement and freedom but also unexpected sadness and fear of the unknown.

After years of pouring his energy and focus into his job, he wonders how he'll fill his days. Would he be bored and desperate for a social outlet without his daily work structure and coworkers to chat with? Would he feel a lack of identity and purpose no longer carrying a job title? His significant life change has him feeling overwhelmed, confused and lost.

After weeks of drifting rudderless, disoriented, and unmotivated, the feelings of uncertainty begin to fade as he resolves to adapt to his new way of life. Instead of focusing on what was, he focuses on this fantastic opportunity for what it is. It's a chance to reconnect with his past hobbies and interests and pursue new experiences that will enrich his life in a way that his busy career never could. He may have retired from work, but not from life, he thinks to himself.

He sets out to fill this new chapter in life with his passions and purpose. After decades of hard work, he finally has the time and resources to live on his own terms and follow his dreams. He's in control, ready to make the most of this exciting new adventure, only limited by his imagination. He's filled with energy but wonders what is possible and where to begin....

Someday Finally Came

This book is for the newly retired, like Jamie, who, instead of continuing to feel bored, lost, and isolated by his monumental lifestyle change, has decided to seek solutions and ideas for how to spend the rest of his life in the most enjoyable and fulfilling way possible. This book is a roadmap and inspiration for planning an exciting, active, happy, healthy, and mentally sharp life after work. It's filled with more possibilities to explore than could be experienced in 1000 lifetimes. It's a glimpse into the countless ways people spend their days, from the simple to the sublime. Take your pick!

You'll find hundreds of ideas to spark your imagination and ignite your next passion. These pages have so many fun things to do in retirement, including new hobbies, travel inspiration, social ideas, health and longevity tips, technology benefits, fun games, relaxation ideas, stress management techniques, volunteering opportunities, food tips, home improvement projects, fun ways to make or save money, and more.

And because this is the ultimate book of fun things to do in retirement, you won't just get plenty of ideas. By going much more in-depth on some recommended topics, you'll get useful insider tips, resources, fun facts, and simple steps to get started on your new interest as efficiently as possible.

Rather than diving right into things to do in retirement, the book starts by focusing inward on the big picture of what a fulfilling retirement will look like to *you*. It provides some practical advice and best practices for recalibrating your mindset to take advantage of this huge life change for the better.

With so much free time, deciding how to spend each day can be overwhelming. To help prioritize and build new healthy habits, we go over some great ideas for staying physically and mentally fit while aging gracefully. We also focus on not only *what* to do but also *why* to do them. By highlighting the benefits of an activity, you'll be able to spend your time on the things that will be the most fulfilling to you, so you'll be able to make retirement the best time of your life.

Time

I'm so excited to share with you these motivational ideas about ways to spend your most valuable resource, time. It's an intangible gift that you can never replenish. Essentially, time is life. And we should not waste it.

When I was young, I enjoyed reading many popular life lessons and "little instruction" type books with tidbits of wisdom sprinkled throughout. One tip that resonated with me was to imagine myself in bed at the end of my life. What regrets would I have or wishes I would have done? Sitting up in bed that night, I projected myself into the future, taking my final breaths and wondering what I would be thinking.

I concluded that my biggest regret would probably be not fully living. I would regret not taking advantage of each season of life and not experiencing all I could with the short time I had on this earth. That clarity has motivated and guided me throughout my life. It's pushed me to explore the world, seek out new experiences, and try everything I could with a strong sense of "you only live once" mentality. Over time, I've found the most satisfaction in the things I do rather than what I have.

Now, I'm thrilled to share with you exciting things to do in retirement and also attempt to shed some light on what might matter to you at the end of this grand adventure.

With the freedom that retirement brings, you'll have more spare time than at any point in your life. What an opportunity! This is the time to dream, explore, experience, and do everything you want. You've earned it. Now let's get busy making retirement the best and most fulfilling time of your life. There's no time to waste!

Chapter 1

Know Where You're Headed

One of my favorite quotes is, "If you don't know where you are going, you'll end up somewhere else" from Yogi Berra. Variations of this truism about the importance of defining your purpose at the beginning can be found everywhere from Lewis Caroll's Alice in Wonderland[1], "Alice: Would you tell me, please, which way I ought to go from here? Cheshire Cat: That depends a great deal on where you want to get to" and "begin with the end in mind" from Stephen Covey's award-winning book, 7 Habits of Highly Effective People[2]. Let's put some thought into where you're headed.

So where do you want to go?

Life is full of seemingly endless possibilities and ways to spend your time, and it can be confusing and overwhelming to figure out what you should do. How do you sort out the trivial, meaningless time wasters from the purposeful, meaningful activities?

. . .

What is important to you?

Reflect on what's important to you, then prioritize those things. Because if you don't care about anything, then it doesn't matter much what you do. Any road will lead you nowhere. Skip ahead from this chapter on living purposefully and just start doing stuff. I highly doubt there are many, if any at all, that don't care about anything.

You may have many things that come to mind as important to you. It could be preserving the environment, caring for animals, giving to charity, or practicing your faith. Or perhaps it's family, friends, your health, or simply happiness. There are no right or wrong answers because every individual is unique.

Please take a few minutes to reflect thoughtfully upon the things you care about and write them down somewhere now. Go ahead. Just list anything and everything important to you without judging it. It might seem weird, but later you'll find out why it's essential. Pause now, and come back when your list is complete.

What regrets will you have?

Now that you've got your "things I care about" list, let's turn up the heat and build upon it with some added clarity by jumping ahead to game over. Yup, let's get introspectively morbid. We're all going to get there someday, so there's no point in denying it. Let's free ourselves from the fear of thinking about it and accept our future fate at an uncertain date. Acceptance is freeing.

Now imagine yourself sitting in bed reflecting upon your life before your number is almost up. What regrets will you have, or is there anything you would do differently? Stop and write it down, or spend some time tonight going deeper into the things that will truly matter to you in the end.

Certainly, it's hard to imagine our biggest regrets if this were our last day of life. Below is a list of the top regrets people express at the end of life, according to research and surveys[3].

. . .

Top Regrets

1. **Not pursuing their dreams and passions:** Many people regret not following their hearts and pursuing their true passions.
2. **Not spending enough time with family and loved ones:** People often regret not spending more time with their family, loved ones, or once close friends, especially as they grow older and drift apart.
3. **Not traveling more:** Many people wish they had traveled more and experienced more of the world.
4. **Not taking care of their health:** People often regret not taking better care of their health, whether through exercise, eating a healthy diet, or quitting smoking.
5. **Not having the courage to express themselves:** Many people regret not expressing themselves fully and honestly, whether it's in their personal or professional lives. Some developed illnesses related to carrying bitterness and resentment.
6. **Not having the courage to take risks:** People often regret not taking more risks in their lives, whether it's in their careers, relationships, or personal pursuits.
7. **Not being kinder or more compassionate to others:** Many wish they had been kinder and more compassionate to others, whether to family, friends, or strangers.
8. **Not prioritizing their happiness:** Many people realized they took life too seriously, worked too hard, and wished they'd spent more time having fun and doing the things that made them happy.

Let go of regrets.

It's never too late to change course. If something jumps out at you, the best advice is to let it go because holding onto a past regret is detrimental to your health. If possible, make up for the time lost with your loved ones or work towards fixing something.

The above wisdom, such as being authentic and true to yourself; following your dreams; cherishing and preserving the freedom bestowed upon you by maintaining good health; repairing relationships that weren't given the time or effort they deserve; being open with our feelings and not holding onto past grievances; prioritizing our happiness; stepping out of our comfort zone and experiencing the world; and finding our courage; is excellent advice for any age or stage of life.

What aspirations do you have?

If you have additional insight into what's truly important to you after considering potential regret, add it to your list now. Finally, let's lighten the mood and add things you'd like to do or accomplish, no matter how insignificant they might seem. It can be little things like learning to play the piano or attending an event or bigger things like making a cookbook or traveling around the world. Whatever it is, big or small, write it down. Think hard. This is going to help you going forward.

Lists force us to think concretely.

Writing things down on a list is important. It forces us to think concretely. It's the first step in making shapeless unformed thoughts in our heads, concrete actionable ideas. If we can't physically get ourselves to take the smallest of steps, such as writing something down that we hope to accomplish, we really don't care about it. We subconsciously know we'll never do anything with it, and it will just be a reminder of something that will go unfulfilled. Inversely, by taking the micro-step action like writing it down, it proves to ourselves that this is something we care about, something we're willing to put effort into, and we're now in motion in the direction of making that happen. Every day we don't make progress, our goals get further away because we have less time to achieve them.

Prioritize

Now that you've looked inward and pulled out your list of important things, sort through them and put the most important ones at the top. These will be your biggest regrets if things don't work out or you cannot actualize them.

> *With this bucket list of sorts, you've now got a rudder to help guide your decisions on what to do with your time.*

Put your list on a wall or somewhere you'll see it often.

Humans are a forgetful bunch. With time, everything fades. The ebb and flow of everyday life creates new memories, constantly piling on top of old ones. We need reminders to help us remember and stay focused on the things that matter. Putting your list on a wall or somewhere you'll see also creates a dream board. Many people who use dream or vision boards say they work because they are visual reminders of our intentions that will help shape our thoughts and actions. Subconsciously our brains will prioritize the things on our dream board and work in the background to recognize opportunities and nudge us toward making our goals a reality. Give it a try. What do you have to lose?

Micro-steps

Take small steps in the direction of the things important to you, and put the most effort into your priorities at the top of your list. Before you know it, you'll be exactly where you hope to be and doing the meaningful things you care about because you'll be following your heart.

Be Open to Change

Just like the world around us, we are not static creatures. Who we are now (what we know, our values, our goals, our interests, our experiences, our habits, our preferences) is not and should not be set in stone. We change. We grow. We learn. The person we were as kids (what we liked, what we thought, what we did) is very different from who we are now.

Change is a good thing, not something to fear. Being open to change allows us to avoid getting stuck in our ways and becoming rigid creatures of habit. It frees us to have new experiences and consider new ideas, which will change how we think and who we are.

"The only true wisdom is in knowing you know nothing." This famous quote from Socrates reminds us to stay humble and that a wise person is open-minded. We don't know everything. We should have the desire to continually learn, ask questions, and grow inwardly and outwardly. When we grow, we change.

Don't be afraid to periodically reexamine your goals, interests, and the "things that are important to you" list to make any necessary changes for who you are at present.

The Fantastic Five

How we *spend our days* will ultimately become how we *lived our lives*. When deciding how to spend your days, consider if the activity fits into what we're going to call "the fantastic five." These are the things that, at the end of the day (our lives), most people would be happy saying they spent their time in these meaningful pursuits.

- Fulfilling
- Purposeful
- Happy

- Involved
- Balanced

Fulfilling

Being satisfied or content with the action. Will you feel good about doing this thing? Will it fulfill you? This is a personal feeling that only you have the answer to. If it's fulfilling, it means you're following your inner voice, and it's a worthwhile endeavor. Knowing yourself and doing the things that are your strengths and that you're most passionate about leads to high levels of fulfillment.

Purposeful

Having a clear aim or purpose in mind. Being intentional, aware, and deliberate. Is this activity useful or meaningful in some way? Is it related to your "things that matter" list?

Happy

A mental state of well-being with positive feelings and joy. Happiness is a choice, a mindset to keep regardless of external factors, but certainly, some things can fill you with more good feelings than others. However, don't rely on external things or experiences to make you happy. Some people have everything and are still unhappy. And due to the law of reciprocity, some people believe that happiness doesn't result from what we get but from what we give.

Involved

Actively connecting with people socially, building meaningful relationships, helping others, and putting yourself out into the world. Staying active. Doing new things, taking risks, learning, and growing from your experiences. Being involved in life is the difference between living fully and not really living at all.

Balanced

Make sure to spend some time on all facets of your life (physical health, mental health, spiritual, relationships, finances, family, creativity, cleanliness, goals, charity, happiness, etc.). If you neglect something, that's the thing that will probably cause you pain in the future, one way or another.

* * *

A New Beginning

Few events are as life-changing as retirement. Suddenly the daily routines and old habits built up from decades of focus on work are gone. Deadlines are gone, the boss is gone, the alarm clock is gone, and the tension is gone. Can I get an Amen? Hallelujah!

So what's left? You and the freedom to live your best life in this new exciting chapter you're beginning. This fresh start is the perfect opportunity to reexamine, reset, and recalibrate your inner thoughts to adjust and make the most of your time. Our attitude and outlook on life can be our biggest strength or our greatest weakness. Our mind can give us freedom, motivation, joy, and vibrancy while raising our focus on the things that matter, or it can keep us confined, limited, unhappy, and lost. It's essential to periodically reexamine our thought patterns to positively affect our lives.

Focus on Mindset

- **Don't fear change.** It's inevitable. Embrace it as an opportunity for personal growth.
- **Let go of the past.** Don't worry about the future. Live fully in the moment.

- **Be open-minded.** Cultivate a receptive attitude that opens us to new perspectives, people, knowledge, and experiences.
- **Be optimistic.** The world tends to look the way we think it does. View the glass as half-full rather than half-empty. Look for the good, and you'll see the good.
- **Be curious.** Combat boredom with a strong urge to explore, discover, and know.
- **Be active.** Life is an action. Try everything.
- **Be kind.** Spread love, not anger.
- **Be yourself.** Forget what anyone else thinks or expects of you. Be unique.
- **Follow your passions.** Do what excites you most.
- **Be grateful.** Count your blessings often.
- **Be balanced.** Give attention to all areas of your life.
- **Accept your mortality.** Give thought to what might come next.
- **Have fun.** Humor, playfulness, and laughter are seriously important.
- **Eliminate distractions and negativity.** Rise above the dark clouds to focus on the things that matter to you.
- **Prioritize your mental and physical health.** Your life depends on it.
- **Fully appreciate and take advantage of each day like it is your last.** Live life to the fullest. Do everything you can while you still can. Don't waste your precious time. Seize the day!

First Steps To Rockin' The Retired Life

We're just about ready to dive into the fun stuff to do in retirement sections, but before we do and you potentially become overwhelmed with exciting new ways to spend your time, here's a suggestion on the first steps to take for rockin' your new retired life.

1. **Celebrate, celebrate, celebrate!-** Seriously. You probably don't need me to tell you how amazing this moment is. It truly is an accomplishment worthy of basking in your new glow of freedom for as long as you like. Soak it up. Get dressed up and go to a fancy dinner. Pop some bubbly and stay up all night if you want. Get used to how great you feel and how good this future will be.
2. **Relax-** Don't stress. A lot will change, which can feel scary as you head into the unknown, but now is not the time to worry about it. Put your mind at ease. There is no rush to do anything stressful. Sleep in all day because you can. Drive all around and go to the park or shopping when most people are stuck at work. The years of anticipation building up to this moment can weigh heavy on you. Take some time to unload and settle in.
3. **Exercise more**- Your busy daily schedule just opened wide up. You have no reason not to start or double down on your health. Use it or lose it is no joke. The benefits of caring for your mind, body, and spirit are significant. On one end, there is freedom and happiness. On the other, there is pain and suffering. Work on your diet. Shed some unwanted pounds. Sleep fully. Stay active and mentally stimulated. Recognize and look for ways to reduce stress. Make it a point to fight back against aging with regular exercise.
4. **Prioritize fun-** Remember when we were young, and all that mattered was having fun? Life's endless responsibilities probably got in the way, and we most likely lost touch with our carefree, live-in-the-moment, fun side of us. Play is essential to our health and happiness. Think back to when you were a child and your favorite activities. What did you do for fun? What made you the happiest? Give those activities another shot and connect with the emotions of how you feel while doing them. Chances are you'll still find joy in them. "We don't stop playing because we grow old; we grow old because we stop playing." -George Bernard Shaw.

5. **Set a new budget**- Your new free lifestyle, unfortunately, won't be free. You'll want to do many fun things, but blowing through your nest egg all at once shouldn't be one of them. Know how much money you're comfortable spending each year with a budget, then maximize your fun with the amount you have set aside to play.
6. **Make plans and set goals**- This is where you whip out your bucket list and "things I care about" list from earlier and plan to take action. Consider your future mobility may decrease, so put your most physically active and important things as the first to accomplish. If you are married, discuss with your spouse and decide on the things you'll be doing together. Create a rough timeline for visiting the once-in-a-lifetime places you've been dreaming of. Consider the long-term steps you'll need to take and create a timeline.
7. **Create new daily habits**- Freedom can become a double edge sword, and boredom can follow closely behind. You'll be tempted to just stay in bed some days because no one is breathing down your neck to get to work (if you're married, unfortunately, disregard this sentence). It can become easy for one unproductive day to snowball until you're in a rut doing nothing worthwhile most days. Before that happens, create a daily or weekly schedule balanced with the things you care about and some healthy habits like exercise, reading, socializing, small steps working towards goals, etc., to keep you moving in the right direction even when you lose some motivation. Independence isn't as easy as you might have dreamed. It takes strong willpower to stay active and productive. Start with a solid plan to structure your days, so they don't slip away.

* * *

Finding Your Spark

As you read through the fun things to do, note your potential interest in that activity by dog-earing the page or writing down the page number or topic. With so many things, it's easy to forget something you might be curious about as you continue reading.

Think of this as not just a book to read but a book to do. Try to read with intention, looking for something that will spark your imagination and lead to you actively pursuing your next passion. Find that interest that will have you staying up at night thinking about it with excited anticipation. Find something that might fill your heart with joy as you decide to learn, practice, or do it.

If you're not the kind of person who becomes overly passionate about your hobbies, go in with an open mind and look for something fun or simply new to try. The only way you'll know if it's for you is to try it. If you find yourself in a rut, just pick something different to try. If it's not for you, slash it off your list (and pat yourself on the back for the new life experience), then move on to something else. A new experience is better than no experience. Eventually, you'll bump into an activity you love and be off on your new adventure.

Fun is not universal.

It probably won't surprise you that people are all different, and as such, there are many ways people choose to spend their time, from the mainstream to the obscure. I took a broad definition of fun to include the things that at least some people willingly choose to spend their precious free time on.

You're only as old as you feel.

I omitted some fun things to do that a retired person probably won't be interested in because they are probably no longer 25. If you are 25 and retired, all I can say is, well done. However, I kept a few more physically demanding activities because someone might be in fantastic shape and be interested in that more challenging endeavor. Alternatively, one might not be interested in participating (such as mixed martial arts combat) but could still be interested in getting involved in another way, such as attending events and watching them on tv.

Categories for fun

There are a million ways to categorize fun things to do. Some items might be found in a different section than you'd expect to keep a grouping of items from getting too long. Sections are not all-inclusive. Also, some ideas might be found in multiple areas to make them easier to stumble upon for someone who might not think to look in the other category. The bottom line is don't get too caught up with the categories. There is good stuff to do everywhere and where you might not expect it.

Additional Info

Some "fun things to do" are pretty well-known and self-explanatory, so the reference might not have much explanation. Others, particularly the ones that might have a lot of benefits for seniors, have much more written about them. Some entries have "simple steps" to get started to help alleviate the fear of the unknown that someone might have as they consider learning something new. Finally, if something piques your interest, but you're unsure what it is exactly, or maybe you'd like more info, don't hesitate to type the topic into a search browser.

Printed Book Website Links

To make exploring additional information on a topic easier, this book contains 554 links to websites, books on the subject, or products that could be fun or useful. To avoid cluttering the book with long ugly websites, we've simplified accessing the websites with any of the three options below.

To access the website links on the ***printed version*** of this book, either;

1. Use a smartphone camera or QR scanner app on the Chapter Title QR code image and go directly to our website with all the links for the chapter. (Basically, the QR code is a shortcut, so you don't need to type the full web address in an internet browser. Just point your camera phone at the image, then tap the QR code on the screen).
2. Go to www.funretirementbooks.com/v1-links for all the helpful links.
3. Or email us at links@funretirementbooks.com for a free PDF with easy access to all the clickable links.

QR Link to All Website Resources in Book

Go for it! Simple Start Steps

I frequently hear, "I'd love to do that, but I have no idea where to start." I'm not sure whether it's the truth or just an excuse to rationalize not taking action. With sufficient motivation, I believe even the seemingly most daunting things can usually be achieved by breaking the goal into more manageable and attainable little steps. It's less intimidating. It's also motivational because you can see yourself getting closer to your destination with each tiny step you complete.

Taking the time at the start to brainstorm the steps you'll need to take and then breaking each step down into as many simple actionable steps as possible is extremely helpful. There is no one way to get somewhere, so the plan doesn't need to be perfect or even complete. It just needs to be *a* plan, *your plan*, to get where you want to go.

The plan will usually start with steps related to figuring out how to find information to learn about what you don't know. The following steps in your plan should continue with the assumption that you'll find out what you need to know and will take action on that info, leading to the next step, and so on. As long as each step gets you closer to your goal, you're heading in the right direction, even if you don't have it all figured out at that moment.

I've used the simple steps strategy to plan extended travel, start businesses, and accomplish many other things that seemed intimidating initially. It works. I've included simple start steps for some of the things to do to help get you started. The steps are usually pretty obvious when you see them, but they might be just what someone needs to go from an excuse of "I'd love to do that, but I have no idea where to start" to "I can't believe I did that!"

It's been said that boredom is really just a lack of imagination. Without further ado, let's find something to do! Since a healthy retirement is a happy one, let's begin our journey with the most important aspect of retirement, our health.

Chapter 2

Focus on Health and Wellness

Retirement is the reward for a life of hard work and dedication, but it can be so much more than a time of rest. The key to a truly fulfilling retirement is to make a commitment to lifelong health and wellness. To ensure a happy and healthy retirement, we should focus on physical, mental, and spiritual health.

Exercise is one of the most important aspects of health and wellness. Not only does it help to keep our bodies strong and flexible, but it also releases endorphins that make us feel good. Staying physically active can reduce the risk of chronic illnesses, heart disease, and cancer and even help us age more gracefully.

Mental health is just as important as physical health. It is essential to stay engaged and challenge your mind with puzzles, games, and other activities that can help to keep your memories sharp and your brain healthy. Finding ways to relax can be equally beneficial, like meditation, yoga, or something as simple as taking a walk or reading a book. Having a social network also improves your overall mental health.

Spiritual health is also a key part of health and wellness. Taking the time to nurture your spirituality can give you a sense of purpose and satisfaction and provide a sense of peace and comfort. Whether participating in religious activities, volunteering in your community, or simply taking time to appreciate the little things in life, developing your spiritual side can have great benefits.

Neglecting health and wellness in retirement can lead to a number of negative consequences. Poor physical health can lead to chronic illnesses, depression, and an overall decrease in quality of life. Lack of mental stimulation can lead to memory loss and an increased risk of dementia. And neglecting spiritual health can lead to feelings of isolation and a lack of purpose and meaning.

So make sure to take the time to focus on your health and wellness in retirement. Make exercise a part of your daily routine, challenge your mind with activities that engage and stimulate your brain, and find ways to nurture your spiritual side. Doing so will help you enjoy your retirement years to the fullest.

In this chapter, we'll jump into some fun ideas on staying healthy and living our best lives in retirement.

Chapter 2 Website Links

* * *

Start a Wellness Journey

Strengthen your overall health

Wellness is a holistic approach to health and well-being, encompassing physical, mental, emotional, and social aspects of life. It focuses on achieving balance and optimal functioning in all these areas, leading to a fulfilling and happy life.

For a retired person, wellness takes on a special significance. After a lifetime of work and responsibilities, retirement provides an opportunity to focus on one's own well-being and improve quality of life. It is a chance to prioritize self-care, engage in meaningful activities, and maintain social connections.

Wellness in retirement means taking care of physical health through exercise, nutritious eating, and sufficient rest. It also involves mental wellness through engagement in activities that bring joy, learning, and stimulation. It's also important for a retiree to prioritize social connections with loved ones, as these provide support, companionship, and a sense of belonging.

In the end, wellness is not a destination but a continuous journey. A journey that requires dedication, patience, and self-awareness but ultimately leads to a rich, fulfilling, and joyful life. For a retiree, it is the key to aging gracefully, living with purpose, and finding happiness every day.

Mental Wellness

Mental wellness refers to the state of being mentally and emotionally balanced, with a positive outlook on life. It is an important aspect of overall wellness and can significantly improve the quality of life for a retiree. The following activities can help maintain good mental health, reduce stress and anxiety, and find joy and purpose in retirement.

37 Ideas for Improving Mental Wellness

1. **Gratitude journal-** Writing down daily gratitudes can help reframe one's perspective and increase overall happiness and positivity. It's like giving your brain a daily dose of sunshine.
2. **Practice mindfulness-** By becoming more aware of the present moment and focusing on one's thoughts, feelings, and sensations without judgment, mindfulness can help

reduce stress and improve mental clarity. It's like taking a break from life's chaos and just being in the now.

3. **Meditate-** Regular meditation can help quiet the mind, improve mental clarity, reduce stress and anxiety, and increase happiness and well-being. It's like hitting the reset button on your brain.
4. **Listen to music daily-** Listening to music can have a powerful effect on mood, reducing stress and anxiety and promoting feelings of joy and happiness. It's a sonic therapy that can soothe your soul, lift your spirits, and transport you to a happier place, all while feeling like a rockstar ready to conquer the day and inspire you to dance like nobody's watching.
5. **Eliminate distractions-** By reducing distractions and creating a calm, focused environment, one can improve concentration, reduce stress, and increase productivity. It frees up space in your brain for more important things.
6. **Work to reduce stress-** By reducing stress through activities such as exercise, therapy, or stress-management techniques, one can improve mental well-being and overall happiness. It's like giving your brain a well-deserved break from the daily grind in search of inner peace. You'll feel like a zen warrior ready to conquer any stressful situation.
7. **Adopt an animal-** Caring for a pet can bring joy and purpose to one's life, reducing feelings of loneliness and stress. They'll be your loyal companion, providing comfort and joy. They will always be there to snuggle away your worries or lick your face with unconditional love - it's like having a therapy session, but with added cuddles and adorable antics to keep you smiling even on the toughest days.
8. **Ikigai, the Japanese secret to aging-** Discovering one's ikigai, or purpose in life, can bring a sense of fulfillment and satisfaction, improving overall mental wellness. It's like finding the compass that guides you through life's journey.

9. **Study happiness-** Learning about the science of happiness (positive psychology) and ways to cultivate it in daily life can boost mood and reduce stress. It's like unlocking the secrets to a brighter and more joyful life.
10. **Brain training-** Engaging in cognitive exercises and activities that challenge the brain can improve cognitive function and stave off age-related mental decline. It's like giving your brain a workout to keep it in top shape.
11. **Massage-** Regular massage can reduce stress and improve mood, promoting relaxation and overall well-being. Imagine a dance of fingertips and muscles, a symphony of kneading and pressing, a tantalizing tango of relaxation and rejuvenation, where your aches and pains will take a bow and exit stage left, and your mind will sing with delight, "encore, encore!" as you blissfully float on the cloud of serenity.
12. **Brain aging-** Understanding the changes that occur in the brain as we age, and learning how to maintain brain health and function, can help maintain mental well-being and reduce the risk of age-related mental decline. It's like taking a proactive approach to keeping your mind sharp and resilient.
13. **Balance chakras-** Balancing the body's energy centers, or chakras can promote feelings of peace and well-being, reducing stress and anxiety. It's like giving your mind and body a harmonious tune-up.
14. **Self-realization-** Engaging in self-reflection and exploration can bring greater understanding and acceptance of oneself, improving mental well-being. It's like peeling back the layers to discover the true self.
15. **Buddhist mindfulness-** Mindfulness meditation is one of the most important elements of the Buddha's "noble eightfold path" to end suffering and instill wisdom. It's like taking a deep breath of fresh mountain air, letting go of your thoughts like a bird leaving its nest, and being fully present in the moment - it's like having a zen master in your mind, reminding you to stay calm and centered amidst the chaos

of daily life, and bringing a sense of peace and serenity that's almost as good as a day at the spa but with fewer cucumbers on your eyes.

16. **Learn to manage difficult times-** Learning coping mechanisms and strategies for managing difficult times can improve resilience and mental well-being. It's like arming yourself with the tools to navigate life's challenges.
17. **Acupuncture-** This ancient healing practice can reduce stress and improve mental wellness by balancing the body's energy. It's like giving your body a natural reset. An old poem says it best; Tiny needles, a little poke, a thousand-year-old art of the oriental folk. With skillful hands, the acupuncturist will work, balancing your chi and fixing your quirks. It's not as scary as it may sound. Just lie down, relax, and let the needles surround.
18. **Cupping-** This traditional holistic treatment of putting suction cups on your skin can improve circulation and reduce stress, promoting physical and mental relaxation. It's like giving your muscles a deep-tissue massage while bringing balance to your energy within.
19. **Trigger point therapy-** This targeted therapy can relieve pain and tension, improving physical and mental relaxation. It's like a game of whack-a-mole, where the therapist uses their magic fingers to find the sneaky little knots in your muscles and then smashes them with ninja-like precision, leaving you feeling as loose and wiggly as a bowl of jello at a dance party.
20. **Aromatherapy-** Using essential oils and scents can improve mood and reduce stress, promoting relaxation and well-being. It's like taking a sensory journey to calmness through an enchanting garden of fragrant blooms and herbs. Where the scents of lavender, peppermint, and eucalyptus swirl around you like a sweet embrace, soothing your soul and caressing your senses as you blissfully inhale the essence of relaxation and rejuvenation.

21. **Sound therapy-** Various sounds and vibrations can reduce stress and promote relaxation, improving mental well-being. It's like a musical escape from daily life.
22. **Human energy field therapy (aura)-** This therapy aims to balance and harmonize the energy field around the body, improving overall physical and mental well-being. It's like giving your aura a boost.
23. **Seeking support through therapy or counseling-** Reaching out for professional support through therapy or counseling can provide a safe and confidential space to process emotions, reduce stress and improve mental health. It's like having a trusted friend to confide in.
24. **Engaging in spiritual or religious practices-** Practicing spiritual or religious practices can bring a sense of peace, purpose and provide a support system, positively impacting mental wellness. It's connecting with a higher power to find peace within.
25. **Reiki-** This energy healing practice can reduce stress and promote relaxation, improving mental and physical well-being. Imagine a magical energy flow, swirling and twirling like a graceful dancer around your body, as a gentle touch from the Reiki master's hands awakens your inner glow and melts away the stresses and woes, leaving you feeling as light and airy as a cloud, and as bright and sparkly as a disco ball.
26. **Spa or hot spring-** Indulging in a spa or hot spring can promote relaxation, reduce stress and improve mental wellness. It's a blissful oasis of peace and rejuvenation to soothe the mind, body, and spirit.
27. **Write a forgiveness letter-** Writing a letter to forgive someone or yourself can bring emotional release and reduce stress, improving well-being. It's like freeing yourself from the burden of resentment.
28. **Fix a mistake-** Taking steps to rectify a mistake can bring a sense of closure and improve self-esteem, positively impacting mental wellness. It's like righting a wrong and feeling empowered.

29. **Lift up your worries-** Releasing worries and trusting in a higher power to handle the burden can reduce stress and bring peace. It's like handing over control and finding comfort.
30. **Focus on your posture-** Improving posture can reduce physical discomfort and improve confidence, positively impacting mental well-being. It's like standing tall and feeling empowered.
31. **Surround yourself with positive, healthy people-** Like a sunflower that follows the sun, surrounding yourself with positive, healthy people will help keep your mind bright and shining and your spirit full of joy. It's like having a team of cheerleaders on your side.
32. **Distance yourself from negative, draining people-** Limiting or avoiding time with negative, draining people can reduce stress, improve mood and protect mental well-being. It's like shielding yourself from negativity.
33. **Reduce or eliminate consuming unhealthy things (food, shows, news, etc.)-** Consuming unhealthy things can have a negative impact on mental well-being by creating stress, anxiety, and depression. Therefore, reducing or eliminating these things can help to maintain a healthy mental state and promote positive emotions.
34. **Sit in the sun-** Spending time outside in the sun can boost mood, improve sleep and promote a sense of well-being. It's like a natural dose of happiness.
35. **The importance of laughter-** Incorporating laughter into daily life can reduce stress, improve mood and strengthen relationships, promoting overall mental wellness. It's like a prescription for happiness.
36. **Using apps such as Headspace and Calm-** Meditation and mindfulness apps like Headspace and Calm can reduce stress, improve focus and promote relaxation, positively impacting mental wellness. It's like having a personal mindfulness coach in your pocket.

37. **Acceptance-** Embracing and accepting life's challenges and changes can bring a sense of peace and reduce stress, positively impacting mental well-being. Acceptance is the act of recognizing and understanding the reality of a situation and taking responsibility for it rather than trying to resist or deny it. It is crucial for mental well-being because it allows us to move forward from difficult or stressful situations instead of dwelling on them and getting stuck in negative thought patterns. It's like finding peace in the journey, no matter what comes your way. Accepting your new way of life during retirement is essential for optimizing joy in your golden years.

Books

1. Gratitude: A Day and Night Reflection Journal (90 Days) by Insight Editions link
2. Ikigai: The Japanese Secret to a Long and Happy Life by Héctor García link
3. Keep Sharp: Build a Better Brain at Any Age by Sanjay Gupta M.D. link
4. The Path to Longevity: The Secrets to Living a Long, Happy, Healthy Life by Luigi Fontana link
5. Chakra Healing: A Beginner's Guide to Self-Healing Techniques that Balance the Chakras by Margarita Alcantara link
6. Living Untethered: Beyond the Human Predicament by Michael A. Singer link
7. You Are Here: Discovering the Magic of the Present Moment by Thich Nhat Hanh link
8. When Things Fall Apart: Heart Advice for Difficult Times by Pema Chodron link
9. Acupuncture Points Handbook: A Patient's Guide to the Locations and Functions of over 400 Acupuncture Points by Deborah Bleecker link
10. The Complete Book of Essential Oils and Aromatherapy, Revised and Expanded: Over 800 Natural, Nontoxic, and

Fragrant Recipes to Create Health, Beauty, and Safe Home and Work Environments by Valerie Ann Worwood link
11. Sound Medicine: How to Use the Ancient Science of Sound to Heal the Body and Mind by Kulreet Chaudhary M.D. link
12. Essential Reiki: A Complete Guide to an Ancient Healing by Diane Stein link

* * *

Prioritize Physical Health

Keep strong and healthy

We're all just one doctor visit away from our world changing forever. It's easy to think when we get older, our health may just gradually decline, and we'll have a chance to do all the things we want before it's too late. Unfortunately, that's not always the case. We could be seemingly healthy one day and suddenly sick or demobilized the next. Whether it's an unexpected diagnosis that puts us into an emergency treatment plan, a heart attack or stroke, or something else, our freedom and health can disappear in an instant. If that happens, it may be too late to adjust our habits and regain our healthy lives.

While we can't know what our future holds, we can certainly see the direction we're heading. If we have unhealthy habits, we're headed down a short road leading to problems. On the other hand, if we take the more difficult path, stay focused on our health, and put in the effort, we have a much better chance of enjoying a long winding trek with many beautiful sunsets.

3 7 Ways to Focus on Physical Health

1. Start your day with a gentle walk in nature to help invigorate your body and feel the rejuvenating effects of the fresh air.

2. Develop a healthy, balanced diet to ensure you get all the vitamins and minerals your body needs.
3. Take time each week to practice yoga or stretching and experience a newfound sense of flexibility and strength.
4. Stay hydrated by drinking plenty of water, and feel the positive effects of increased energy and clarity.
5. Join a fitness class to challenge yourself and connect with others who share your same goals.
6. Challenge yourself with a new physical activity each month, and reap the rewards of enhanced physical and mental health.
7. Incorporate a regular strength training routine and experience improved posture and balance.
8. Schedule regular check-ups with a healthcare professional to monitor and manage your health.
9. Take time to relax in a hot bath and unwind from the stress of the day, allowing your body and mind to reset.
10. Get plenty of quality sleep each night, and wake up feeling refreshed and invigorated.
11. Visit your local farmer's market and stock up on fresh, nutritious fruits and vegetables to fuel your body.
12. Take a scenic bike ride with friends and get your heart rate up while taking in the beauty of nature.
13. Commit to a daily practice of gratitude and mindfulness to prioritize your physical and mental well-being.
14. Try a new recipe each week and explore the delicious world of health-focused meals.
15. Get outdoors and explore new places to stay active and experience the joys of new adventure.
16. Sign up for a 5K or another running event to track your progress and celebrate your accomplishments.
17. Schedule regular massages to alleviate stress and tension in your body and mind.
18. Make time for fun activities like swimming or tennis to add variety to your fitness routine.
19. Enjoy a restorative picnic in the park to nourish your body and soul with good food and fresh air.

20. Joining a local gym can help you reignite your vigor as you embark on a journey to strengthen and tone your body.
21. Breaking unhealthy habits can tremendously impact your physical health, as you give your body the chance to rejuvenate and re-energize.
22. Losing weight through intermittent fasting can be incredibly rewarding as your body adjusts to a new lifestyle of healthy eating and exercise.
23. Senior martial arts can be an invigorating and empowering experience as you become more flexible and agile while also increasing strength and endurance.
24. Water aerobics can be a refreshing and invigorating way to get your body moving as you burn calories while improving cardiovascular and muscle strength.
25. Learning about longevity is a great way to stay informed about what you can do to increase your quality of life and potentially extend your lifespan. You'll gain a better understanding of the benefits of nutrition, exercise, and other lifestyle choices that can keep you living a healthy and active life.
26. Developing a home fitness routine is an easy way to stay fit and healthy without leaving your home. Whether you want to focus on strength training, cardio, or both, you can customize the program to fit your needs and preferences. It's a great way to stay active without going to a gym.
27. Zumba classes offer a fun and exciting way to get some exercise. You'll be able to learn some new dance moves while also burning calories and improving your cardiovascular health. Plus, you can enjoy the music, socialize with other participants, and have a great time while you're at it.
28. By learning about gut health, you'll better understand how the foods you eat and your lifestyle choices can impact your overall well-being. You'll be able to adjust your diet and lifestyle to help improve your digestive health and keep your body functioning optimally.

29. A spin class, or indoor cycling class, can be a great way to get a full-body workout. By working on your cardio, strength, and endurance, you'll be able to improve your physical health and enjoy the energy boost and endorphin rush that comes from a great session.
30. Smart mirror workouts are an innovative way to stay active, with the bonus of having a virtual coach to monitor your progress and encourage you. It's a great way to stay engaged and motivated.
31. Skipping rope is an excellent way of keeping fit as it increases your heart rate, strengthens your muscles, and improves balance – all without leaving home. It's a fun and easy way to exercise.
32. Using a park's fitness stations is a fantastic idea for older people who want to keep active. Not only do you get to enjoy the outdoors, but it's also a delightful way to stay healthy and build muscle strength.
33. Jogging is an effective and accessible form of exercise, perfect for retirees who want to stay in shape. It helps to keep the heart healthy and improve your stamina, and it's a great way to enjoy the outdoors.
34. Kung Fu is a great way to stay active, improve your physical and mental health, and learn self-defense techniques. It's a fun way to have a full-body workout and develop your Bruce Lee coordination skills.
35. Fast walking is an easy and convenient way for retirees to get moving and stay healthy. It's a low-impact exercise that can help to improve balance and coordination and can be done anywhere.
36. Tai Chi is a great way to relax and improve physical and mental well-being. It can help to reduce stress, improve balance, and increase flexibility. It's a tremendous way to improve physical and psychological health.
37. Pilates is a fabulous form of exercise, perfect for older people who want to increase their range of movement and strengthen their core. It's low impact but an effective way to stay fit and healthy.

Books

1. 6-Minute Fitness at 60+: Simple Home Exercises to Reclaim Strength, Balance, and Energy in 15 Days by Jonathan Su link
2. Medical Medium Cleanse to Heal: Healing Plans for Sufferers of Anxiety, Depression, Acne, Eczema, Lyme, Gut Problems, Brain Fog, Weight Issues, Migraines, Bloating, Vertigo, Psoriasis by Anthony William link
3. Complete Guide To Fasting: Heal Your Body Through Intermittent, Alternate-Day, and Extended Fasting by Dr. Jason Fung link
4. Lies My Doctor Told Me Second Edition: Medical Myths That Can Harm Your Health by Ken Berry link
5. The Complete Ketogenic Diet for Beginners: Your Essential Guide to Living the Keto Lifestyle by Amy Ramos link
6. Practical Paleo, 2nd Edition (Updated And Expanded): A Customized Approach to Health and a Whole-Foods Lifestyle by Diane Sanfilippo link

* * *

Stress Less

Reduce the mental baggage

Stress is an inevitable part of life, but managing it effectively can make a world of difference in our overall well-being. Ignoring or avoiding stress can lead to a host of physical and mental health problems, negatively impacting our relationships, productivity, and quality of life.

Think of stress as a small flame that, if left unattended, can turn into a raging fire and consume everything in its path. By taking control of stress, we can turn that flame into a warm and comforting glow, bringing peace and balance to our lives.

Managing stress can help us maintain our physical health, with studies showing that individuals who effectively manage stress have lower rates of heart disease, stroke, and other health problems. Moreover, managing stress can improve our mental health, boosting our mood and reducing feelings of anxiety and depression.

But the benefits of stress management go beyond just physical and mental health. It can also lead to increased productivity and efficiency, better relationships, and a more fulfilling life. When we effectively manage stress, we open the doors to new opportunities and experiences, allowing us to live life to the fullest.

So, let's take control of stress and transform it into a source of strength and balance. By doing so, we'll not only improve our health and well-being, but we'll also enrich every aspect of our lives.

What is stress?

Stress is an emotional, physical, and psychological response to changes in a person's environment or life that are perceived as a challenge or threat. It is the body's way of responding to a stressor, such as a physical or psychological demand. Stress can be both positive and negative. Positive stress can help a person to stay motivated and alert, while negative stress can be harmful.

How Stress Affects the Body

Stress occurs when the demands placed upon an individual exceed their ability to cope. When this happens, the body responds with a "fight-or-flight" response, an automatic physiological reaction to danger, by releasing hormones such as cortisol and adrenaline. Cortisol helps the body prepare for danger by increasing heart rate and blood pressure, suppressing the immune system, and increasing the availability of energy. Chronic stress can negatively affect the body, as elevated cortisol levels can lead to various physical and mental health issues.

. . .

9 Harmful Effects of Stress[4]

1. **Physical health-** Chronic stress can lead to a number of physical health problems, such as headaches, muscle tension, chest pain, fatigue, digestive issues, sleep disturbances, and a weakened immune system.
2. **Mental health-** Prolonged stress can lead to anxiety, depression, irritability, mood swings, and decreased motivation.
3. **Cognitive function-** Stress can negatively impact memory, attention, and decision-making abilities, leading to decreased productivity and efficiency.
4. **Relationships-** Stress can strain personal relationships, cause conflicts, and lead to feelings of isolation.
5. **Heart health-** Chronic stress can increase heart rate and blood pressure, increasing the risk of heart disease and stroke.
6. **Substance use-** Stress can increase the likelihood of substance abuse or addiction as a way to cope.
7. **Weight changes-** Stress can cause overeating or loss of appetite, leading to weight changes and health problems.
8. **Sexual functioning-** Stress can cause sexual dysfunction and reduce intimacy in relationships.
9. **Aging-** Chronic stress can hasten the aging process and increase the risk of age-related health problems.

As you can see, stress is a major cause of health problems and should be managed effectively to maintain overall well-being. Stress is inevitable, but it doesn't have to control us. By incorporating stress-management techniques, we can turn stress into a manageable force rather than a destructive one.

28 Stress Management Techniques

1. **Exercise-** This doesn't have to mean hitting the gym for hours every day. Simply taking a walk or doing some light stretching can help reduce stress and improve overall well-being.
2. **Deep breathing-** Taking deep breaths can help calm the body and mind, reducing feelings of stress and anxiety. Use deep breathing techniques like 4-7-8 breathing.
3. **Meditation-** This practice involves mental techniques such as focusing on the present moment and accepting it without judgment, helping to reduce stress and increase mental clarity.
4. **Laugh-** Laughter is truly the best medicine, and incorporating humor and fun into our lives can help reduce stress and improve our overall mood.
5. **Write it out-** Writing down our thoughts and feelings can help us process them and release pent-up emotions, reducing stress in the process.
6. **Connect with others-** Spending time with friends and loved ones can help boost our mood and reduce stress and anxiety.
7. **Get organized-** Having a structured schedule, and a clean living space can reduce feelings of overwhelm and improve our ability to manage stress.
8. **Get enough sleep-** A good night's sleep can help improve our mood and overall well-being, reducing stress and increasing our ability to handle life's challenges.
9. **Practice gratitude-** Taking time to focus on what we are grateful for can help shift our perspective and reduce feelings of stress and negativity.
10. **Find a hobby-** Engaging in a favorite activity can provide a sense of accomplishment and take our minds off of stress and worries.
11. **Practice mindfulness-** Mindfulness techniques like deep breathing, meditation, and yoga can help you stay centered and calm, even in the face of stress.

12. **Connect with nature-** Spending time in nature can help soothe the mind, reduce anxiety, and improve overall mood.
13. **Try aromatherapy-** Certain essential oils, such as lavender, are known for their calming effects and can help reduce stress levels when smelled.
14. **Seek support from loved ones-** Talking to friends and family about what's bothering you can help you feel better and reduce stress levels.
15. **Practice self-care-** Taking care of yourself is important for managing stress, whether through activities like getting a massage, taking a relaxing bath, or simply taking a nap.
16. **Set boundaries-** Make sure you're not overextending yourself and taking on more than you can handle, which can lead to increased stress levels.
17. **Prioritize your tasks-** Make a to-do list and prioritize the most important tasks first to avoid feeling overwhelmed by too many responsibilities.
18. **Take breaks-** Taking short breaks throughout the day can help reduce stress and improve your ability to focus and stay productive.
19. **Acceptance-** Acceptance means acknowledging and embracing your current reality instead of trying to resist or change it. Practicing acceptance can help you let go of stress and frustration and instead find peace and contentment in the present moment.
20. **Don't procrastinate-** Putting things off only adds to stress and anxiety, so make a to-do list and tackle tasks one by one.
21. **Focus on things you can control-** Instead of dwelling on things that are outside of your control, focus on what you can influence and change.
22. **Understand when we're emotional, we have limited rational thought-** Being aware of our emotional state can help us avoid making impulsive decisions or overreacting.

23. **Practice Tai Chi-** Tai Chi is a gentle form of exercise that helps you focus on your breathing, improves balance and flexibility, and reduces stress.
24. **Make your bathroom a relaxing spa-** Create a calming atmosphere with candles, bath salts, music, bubbles, essential oils, and a sparkling drink. A relaxing spa-like atmosphere can help you unwind and de-stress after a long day.
25. **Positive self-talk-** Positive self-talk can help shift our negative thought patterns into a more optimistic and empowering perspective. By consistently reminding ourselves of our strengths and abilities, we can boost our self-esteem and confidence, which in turn can help reduce stress levels. Additionally, speaking kindly to ourselves can also improve our overall mood and outlook on life.
26. **Keep things in perspective-** Keeping things in perspective can be a helpful tool for avoiding overreactions and managing stress. By taking a step back and looking at a situation objectively, you can gain a better understanding of what's really happening and make decisions based on rational thought rather than knee-jerk reactions. When you approach challenges and conflicts with a clear mind, you can better address them and find solutions that are in your best interest.
27. **Reframing-** Reframing involves changing your perspective of a stressful situation and looking at it in a more positive light.
28. **Self-compassion-** Being compassionate with yourself means treating yourself with kindness and understanding instead of criticizing yourself when things go wrong. This can help reduce stress and increase resilience.

Resources

1. 15 Simple Ways to Relieve Stress link
2. 25 Quick Ways to Reduce Stress link
3. Top Ways to Reduce Daily Stress link

Books

1. Stop Overthinking: 23 Techniques to Relieve Stress, Stop Negative Spirals, Declutter Your Mind, and Focus on the Present (The Path to Calm) by Nick Trenton link
2. The Subtle Art of Not Giving a F*ck: A Counterintuitive Approach to Living a Good Life by Mark Manson link
3. The Art of Letting GO: How to Let Go of the Past, Look Forward to the Future, and Finally Enjoy the Emotional Freedom You Deserve! by Damon Zahariades link

* * *

Get in Touch with Your Spiritual Side

Find your higher purpose

Religion or spirituality can provide great comfort and solace in retired life. When we're retired, we often have more time to reflect on the bigger picture of our lives, think about what matters, and ask questions about our purpose and place in the world. Religion or spirituality can answer these questions and help us make sense of our lives.

It can also bring a sense of community and connection to our lives, especially as we age and our social networks may shrink. Participating in religious or spiritual activities allows us to meet new people, form meaningful relationships, and feel part of something larger than ourselves. Whether through worship services, volunteer work, or community events, religion or spirituality can give us a sense of purpose and fulfillment.

It can also provide us with guidance and support as we navigate the challenges of aging and retirement. Whether facing health problems, dealing with financial stress, or coping with the loss of loved ones, religious or spiritual beliefs can offer comfort, encouragement, and hope in difficult times.

Finally, religion or spirituality can bring a sense of peace and contentment to our lives. By focusing on our faith and relationship with the divine, we can find meaning and purpose and experience a deep sense of joy and fulfillment. So if you're looking for a way to bring more peace, purpose, and joy into your retired life, exploring religion or spirituality could be the perfect place to start.

Books

1. The Purpose Driven Life: What on Earth Am I Here For? by Rick Warren link
2. The Untethered Soul: The Journey Beyond Yourself by Michael A. Singer link
3. Mere Christianity by C. S. Lewis link

* * *

Go Fancy Picnicking

Enjoy nature in style

One day I was biking near the coast and stopped to take in the fantastic cliffside scenic ocean view. Tucked away from the main walkway and nestled among nature, I ran into a young couple having a picnic. But this was no ordinary picnic. They were dressed in old-fashioned clothes and had a very comfortable and fancy picnic setup. They had a picnic basket with cheese, wine, and snacks. A semi-decorated picnic blanket with a roped-off area, candles, and sheer linen. Relaxing old-style chairs, a small coffee table, and some games. They were enjoying nature in a comfortable, unrushed, and fun way. Brilliant, I thought! The young Japanese couple said they were "forest bathing."

Forest Bathing

Forest bathing, or shinrin-yoku, means "to soak up the forest with all your senses." Originating in Japan in the 1980s, it's a practice of simply being mindful and present in nature, connecting with it through our senses of sight, sound, smell, touch, and taste. There is no destination or goal other than to notice and appreciate your surroundings. Opening our senses bridges the gap between us and the natural world, promoting our well-being.

7 Benefits of Spending Time in Nature

Studies[5] have shown that spending time in nature has many benefits.

1. Boosts mood
2. Reduces stress
3. Improves creativity and problem-solving
4. Protects against anxiety and depression
5. Health benefits when active
6. Stimulates your senses (sights, sounds, smells, etc.)
7. Promotes calm and relaxation

Slowing Down

When I go outside into nature, I'm typically doing an activity like hiking, biking, walking, kayaking, or something else that takes up most of my attention. I'll stop briefly to enjoy a nice view or notice something beautiful while passing by, but I've never really stopped and made nature the main event. Seeing this couple's fancy picnic, I realized it's a perfect way to slow down, immerse myself in, and appreciate nature.

Go for it! How to Fancy Picnic:

Step 1 - Scout out your future spot

1. **Look in advance-** Don't deal with the stress of searching for the perfect picnic spot on the day of the fancy picnic, do it days in advance without any gear.

2. **Secluded or not?-** Search for a secluded or semi-secluded spot away from human distractions. Or, perhaps, you'd enjoy the attention of people curiously envious of your little setup. Then, by all means, find a spot a little more visible.
3. **Near parking-** You'll have a wagon full of goodies and not want to haul it far.
4. **Nature-** Look for a little flat clearing beneath attractive trees with a nice view, around flowers, near colorful plants. Large parks, near the ocean, in the woods, or off trails might have a great spot somewhere.
5. **Hazards-** Once you find your potential spot, keep an eye out for picnic party poopers such as bugs (ants, mosquitos, flying annoyances, etc.), uncomfortable ground if sitting on a blanket (rocks, holes, uneven ground, etc.), unwanted animals (anything dangerous like snakes, etc.), and wetness (get a picnic mat that is waterproof for a piece of mind).

Step 2- Get Ready

1. **Gear up-** Purchase or assemble your picnic gear, such as a blanket, chairs, small table, picnic basket, umbrella (if desired), and wagon (to carry everything).
2. **Get fancy-** Get together a fun, old-world style outfit (victorian style hat, bowtie, etc.) and decorative touches (flowers, candles, ribbons, pillows, etc.).
3. **Snack up-** What's a picnic without some yummy treats? Fancy picnics take things up a notch with things like meats, cheese, crackers, fruits, wine, or champagne.
4. **Pack some fun-** While you'll want to spend most of your time admiring nature's wonders, you may want to add a small game (cards, board game, etc.) or entertainment (book, music, puzzle, instrument, etc.) to break up your picnic.
5. **Practical items-** Don't forget things like sunscreen, bug spray, sunglasses, water, a flashlight, or a light jacket you may need.

Step 3- Go for it

1. **Timing-** Plan for 1-3 hours, so you don't feel rushed. Consider the time of day because you might want to be there for sunset if the location has a great view.
2. **Mindset-** Your purpose is to use all your senses to heighten your awareness of the beauty of the natural world you are immersed in. Relax, notice, and appreciate your surroundings. Become fully present in the moment without outside distractions.
3. **Keep it silly-** Have fun with it! You're all dressed up and having a fancy picnic in the middle of nowhere. How absurd! Imagine you're living 200 years ago and have a strange Victorian accent, that you live in the Downton Abbey mansion and are out for a picnic or anything else that makes you laugh.
4. **Photo-** Don't forget to set up a small retractable tripod and take a photo of your fancy picnic (everyone in it) to remember and impress your friends and family!

Resources

1. Creative Ideas for a Romantic Picnic link
2. Meat and Cheese Basket Ideas link
3. Gourmet Picnic Ideas link

Products

1. Picnic Basket for Two link
2. XL Waterproof Picnic Blanket link
3. Portable wine and cheese folding picnic table link
4. Compact extendable phone tripod link

Books

1. Forest Bathing: How trees can help you find health and happiness by Dr. Quing Li link

2. The art of picnics by Alanna O'Neil link
3. Beautiful Boards: 50 Amazing Snack Boards by Maegan Brown link
4. The Power of Now by Eckhart Tolle link

Pairs well with: Wine and cheese platters, painting, card games

You might also like: Tai Chi, yoga, meditation

Chapter 3

Connect with Others

Retirement can be an exciting and fulfilling chapter in a person's life, but it can also be a time when social connections and a sense of purpose are lost. Without the daily routine of work and the interactions with colleagues, it's vital for retired individuals to find new ways to connect with others and stay socially active. Social connection plays a critical role in mental and emotional well-being, especially as we age. It provides a sense of community and helps to prevent feelings of loneliness and isolation.

One of the best ways to stay socially connected as a retiree is to get involved in volunteer work. Whether it's volunteering at a local community center, helping to restore a park, or lending a hand at a food bank, there are countless opportunities to give back and make new friends in the process. Traveling to volunteer can provide a sense of purpose and an opportunity to see the world while making a positive impact.

Another great way to stay connected is to explore new hobbies and interests. Many retirees find joy in taking up gardening, photography, painting, or learning a new language. Joining a class or group centered around these interests provides a social outlet and an opportunity to learn from others and make new friends.

Staying physically active is also crucial for staying socially connected. Exercise classes, walking groups, and community sports teams provide opportunities to stay active, improve health, and connect with others. For retirees who enjoy travel, embarking on adventure vacations, such as hiking trips, can be a great way to explore new destinations and make new friends along the way.

Staying socially connected is an essential aspect of a happy and fulfilling retirement. From volunteering and exploring new hobbies to traveling and staying physically active, there are many opportunities to connect with others and maintain a sense of purpose. By embracing these opportunities, retirees can ensure a lively and enriching retirement filled with new experiences and lifelong friendships.

Retirement may mean leaving the workforce, but it doesn't mean you have to give up an active social life. In this chapter, we'll discover some fun ideas for growing and maintaining your social network in retirement.

Chapter 3 Website Links

* * *

Find Friends Online

Try senior dating or friendship-finding websites

Remember when meeting like-minded people meant cramming into a loud questionable bar, hoping to bump into someone compatible?

With the internet, there's a much better and more efficient way to find that special someone. It's what the younger generation does, and it's a perfectly normal way of getting out there without the hassle of going anywhere.

Picture this: You're retired, and you have all the time in the world, but you find yourself spending your days twiddling your thumbs and staring out the window, waiting for something to happen. You've watched every TV show on Netflix, read every book on your shelf, and even tried knitting, but you still feel like something's missing. You long for companionship, someone to share your stories and interests with, but you're unsure where to find like-minded people your age. Enter senior dating and friendship-finding websites.

At first, you might think, "Oh, those websites are for desperate people," or "I'm too old for that kind of thing," but hear me out. These websites are not just for finding a romantic partner but also great for finding new friends with similar interests and experiences.

For starters, these websites allow you to connect with people from all over the world who are also retired and looking for companionship. You can browse through profiles and find people with similar hobbies and interests. Who knows, you might even find someone who shares your love of astronomy or your obsession with gardening!

Plus, using these websites can be a lot of fun. It's like a game of "Who's Who," but for seniors. You get to put your best foot forward and show off your personality. You can upload photos, write witty bios, and even send virtual gifts to people you're interested in. It's like being back in high school but without the drama.

And let's not forget the convenience factor. With these websites, you can chat with people from the comfort of your own home. You don't have to worry about getting dressed up or going out to social events to meet people. Instead, you can log in, chat with people who catch your eye, and then decide if you want to take things to the next level.

Senior dating and friendship-finding websites are not just for finding romantic partners but also for finding like-minded retirees who share your hobbies and interests. Using these websites can be a fun, engaging, and completely normal way to meet new people and add some excitement to your retired life. So what are you waiting for? Take a look at the list below and start exploring the possibilities!

12 Senior Dating or Friendship-finding Websites

1. **SilverSingles** (www.silversingles.com): This site is specifically designed for seniors over 50 and has a personality test to help match you with compatible partners. Plus, they have a blog with articles about senior dating and lifestyle, which can be a fun read.
2. **Amintro** (www.amintro.com): Amintro is a senior friendship-finding website that's all about connecting retirees with others who share their interests, values, and experiences. It's a great option if you're looking for companionship, support, or just someone to chat with. With its focus on friendship, community events, and user-friendly interface, Amintro can help you find meaningful connections with like-minded seniors in your area.
3. **OurTime** (www.ourtime.com): OurTime is another popular dating site for seniors, with a large user base and easy-to-use interface. They also have a section for online safety tips, which can be helpful and informative.
4. **SeniorMatch** (www.seniormatch.com): With a community of over 1 million members, SeniorMatch is a great place to find friendship or romance. They also have a "let's meet" feature that suggests potential matches for you based on your preferences.
5. **Stitch** (www.stitch.net): Stitch is a social networking site that connects seniors for friendship, companionship, and activities. They have groups for all sorts of interests, from hiking to book clubs, so you can easily find like-minded people.
6. **EliteSingles** (www.elitesingles.com): EliteSingles is a dating site for seniors seeking a more serious relationship. They use a matchmaking algorithm to match you with

compatible partners, and they have a blog with dating tips and success stories.

7. **SeniorFriendFinder** (www.seniorfriendfinder.com): SeniorFriendFinder is a social networking site that aims to connect seniors for friendship and activities. They have a section for senior news and events, which can be a fun way to stay up-to-date on what's happening in the community.
8. **AgeMatch** (www.agematch.com): AgeMatch is a dating site for seniors that caters to people looking for both older and younger partners. They have a "Let's Meet" feature that suggests potential matches for you based on your preferences, and they also have a blog with dating tips and advice.
9. **Singles50** (www.singles50.com): This site is specifically designed for singles over 50, so you know everyone on the site is in your age range. They also have a personality test that helps you find matches based on your interests and values.
10. **OkCupid** (www.okcupid.com): While OkCupid isn't specifically for seniors, it's a popular dating site with a large user base. The site has a fun and quirky personality test that helps you find matches based on shared interests and values.
11. **ChristianMingle** (www.christianmingle.com): If you're a Christian looking for love or friendship, ChristianMingle could be the site for you. They have a large user base of Christian singles, and their matching system considers factors like faith and values.
12. **eharmony** (www.eharmony.com): Not only for seniors, this popular dating site has been around for over 20 years with a large user base and a compatibility matching system. They also have a section on their site for senior dating tips, which can be helpful if you're new to online dating or just looking for some advice.

Go for it! Simple start steps:

1. Search online for "senior friendship-finding websites."
2. Browse a few sites that seem interesting.
3. Put yourself out there and have fun! You might be just the person someone's been hoping to meet. Give someone the gift of you!

Resources

1. Forbes Best Senior Dating Sites of 2023 link
2. 15 Best Apps For Making Friends in 2023 link
3. Helpful Apps For Seniors Looking To Make New Friends link

* * *

Activities to Stay Social

Find reasons to connect socially

Sometimes it's not about what you do but who you do it with. At times we just need an excuse or opportunity to connect with others. Whether you have a group of friends you'd like to do things with or are looking for ways to meet others, below are some ideas to bring you closer to people.

43 Ideas for Social Connection

1. **Dog park/walk dog-** Walking a dog at a local park or joining a dog walking group provides opportunities to strike up conversations with other dog owners and build new relationships.
2. **Group travel-** Group travel is a fantastic way to connect with others, explore new places, and create memories together.

3. **Volunteer at a place of worship-** Volunteering provides opportunities to connect with others and make a difference while finding spiritual fulfillment.
4. **Paint and sip classes-** Participating in paint and sip classes can provide a social and creative outlet for making new friends and bonding over art and wine.
5. **Fantasy football-** Fantasy football is a thrilling journey of suspense and excitement, a perfect blend of strategy and chance that makes it an exhilarating experience as you watch your team battle for victory each week. It's an enjoyable way to stay connected with friends and feel a part of an exciting sport each week.
6. **Host a dinner party-** Hosting a dinner party allows you to bring together people over a shared meal, fostering a warm and inviting atmosphere for making new friends and reconnecting with old ones.
7. **Join a book club-** Joining a book club allows one to connect with like-minded individuals over a shared love of literature.
8. **Throw a surprise party-** Throwing a surprise party for someone can be an entertaining way to bring joy to someone's life and build connections with others through fun and celebration.
9. **Join a Toastmaster group-** Joining a Toastmaster group provides a space to practice public speaking and form new relationships.
10. **Join Facebook groups dedicated to your interests-** Joining Facebook groups dedicated to one's interests can be a great way to connect with others who share the same passions.
11. **Charades game-** Playing charades can be an entertaining, interactive way to connect with others and engage in social play.
12. **Card games-** Playing cards provides a casual, shared activity that encourages conversation and a bit of friendly competition.

13. **Board games-** Playing board games is an enjoyable way to spend time and build relationships with family, friends, and neighbors.
14. **Mahjong-** Playing mahjong with friends can be an exciting way to connect with others, where strategizing, laughing, and bonding is just as important as winning.
15. **Online gaming-** Online gaming can provide a social outlet and an opportunity to connect with others who share similar interests and competitive spirit.
16. **Scavenger hunts-** Scavenger hunts are a fun and interactive way to bond over a shared experience.
17. **Cosplay-** Connect with others who enjoy a similar passion for creating and showcasing costumes based on their favorite characters.
18. **Plan a costume night-** Spice up the night with a costume party, and have some fun connecting with others by guessing each other's costumes and letting your creative sides show.
19. **Play music together-** Making music together is the perfect way to connect socially, as everyone can enjoy each other's vibes and melodies. Learn a new instrument or improve your skills with a group.
20. **Regular weekly friends activities-** Organizing weekly friends activities can be a great way to make social connections and build camaraderie as you join together to share in the joys of an outdoor outing, a sporty challenge, or a friendly game.
21. **Breakfast meetup for senior specials-** Attend a weekly breakfast meetup to take advantage of special discounts and connect with other seniors in the community.
22. **Season pass to a sports event-** Attending a sports event with a season pass is a wonderful way to connect with fellow fans sitting next to you each week and experience the spirit of camaraderie.
23. **Open mic night-** Attending open mic night is a splendid way to meet people and show off your creative talents in a fun, welcoming atmosphere.

24. **Learn one perfect karaoke song-** Learning one perfect karaoke song and going somewhere to perform it can provide a delightful, lighthearted opportunity to connect with others and make new friends who enjoy a good time with tunes.
25. **Become a street performer-** Becoming a street performer is an amusing way to engage with others and share your talents with the community.
26. **Look for acting or drama opportunities-** Joining acting or drama opportunities can provide a stage to showcase creativity and connect with others who share the same passion.
27. **Puppetry-** Puppetry can be a terrific way to unite people, creating a sense of connection and entertainment as they laugh, sing, and tell stories together.
28. **Go to a nudist colony-** Visiting a nudist colony can be a liberating, eye-opening experience that removes anything in the way of connecting authentically with like-minded individuals.
29. **Attend a support group-** Attending a support group can provide a sense of community and an opportunity to connect with others who share similar experiences or struggles.
30. **People watching-** Observing others and their interactions in public can be a fabulous way to connect with a place's culture and gain insight into any given community's social dynamics.
31. **Search for love or companionship-** Attending a speed-dating event can help you find that special someone and open yourself up to a world of new friendships and potential romance.
32. **Make friends in different age brackets-** Making friends in different age brackets provides opportunities to learn and exchange life experiences, broadening perspectives and fostering social connections.

33. **Reconnect with old friends-** Reconnecting with old friends can help reignite and strengthen relationships from the past, bringing joy, laughter, and a sense of community.
34. **Connect with siblings-** Connecting with siblings through shared experiences and memories can strengthen familial bonds and bring joy to life.
35. **Bond with grandkids-** Bonding with grandkids creates opportunities to share stories, create new memories, and strengthen family bonds.
36. **Share your life lessons with someone-** Sharing life lessons with someone can create meaningful connections and opportunities for mentorship and friendship.
37. **Create family moments-** Creating family moments provides opportunities for social connection and bonding with loved ones.
38. **Bond with your spouse-** When we're around someone always, it's easy to fall into comfortable routines and not prioritize the relationship. Reenergize your relationship with your spouse by doing something unexpected that they would enjoy.
39. **Volunteer-** Volunteering allows you to give back to your community while making lifelong friends.
40. **Become an Airbnb host-** Becoming an Airbnb host provides a unique opportunity for retired individuals to connect with travelers worldwide and share their experiences and local insights.
41. **Adult summer camp-** Attending an adult summer camp can be a fun and unique way to connect with others and make new friends through shared outdoor activities and bonding experiences. Search "Senior adult summer camp + [your city].
42. **Taking classes-** Taking classes can be an entertaining and educational way to meet new people, broaden your horizons, and learn something new.
43. **Joining clubs or groups-** Participating in local clubs or groups allows you to meet new people and expand your

social circle. Some popular clubs include hiking, art, craft, car, RV, cooking, etc.

Resources

1. Best Places For Seniors To Socialize link
2. Beyond Bingo: 14 Activities for Elderly People That Aren't Boring link
3. Fun Activities for Seniors: Over 100 Ways to Play link

* * *

Do Things for Others

Engage socially by helping

Doing things for others is one of the surest ways to make meaningful connections with others. Whether volunteering at a local charity, helping a neighbor in need, or simply taking time out of your day to lend a helping hand - it's incredible how much joy can come from selflessly giving back.

Volunteering is a great way to put others first and learn more about the world around you. You can use your unique talents to better the lives of those less fortunate. Whether it's cooking in a soup kitchen, helping at a local animal shelter, or painting a mural at a school - there are hundreds of opportunities to make a difference. Not only will you be connecting with people you may have never met, but you'll be building important skills like teamwork, leadership, and problem-solving.

If you don't have time to volunteer, you can still find ways to reach out and make an impact. Helping a friend move into a new residence, bringing food to an elderly neighbor, or mowing someone's lawn – all these little acts of kindness can be very meaningful for others. A little kindness is never really little. You don't need much money or time to connect with people and share your skills – sometimes, the best connections are made with a simple smile or a few kind words.

By putting others first and showing that you care, you can create meaningful relationships and positively impact the lives of those around you. Doing things for others is a powerful way to create meaningful social connections.

20 Ways to Engage Socially with Kindness

1. **Plan a surprise for someone-** Organizing a surprise for someone can be a great way to show them how much you care and bring people closer together.
2. **Be a mentor-** Use your knowledge to help others learn and grow, building strong relationships as you help them reach their goals.
3. **Support a loved one-** Helping a loved one with something can be a great way to show them your appreciation and create a strong bond of friendship.
4. **Coach a team-** Coaching a team provides a unique opportunity to connect with others through a shared pursuit of success.
5. **Smile at every stranger-** Smiling at every stranger you encounter is an easy way to spark meaningful conversations and make social connections with those around you.
6. **Pick up litter-** Joining a local litter-picking group can help you meet like-minded people and contribute something positive to your community.
7. **Send an unexpected card to someone-** A thoughtful and creative way to brighten up someone's day and connect with them on a more personal level.
8. **Read a thank you note to someone-** Expressing gratitude to those around you is a beautiful way to foster meaningful connections and bond with others socially.
9. **Read to a child or someone-** Curl up with a good book and let your imagination take you on a journey while connecting with a loved one through the shared experience of storytelling.

10. **Make or cook something for neighbors or a friend-** Making something with your own two hands and offering it to someone else is the perfect way to show that you care enough to put effort into strengthening your social connection.
11. **Be a free hugs person-** Giving free hugs is a great way to make someone feel loved and connected to the world around you.
12. **Help in your neighborhood-** Getting involved in your local community is a great way to meet new people and make meaningful connections.
13. **Teach music to grandkids-** Bringing music into the home together can create a magical bond between grandparent and grandchild, making a new and delightful way of connecting.
14. **Complement every person you meet-** Make a lasting impression by offering sincere compliments to everyone you encounter and watch your social network blossom before your eyes.
15. **Do a random act of kindness-** Giving a stranger a heartfelt act of kindness is a great way to connect with people and spread joy in the world.
16. **Create a treasure box for grandkids-** A treasure box filled with little surprises is a great way to form meaningful connections with grandkids and strengthen family bonds.
17. **Get a head start on Christmas or birthday shopping-** Make holiday shopping easier and more enjoyable with a head start on finding thoughtful and unique gifts that will bring joy to your loved ones.
18. **Bring toys to a homeless shelter-** Bringing toys to a homeless shelter can be a great way to bridge the gap between people, bringing smiles and laughter to the faces of those who need it most.
19. **Take 10 minutes to really listen to someone-** Listening is a powerful way to connect with someone; taking 10 minutes of undivided attention shows a level of

respect and understanding that is sure to open up new and meaningful conversations.

20. **Volunteer-** Volunteering can be a fantastic way to meet new people and form meaningful connections. You can make a lasting impact by donating your time and resources and finding a community of like-minded individuals who share your passion and dedication. Whether you're helping to build homes, cleaning up a park, or organizing a fundraiser, volunteering can provide a sense of purpose while also allowing you to get to know others. You may even create lasting friendships that will enrich your social life for years to come.

Resources

1. 101 Best Random Acts of Kindness Ideas link
2. 75 Random Acts of Kindness link
3. 51 Fun And Painless Ways To Meet New People link
4. Find The Best Volunteer Opportunities Near You link

* * *

Social Sports and Games

Connect through the camaraderie of competition

Sports and competitive games offer an easy and fun way for people to connect with others in the social sphere. Participating in a team sport or game provides a great reason to get together and share a common interest.

Whether playing or watching, sports and game-playing can provide an incredible social experience. For those seeking to make new friends, participating in a pick-up game of basketball or a rousing game of charades can be a great way to break the ice and have fun. Even if you don't win, something about sharing a few laughs and competing quickly builds bonds.

On the other hand, inviting friends to watch a sporting event can also be a great connection opportunity. Sharing a plate of nachos or a pitcher of beer while cheering on your favorite team builds a sense of camaraderie that can't be found anywhere else. Plus, there's nothing quite like watching a game with a crowd of passionate fans screaming and singing along to the national anthem. It's an experience that's sure to bring even the most reserved of people out of their shells.

No matter the type of game or sport, the social opportunities that come with it are unparalleled. Whether you're looking to make new friends or strengthen an existing relationship, participating in or watching a game is a fantastic way to do just that. Some sports below might not be recommended for seniors to participate in, like roller derby, but they might be entertaining to watch with friends.

42 Ideas To Socialize Through Sports

1. **Golf-** Whether it's on the course or at the range, golfing is the perfect way to tee off a social connection - with each stroke, you can strike up a conversation and drive relationships.
2. **Miniature golf-** Putt-putt your way to glory and feel like a kid again with a few rounds of miniature golf.
3. **Snow golf-** Experience a totally new kind of golfing adventure: hit the links while snowshoeing through a winter wonderland.
4. **Basketball-** Basketball is the ideal sport to shoot the breeze, sink a few shots in the social court, and make some slam-dunk connections.
5. **Baseball/Softball-** The perfect way to hit it out of the park in terms of socializing, team up with new friends, and enjoy some quality time in great company.
6. **Over the line-** Forget crossing the street - you can literally go 'over the line' on this exciting home run derby-like sport, guaranteed to keep everyone on their toes.

7. **Soccer-** Soccer is the ultimate way to kickstart your social life, score some goals with new acquaintances, and pass the time in friendly company.
8. **Cricket-** Cricket is the sport to bat away the blues, bowl people over with your charm, and put yourself in the social lineup.
9. **Tennis-** Playing tennis is the perfect way to serve up an ace conversation with a partner, rally your social life, and score a few new friends.
10. **Pickleball-** Pickleball is the perfect way to make a racket and rack up connections - it's a double whammy of social interaction.
11. **Badminton-** Badminton is the sport to shuttle your social life into the stratosphere, send some friendly banter over the net, and rally up some new acquaintances.
12. **Racquetball-** Playing racquetball is a great way to break the ice and make new friends quickly, as you get your heart pumping and practice some friendly competition.
13. **Squash-** The game that'll have seniors dashing around the court to prove that agility and speed aren't reserved only for younger generations - a fun and challenging way to stay active.
14. **Handball-** Playing handball offers a terrific way to connect as they bounce the ball off the wall and share a few laughs along the way.
15. **Roundnet-** Roundnet offers a wonderful way to rally and roll their way to well-deserved fun.
16. **Shuffleboard-** Shuffleboard is the pastime to shuffle off your loneliness, slide into a few new friendships, and make some ace companions on the court.
17. **Volleyball-** Volleyball is an activity to spike your social life, bounce off some friendly banter, and dig up a few new friends.
18. **Beach volleyball-** Head to the beach and make friends while playing a competitive game of beach volleyball - a great way to build relationships while having fun in the sun.

19. **Water volleyball-** For seniors, the volleyball pool becomes a bubbling cauldron of laughter when the grandmas and grandpas spike it home.
20. **Snow volleyball-** Try conquering the snow by playing a friendly round of volleyball with friends - an exhilarating take on a classic game.
21. **Frisbee golf-** Frisbee golf is the game to send your social life soaring, ace a few conversations, and make some eagle friends on the course.
22. **Ultimate frisbee-** Feel your age fly away as you leap for the ultimate frisbee, just like a teenager, but with much more grace.
23. **Cornhole-** Playing a game of cornhole is sure to bring hours of fun and laughter, making it the perfect way to connect socially.
24. **Darts-** Throw your cares away and connect with your friends over a game of darts, a classic way to make some new connections.
25. **Pool or billiards-** Playing a game of pool or billiards can be a fun and inviting way to bond with friends and strangers alike as you pick up your cues and make a joyful competition out of a game that's been around for centuries.
26. **Bumper pool-** Bumper pool offers an exciting, competitive way to connect with others around the table while avoiding the usual social awkwardness of real pool.
27. **Air hockey-** Challenge your friends to an exciting game of air hockey, and see who has the best reflexes and agility - a thrilling way to stay connected.
28. **Foosball-** The game combines the skill of a grandmaster chess player and the fast-paced reflexes of a professional ping-pong champion - perfect for those who want to challenge themselves.
29. **Table shuffleboard-** Forget bingo. Table shuffleboard is the game that's sure to keep everyone laughing - and engaged - for hours on end.

30. **Table tennis-** Table tennis is the activity to ping your social life, make a few volleys of conversation, and smash your way to a few new friends.
31. **Horseshoes-** A game that brings out the inner cowboy in all of us, no matter how many years have passed.
32. **Lawn darts-** Throw a few rounds of lawn darts and watch as conversations spark and relationships blossom.
33. **Lawn bowling-** Lawn bowling is the way to roll your social circle, strike up some conversations, and get close to good company.
34. **Snowball fighting competition-** Nothing says 'friendship' like a fiercely competitive, snow-filled day of snowball fights.
35. **Curling-** A night of curling is a chance for seniors to bond over their inner Olympians and show that age is just a number.
36. **Fencing-** Where retirees can let their inner swashbucklers out and show that age is no obstacle to being a champion - an exciting and fun experience.
37. **Quidditch/ quad ball-** The game that combines the best of two worlds - the magic of Quidditch and the thrill of basketball - perfect for seniors who want to get their game on.
38. **Roller derby-** The game that shows seniors just how much of a force they can still be in their golden years. Lace up the skates and get ready to power your way to victory.
39. **Rugby-** Rugby is the game to take your social life by storm, tackle your loneliness, and get into a scrum of new friends.
40. **Football-** Football is the ultimate touchdown when it comes to building your social circle, tackling new relationships, and spending time in the company of like-minded retired mates.
41. **Field hockey-** Forget walking the dogs at the park - retirees can take their agility to the field with a game of field hockey, where they'll be laughing and having a blast as they move their way to victory.

42. **Hockey-** Hockey is the game that'll help you slide into a social scene, make some stick-saving connections, and take the ice in fun company.

Resources

1. 10 great sports for seniors link
2. The Best Sports For Older Adults, According To Experts link
3. The Safest Sports for Seniors link

* * *

Play Shuffleboard

Shuffle by or knock off your opponent

A game of touch, feel, and precision, shuffleboard is a fun social sport that's great for people of all ages and mobility levels. It can be played outdoors or indoors.

What is floor shuffleboard?

Players use a cue stick (a pole with a groove at the end) to push (shuffle) their colored disks down a long rectangular court (smooth concrete or wood), attempting to land in the marked scoring areas. Two or four players (in teams of two) alternate turns until their four disks are all played, and the score for the round is counted. The exciting part of shuffleboard is the ability to knock off your opponent's disc from their scoring position and land in a scoring place yourself. Often strategy is involved in defending good discs, and the last disc played, called "the hammer," can change the scoring outcome of the round.

What is a table shuffleboard?

Sometimes found in the corner of bars or recreation centers, table shuffleboard involves sliding small metal pucks, by hand, to scoring positions at the end of the table. Play alternates until the player with the furthest discs down the table is scored at the end of the round. The game ends when an agreed-upon score is reached, such as 21.

Social meet-ups and leagues

Frequently, places with outdoor shuffleboard courts, such as RV resorts, recreation centers, and cruise ships, will have social leagues and meet-up schedules to join a team and get in on the fun.

Go for it! Simple start steps:

1. Search online for outdoor shuffleboard courts near you.
2. Bring a friend to the location and check out the discs and cue sticks from the office.
3. Have fun!

Resources

1. How to Play Shuffleboard link
2. Why Shuffleboard is a Great Game For Seniors link
3. National Senior Games Association Shuffleboard link

Products

1. 9' Shuffleboard Table link
2. 16' Shuffleboard Table link
3. Table Shuffleboard Bowling Pins link

You might also like: Bocce ball, horseshoes, corn hole

* * *

Make Someone Laugh

Be lighthearted and silly

Laughter is one of life's greatest gifts. It can bring joy to a gloomy day, bring a smile to a stranger's face, or lighten the spirits of a room that had been stuck in a funk.

For seniors, in particular, laughter can be an incredibly powerful tool. It can help to create meaningful bonds, relieve stress, increase endorphins, and bring a sense of lightheartedness and joy to life. In fact, a good laugh can be more effective than any medicine for combating loneliness.

Being silly is something we all could use more of. Whether it's something as small as putting a funny face on a picture frame or as joyous as playing tag with the grandchildren, it's important to remember that being silly isn't just for the young and carefree. Being silly can be a powerful way to connect with others and enjoy life.

Studies have shown that when someone laughs, it spreads to those within earshot and can actually elicit the same laughter and joy from them. So don't hesitate to crack a few jokes, share some funny stories, and try to put a smile on someone's face. It could be just the pick-me-up they need.

Life isn't meant to be lived without laughter. Laugh as much as you can, never be afraid to be silly, and do what you can to make those around you laugh and smile. You'll be sure to feel the rewards of doing so.

10 Perks of Laughter[6]

1. **Decreases stress-** Studies have found that laughter lowers stress hormones like cortisol, epinephrine, and dopamine. It can cause the body to produce endorphins, the brain's "natural painkiller," and make us feel happier and more relaxed.

2. **Improves mood-** It's hard to stay in a bad mood if you're laughing. Laughter releases endorphins that make us feel better and help us stay positive.
3. **Boosts immunity-** Research has found that laughing can boost the immune system by increasing immune cells and infection-fighting antibodies.
4. **Improves relationships-** Laughter is contagious and can help strengthen relationships. It can make us feel more connected to friends and family and can help us build stronger relationships with others.
5. **Enhances creativity-** Studies have found that laughter can help stimulate creative thinking and problem-solving. It can also help us stay open-minded and creative when facing challenges.
6. **Enhances memory-** Studies have found that laughter can help us remember new information better, increasing the brain's learning capacity.
7. **Increases energy-** Laughter helps us use oxygen more efficiently, giving us an energy boost.
8. **Alleviates pain-** Laughter helps us produce natural painkillers like endorphins, which can help us cope with pain.
9. **Relieves anxiety-** Laughing can help us relax and release stress and anxiety.
10. **Improves concentration-** Studies have found that laughter can help us stay focused and attentive.

20 Silly Ways to Make Yourself or Someone Else Laugh

1. Talk in an accent to a stranger.
2. Act totally out of character and wacky for a day.
3. Put together a stand-up comedy set for your stuffed animals.
4. Shock challenge. Get a toy shocker, and every time someone is grumpy, they get a shock.

5. Start planning an epic April fool's day prank.
6. Go alone to a faraway park and befriend the trees, pretending not to notice the people looking at you like a crazy person.
7. Write short jokes with sidewalk chalk in the park walkway, then sit back on a bench and wait to see who walks by, reads it, and laughs.
8. Go to a stand-up comedy show.
9. Become a prankster.
10. Create a newspaper comic strip series (Far Side, Peanuts, Garfield, etc.).
11. Play a game of charades with funny actions.
12. Put on a silly hat and start telling jokes.
13. Share funny stories about your childhood.
14. Read funny poems or funny quotes.
15. Have a play-off with funny impressions of each other.
16. Make fun of yourself often.
17. Do some silly dance moves or a silly "exercise" routine.
18. Recount a funny experience you had or have overheard.
19. Break out the karaoke machine and sing some original silly tunes.
20. Make silly faces at each other.

* * *

Social Side Jobs

Have fun making money

For many retirees, work is the last thing on their fun things-to-do list. For others, the social and creative benefits of a casual part-time job or small business can be as fulfilling as the extra spending cash it brings.

Taking on a casual job can provide a sense of purpose and structure to your days. It can be a great way to meet new people and connect with others in your community. Whether working part-time at a local store, taking on a seasonal job, or becoming a consultant, there are plenty of options to explore. It can also be an excellent way to stay mentally and physically active, providing a sense of accomplishment and fulfillment that can be hard to find in other areas of retirement.

Starting a small business can be a fun and creative way to explore your passions and interests. It can be a way to turn a hobby into a profitable venture, providing a source of income and satisfaction. Whether it's starting a blog, selling handmade crafts, or offering consulting services, there are countless opportunities to explore. Additionally, it can be a great way to learn new skills and keep your mind sharp, helping you stay engaged and fulfilled during retirement.

With the rising cost of living, it can be challenging to maintain the same standard of living on a fixed income. By supplementing your income with a part-time job or side business, you can ease financial stress and maintain your lifestyle. It can also provide the opportunity to travel or pursue other activities that may have been out of reach otherwise.

A social side job can be a fun and rewarding way to stay active, engaged, and fulfilled during retirement. It can provide numerous benefits, from social to financial, and help you explore new passions and interests.

38 Ways to Stay Social and Active While Earning Money

1. **Arts and crafts business-** Sell handmade items online or at craft fairs.
2. **Part-time job-** Work a flexible job that provides social interaction and extra income.
3. **Freelance work-** Offer a skill such as writing, photography, or graphic design services online.
4. **Food services-** Start a catering or meal delivery business.
5. **Personal shopping-** Offer personal shopping and errand-running services.
6. **Sell your photographs-** Turn your photography hobby into a money-making opportunity by selling your photos

online. Share your creativity and offer high-quality images for others to purchase.

7. **Lenticular photography-** Combine your love for photography with your technical skills by offering lenticular photography services. This type of photography creates a three-dimensional effect and can be used for special occasions or as unique home decor.
8. **Working at a sporting venue-** A great way to save money is by working part-time at a sporting venue such as a stadium or arena. With free event admission, you'll enjoy some great experiences and make extra cash.
9. **Online tutoring-** Offer tutoring services in a subject you excel in, such as math or a foreign language.
10. **Start a garden-** Grow fruits, vegetables, and herbs to sell at a farmers market or save on groceries.
11. **Offer pet-sitting services-** Pet-sitting for others when they go on vacation can be a fun way to meet some furry new friends and earn a little on the side.
12. **Sell unwanted items-** Clean out your closet and sell clothes, furniture, and other items you no longer need.
13. **Do odd jobs for others-** Offer handyperson services, run errands, or do other simple tasks.
14. **Sell digital products-** If you have expertise in a particular field, create and sell digital products such as e-books or online courses.
15. **Review books-** Get paid for your opinions by reviewing products, books, and other items for websites and companies.
16. **Rodan and Fields business-** Start selling high-quality skincare products through a well-established brand.
17. **Tour guide-** Share your knowledge and love of your city by becoming a tour guide and showing visitors around.
18. **Seasonal job-** Take on a seasonal job, such as working as a pool attendant, Christmas helper, or camp host, for extra cash and social benefits.

19. **Face painting business-** Use your artistic skills to start a face painting business and earn money at festivals, birthday parties, and other events.
20. **Candle-making business-** Create a line of scented candles using natural ingredients and sell them online or at local markets.
21. **Sports photography-** Capture memories and earn money by taking photos at local sporting events, such as Little League games or high school football games.
22. **Teach English online-** Use your language skills to teach English to students worldwide via an online platform.
23. **Nail art business-** Offer unique nail art designs to clients in your area or sell pre-made designs online.
24. **Day trade-** Take advantage of the stock market by analyzing market trends and investing in stocks for short-term gains. With the right skills and research, day trading can generate a steady stream of extra income.
25. **Online sports wagering-** With the convenience of the internet, it's easy to place bets on your favorite sports teams and events. With careful consideration and calculated risk-taking, sports wagering can be a fun and profitable hobby.
26. **Video editing business-** Offer your video editing skills to individuals and businesses looking to produce high-quality content. Utilize your experience and creativity to turn a passion into a profitable business.
27. **Resell old hobby equipment-** Take inventory of unused equipment from past hobbies and sell them to fund new interests or make some extra cash. Turn clutter into cash with a little effort.
28. **Rent out a spare room-** If you have a spare room in your house, rent it out on platforms like Airbnb.
29. **Rent out your car-** Rent out your car when you're not using it to earn extra income.
30. **Rent out equipment-** Rent out items such as power tools or lawn equipment to others.

31. **Metal detecting-** Go on a treasure hunt and search for valuable items using a metal detector. This activity can be a fun hobby, and you may also find valuable items to sell for extra cash.
32. **Online surveys-** Share your opinions and earn money by taking online surveys. Companies value the opinions of seniors and are often willing to pay for their time.
33. **Flipping homes-** Get into the real estate market by flipping homes. This involves purchasing, renovating, and selling a property for a profit. It can be a rewarding and lucrative opportunity for those with experience in the real estate industry.
34. **Dog walking service-** As a senior, you may have the time and love for dogs, making starting a dog-walking business a great opportunity. It's a fun way to make money while exercising and spending time with furry friends.
35. **Thrifting-** Thrift shopping can be a fun and cost-effective hobby that saves you money. With the ability to find unique and one-of-a-kind items, it can also be a way to make a profit by reselling your finds.
36. **Upcycling-** Upcycling is the creative process of taking something old and giving it a new life. With a passion for DIY, starting an upcycling business can save you money and bring in some extra cash by selling your creations.
37. **Music tutoring-** With a lifetime of musical experience, a senior can turn their passion for music into a part-time job by offering music lessons to others. It's a great way to share your love of music and earn extra cash at the same time.
38. **Ride-share driving-** Ride-share driving is a flexible way for seniors to earn extra cash. By using their vehicle, they can choose their hours and pick up passengers on their schedule, making it an excellent option for those looking to supplement their income.

Books

1. Candle Making Business 101: The Simple 8-Step Beginner's Guide to Start, Run, and Grow a Profitable Home-Based Candle Business. From Candle Making to Marketing to Launch in as little as 30 Days. by Grace Holmes link
2. 101 Activities and Resources for Teaching English Online: Practical Ideas, Games, Activities & Tips for ESL/EFL Teachers who Teach Online by Jackie Bolen link
3. Sell Your Crafts Online: The Handmaker's Guide to Selling from Etsy, Amazon, Facebook, Instagram, Pinterest, Shopify, Influencers and More by James Dillehay link

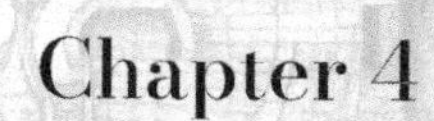

Chapter 4

Go Outside for Fun

Go outside and play! Do you remember hearing that from your parents or saying it to your kids? There's a reason. It's excellent advice! Your perspective shifts when you step outside and can see beyond the walls confining you. The familiar motionless surroundings of the inside can trap you into needing to look inward for excitement. As a child, it can become overwhelming and frustrating to always use imagination for entertainment, so they turn to the only external stimulation, TV, or sit bored. Parents realize that watching TV is like eating sugar. It tastes and feels great but leaves you empty and without nutritional value, the stuff that will help you grow. TV is fantasy. It's not life. It's seeing but not experiencing. It's mostly garbage designed to keep your eyes glued to it and your brain mildly occupied at the expense of doing anything meaningful or healthy. Parents see this and tell their kids to go outside, forcing them to get away from what's restricting them from finding real fun and enjoyment.

It works! Outside the house, the child is surprised to find that things are in motion all around him. He sees the blue sky and puffy white clouds. He feels the cool wind and warm sun on his face. The sweet smell of flowers from the yard fills his nose. Small birds fly over, chirping, and leaves rustle in the wind nearby. His senses are stimulated, and his focus is now outward. He's no longer bored but curious to explore the little world of his backyard that feels so alive. He follows a butterfly to the fence and hears the sound of the neighbors' kids playing. He gets permission and jumps over to spend the day happily playing with his friends. An unexpected outcome came from a little push to go outside and play.

Stimulate the senses and wake the mind with some fresh air. Below are some activities that are fun to do and a great reason to get outside and play. They may take you somewhere unexpected and allow you new experiences that may enrich your life.

Chapter 4 Website Links

* * *

Outdoor Activities to Explore

Stay active outside

When you want to break out of the everyday routine, getting outside and exploring the natural world is one of the best ways to escape it all. Outdoor activities and hobbies offer a plethora of benefits that can help you stay healthy and happy.

The fresh air of the outdoors can help invigorate your body, mind, and soul. It can help you feel re-energized, which can help with daily life stress. Plus, being outdoors can make you feel more relaxed and at peace with the world. It can be an opportunity to reset and refocus, leaving you better equipped to tackle the challenges of day-to-day life.

Outdoor activities and hobbies also give you a chance to get some exercise. Physical activity is essential for physical health and can also help with mental health. Exercise can help reduce stress and improve overall mood while allowing you to concentrate better and think more clearly.

Finally, outdoor activities and hobbies can be a great way to bond with friends and family. Exploring the outdoors together can encourage meaningful conversations and lasting memories. Whether hiking, biking, or camping, you'll have an opportunity to connect with those you love in a whole new way.

58 Fun Outdoor Activities

1. **Golf-** There's nothing quite like the feeling of hitting a perfectly struck golf shot, watching the ball soar majestically through the air, and landing precisely where you intended it to go, all while your friends cheer you on.
2. **Top golf**- A high-tech driving range entertainment venue that offers a unique and interactive golfing experience. It's a fun and challenging way to test one's golfing skills and enjoy friendly competition. Perfect for a group of friends looking to try something new.
3. **Hiking-** A peaceful and rewarding way to immerse oneself in nature and take in the beauty of the outdoors, perfect for those seeking exercise and fun.
4. **Road bicycling-** Road bicycling is an exhilarating way to explore the countryside, offering fresh air, sunshine, and the opportunity to take in the sights and sounds of nature. It is also a great way to get your heart pumping and your endorphins flowing.
5. **Birdwatching-** An entertaining and educational experience, birdwatching allows you to spot and identify different species of birds in their natural habitat.

6. **Gardening-** A relaxing and rewarding activity, gardening is perfect for those wishing to connect with nature and create something beautiful.
7. **Photography-** Capturing a stunning landscape, a moment of joy, or a candid shot of a loved one can be a fulfilling and unique way to express yourself visually.
8. **Astronomy-** Looking up into the night sky and marveling at the majestic stars and galaxies is a peaceful and awe-inspiring experience that can open up a world of possibilities.
9. **Collecting-** Not only is collecting a fun way to remember special moments and find interesting trinkets, but it's also a great way to learn about the history of the places and people you visit.
10. **Roller skating/ rollerblading-** An exhilarating or leisurely activity awaits those who strap on their rollerblades and take to the streets, smooth pavement, and parks providing the ultimate freedom as they glide down the paths. Indoor rinks are nostalgic and outdoor rinks are fun on warm, sunny days.
11. **Swimming-** Whether taking a dip in a freshwater pool, splashing in a lake, or diving into the sea, swimming is refreshing, invigorating, and a great way to get exercise.
12. **Yoga-** Enjoy the blissful feeling of striking a perfect yoga pose while surrounded by nature's beauty, breathing in fresh air, and feeling the sun's warm rays on your skin.
13. **Dog walking-** Take a leisurely stroll with your four-legged friends as they explore the world of sights and smells, an enjoyable and peaceful experience for humans and canines.
14. **Horseback riding-** An adventurous and freeing way to explore the landscape, ideal for any nature lover looking to experience a unique journey.
15. **Fast walk-** Get a breath of fresh air, stretch your legs, and reconnect with the natural world in a brisk, invigorating, fast walk.

16. **Running/ jogging-** Feel the wind on your face and the rhythm of your feet hitting the pavement as an escape from the stresses of life. Jogging is a great way to keep healthy and clear your mind.
17. **Marathon-** Running a marathon is a challenging and rewarding experience that requires determination, perseverance, and a whole lot of heart - but the feeling of crossing the finish line, with the wind in your hair and the cheers of the crowd ringing in your ears, is truly indescribable, and makes all the hard work and training worth it in the end.
18. **Boogie Boarding-** Riding the waves and feeling the rush of the ocean is what boogie boarding is all about. It's a thrilling outdoor activity that's easy to learn and perfect for anyone who loves the feeling of the sun, sand, and saltwater.
19. **Longboard surfing-** Ride the waves with grace and agility, mastering the power of the ocean as you carve and glide through the water, feeling the thrill of the ride.
20. **Sculling/rowing-** Enjoy the peace of the river and the strength of the pull as you glide across the water in this timeless form of aquatic transportation.
21. **Fishing-** Casting your line in the still waters of a glassy lake and patiently waiting for that tug of a bite can provide hours of peaceful enjoyment.
22. **Hunting-** Exploring the great outdoors and searching for that perfect shot of an elusive animal is a rewarding challenge that can be truly satisfying.
23. **Trap/clay pigeon/skeet shooting-** Test your hand-eye coordination and sharpshooting skills in this thrilling outdoor activity that puts your precision to the test.
24. **Knife or ax throwing-** Dare to experience the thrill of precision as you hone your aim and sharpen your blade-throwing accuracy to hit your target with a single throw.
25. **Target shooting-** Test your accuracy and sharpen your aim while challenging yourself to hit the bull's eye at the range and gain confidence as you get better with each round.

26. **Archery-** An up-close and exciting way to test one's focus and sharpen their shooting skills, perfect for the competitive hunter or connoisseur of the bow and arrow.
27. **Bushcraft-** An ideal activity for the outdoorsy type, bushcraft allows you to connect with nature through activities such as shelter-building, fire-lighting, and tool-making.
28. **Taxidermy-** An unusual experience that allows you to admire nature in a way you never thought possible. Taxidermy is a fascinating way to explore the animal kingdom.
29. **Clam digging-** Dig into the sand and uncover hidden treasures as you unearth the succulent delights of a low-tide bounty.
30. **Build sand art at the beach-** Building intricate sand art sculptures at the beach is a fun and creative way to let your imagination run wild, using nothing but your hands, some basic tools, and the natural beauty of the sand and sea to create stunning works of art that will impress and amaze anyone who passes by.
31. **Whale watching-** Step into a realm of wonder as you marvel at the majestic grace of these gentle giants as they dip and dive into the ocean's depths.
32. **Camping-** Feel the thrill of sleeping beneath the stars and reconnecting with the wonders of nature in a secluded and peaceful setting.
33. **Backpacking-** Pack up your essentials and hit the trails, taking in the beauty of nature and the satisfaction of reaching the end of the path. Backcountry hiking can be very peaceful and rewarding.
34. **Float down a river-** Grab an inner tube and plunge into the cool depths of the river, exploring a different side of the world as you drift along.
35. **Forest bathing-** Release your stress and anxiety with a peaceful walk through a lush forest, invigorating your body and soothing your soul.

36. **Coaching sports-** Inspire young athletes to reach their full potential by helping them develop the necessary skills to execute the plays and strategies of their favorite sports.
37. **Duckpin bowling-** The mix between the traditional bowling we know and love with the smaller pins and balls adds a unique twist that can turn a run-of-the-mill evening into an exciting and fun-filled night.
38. **Mushroom hunting-** Search for the hidden gems of the forest, searching for and identifying rare varieties of mushrooms as you marvel at the undergrowth of the wilderness.
39. **Plogging-** Get your heart rate up, and your mood improved as you jog and pick up litter along the way, caring for the environment and feeling the satisfaction of a job well done.
40. **Slacklining-** A combination of yoga, balance, and acrobatics, walking a slackline can be the perfect introduction to a thrilling and rewarding activity.
41. **Butterfly watching-** Be captivated by the kaleidoscope of color as the graceful fluttering of wings provides a mesmerizing show of nature.
42. **Trainspotting-** Enjoy the old-world charm of a vintage locomotive in action, with its distinctive whistle and rumble that conjures up nostalgic memories of a bygone era.
43. **Aircraft spotting-** Get a front-row seat to the sky and marvel at the beauty of a plane taking off or landing in an aeronautical ballet.
44. **Aviation-** Soar through the air and see the world from a new perspective, feeling the rush of freedom and the joy of exploration as you experience the thrill of flight.
45. **Driving-** Explore the roads less traveled, feeling the rush of the open road and the freedom of adventure as you make your way to new and exciting destinations.
46. **Buy a convertible-** Experience the open road like never before in your convertible, the sun beaming down on you as you take in the world around you.

47. **Three-wheel motorcycling-** Feel the wind on your face as you cruise around town in your 3-wheeler, turning heads with your swagger and style.
48. **Metal detecting-** Uncover the history of the land as you search for buried treasure, discovering secrets from times past and experiencing the excitement of the hunt. Who knows what treasures you'll uncover!
49. **Skiing-** A thrilling and exhilarating activity, skiing is ideal for those looking for a fast-paced adventure in the mountains.
50. **Ski season pass-** Enjoy the thrill of conquering the slopes with the freedom of a season pass, which gives you unlimited access to unique snow-filled skiing adventures.
51. **Ice skating-** Nothing is quite as magical as gliding across a frozen lake on ice skates, feeling the cold air against your face.
52. **Snowshoeing-** Explore the winter wonderland with snowshoes, traversing the terrain in a unique way that mixes the fun of a hike with the thrill of an outdoor adventure.
53. **Cross-country skiing-** Imagine gliding effortlessly across a snowy landscape, enjoying nature's crisp air and peaceful stillness as you challenge yourself to explore and discover new trails.
54. **Snowmobiling-** Feel the sheer power and adrenaline rush as you speed across the snow-covered landscape, taking in the majestic vistas and experiencing the thrill of winter adventure.
55. **Hockey/ ice-hockey-** Enjoy the intensity of the game as you battle for the puck, the glory of a well-executed goal, and the camaraderie that comes with playing one of Canada's most beloved sports.
56. **Tour skating-** Feel the exhilaration of ice-skating along a scenic route, admiring the views, and taking in the fresh winter air as you make your way around the track.
57. **Skijoring-** Get the ultimate winter thrill with this unique combination of skiing and horseback riding as you feel the wind rush past you while being pulled by a team of horses.

58. **Make a snowman or ice sculpture-** Let your creativity run wild as you bring snow to life, crafting a unique masterpiece and making lasting memories with friends and family.

Note: See Chapter 3 for many more sports and social outdoor activities.

Resources

1. The 10 Best Outdoor Activities For Seniors link
2. 15 Fun Outdoor Activities for Older People link
3. 19 Exciting Activities for Senior Citizens link

* * *

Ocean and Lake Activities

Have fun by the water

Ah, the ocean and lake activities! Few things can beat the feeling of being surrounded by the vastness and tranquility of these bodies of water. From taking a dip in crystal clear waters to feeling the warm sun on your skin to the soothing sound of waves crashing on the shore, there are many benefits to embracing the ocean and lake activities in your daily life.

For starters, ocean and lake activities offer a unique form of physical exercise, combining the fun of water sports with the health benefits of getting your heart rate up. Whether you prefer kayaking, paddle boarding, or swimming, you'll find yourself invigorated by the challenge and excitement of these activities.

In addition to the physical benefits, bodies of water offer a mental escape from life's daily hustle and bustle. The peacefulness of the water, combined with the breathtaking views, creates an ideal environment for unwinding, relaxing, and recharging your batteries.

Ocean and lake activities are also excellent opportunities to connect with nature and the environment. Whether you're fishing, snorkeling, or just soaking up the sun, you'll appreciate the stunning beauty of these environments and the positive impact they can have on your overall well-being.

18 Exciting Water Activities

1. **Kayaking-** Paddle through serene waters, enjoying the scenic beauty around you. A peaceful kayaking excursion is perfect for getting away from it all and connecting with nature.
2. **Snorkeling-** Put on a snorkel and dive into clear waters to explore the colorful underwater world. This is an opportunity to see exotic marine life up close and personal.
3. **Fishing-** Cast your line and wait for a big catch. Whether you're a seasoned angler or a beginner, fishing is a fun and relaxing activity that can be enjoyed on the ocean or a lake.
4. **Sailing-** Enjoy the freedom of the open sea as you set sail on a sailboat. The gentle rocking of the boat and the sound of the waves will help you relax and soak up the sun.
5. **Surfing-** Imagine the thrill of riding the waves on a surfboard, feeling the rush of wind and water. Surfing is not just for the young. It's an activity that can be enjoyed by anyone who loves the ocean.
6. **Scuba diving-** Scuba diving is the perfect activity if you're looking for an unforgettable ocean adventure. Explore sunken ships, colorful coral reefs, and an array of sea creatures.
7. **Rowing-** Rowing is a classic water activity enjoyed for generations. It is a low-impact and effective way to stay active and enjoy the tranquility of the water. Whether you're out for a leisurely paddle or competing in a race, rowing is a great way to exercise and enjoy the water.
8. **Beachcombing-** Stroll along the shore, looking for interesting treasures such as seashells, driftwood, and colorful stones. This is a great way to get some exercise, fresh air, and a little bit of adventure.

9. **Paddleboarding-** Stand on a paddleboard and paddle your way through calm waters. This is a fun and challenging activity that's perfect for seniors who are looking to explore and exercise.
10. **Swimming-** Dip into the cool, refreshing ocean or lake waters and enjoy a swim. This is a fantastic way to stay active, rejuvenate, and have fun.
11. **Boat tours-** Climb aboard a boat tour and explore the beauty of the ocean or lake. You'll see stunning scenery, wildlife, and maybe even some sites only accessible by water. It's a great way to sit back, relax, and enjoy the ride.
12. **Windsurfing-** Windsurfing is a thrilling water sport that requires skill, balance, and the ability to read the wind. It's exhilarating to harness the wind's power and glide across the water on a surfboard with a sail attached.
13. **Kitesurfing-** Kitesurfing is another exciting water sport that involves using a kite to propel yourself across the water. This sport is a combination of surfing, paragliding, and wakeboarding and provides a unique and adrenaline-fueled experience.
14. **Jet skiing-** Jet skiing is a fast-paced and exciting water activity that involves speeding through the water on a personal watercraft. It's a surefire way to get your adrenaline pumping and explore the waterways.
15. **Water skiing-** A classic water sport that involves being pulled behind a boat while standing on skis. Whether you're a beginner or an experienced skier, water skiing is a great way to get a full-body workout and enjoy the sun and water.
16. **Dive for lobster-** For those who love to dive and explore, diving for lobster is a fun and unique activity. You'll get to experience the beauty of the underwater world and possibly even bring home a delicious treat for dinner.
17. **Outrigger canoeing-** A traditional Hawaiian water sport that involves paddling a canoe with one or more outriggers to provide stability. It's a terrific way to connect with friends, get a workout, and enjoy the scenic beauty of the ocean.

18. **Glow SUP-** This activity involves using a Stand-Up Paddleboard (SUP) that illuminates in the dark. Perfect for calm lakes and bays, this activity offers an exciting way to enjoy the serenity of the water at night. Whether you're an experienced paddler or a beginner, this activity is guaranteed to be an unforgettable experience.

Books

1. Sailing Made Easy by The American Sailing Association ASA link
2. Recreational Kayaking: The Ultimate Guide (Heliconia) Comprehensive Instructional Handbook Covers Equipment, Strokes, Paddling Techniques, Capsize Recovery, Kayak Safety, Paddler's First Aid, & More by Ken Whiting link
3. The Art of Stand Up Paddling: A Complete Guide to SUP on Lakes, Rivers, and Oceans (How to Paddle Series) by Ben Marcus link

* * *

Visit a National Park

Marvel at nature's wonders

I'm a firm believer that travel enhances our lives. It exposes us to new sights, tastes, experiences, people, animals, and ideas that help us grow and feel alive. Visiting one of our country's 63 National Parks is a great way to reconnect with nature and see the places that are so unique or special that they are now protected for future generations.

The diversity of nature within the US Parks system is impressive. From active volcanoes to glaciers, giant sequoias to coral reefs, cascading waterfalls, grand canyons, geysers, massive monolithic rock formations, everglades, and petrified forests, there is so much to see.

. . .

Did you know?

- Yellowstone National Park was the first National Park in 1872.
- 31 states and 2 territories hold our 63 National Parks.
- There are 423 total locations managed by the National Park Service (historic sites, monuments, seashores, cultural heritage, recreation areas, and more).
- 297 million people visited a National Park Service location in 2021.
- At age 62, you can purchase a lifetime pass for $80 or an annual pass for $20.
- Seniors get 50% off campsites within National Parks.
- The National Park Junior Ranger Program awards children with park-specific badges for learning about the park and completing a workbook. Great for when you camp with the grandkids.

Favorite things to do at National Parks

- Photography
- Hiking
- Wildlife Viewing
- Relaxing in Nature
- Kayaking, Canoeing, and Rafting
- Camping
- Backpacking
- Biking
- Snowshoeing
- Climbing
- Stargazing

Top 10 most visited National Parks in 2021

1. Great Smoky Mountains National Park: 14.16 million
2. Zion National Park: 5.03 million
3. Yellowstone National Park: 4.86 million
4. Grand Canyon National Park: 4.53 million
5. Rocky Mountain National Park: 4.43 million
6. Acadia National Park: 4.06 million
7. Grand Teton National Park: 3.88 million
8. Yosemite National Park: 3.28 million
9. Indiana Dunes National Park: 3.17 million
10. Glacier National Park: 3.08 million

Our favorite National Parks ranked

1. Yosemite (California)
2. Zion (Utah)
3. Grand Teton - In fall colors (Wyoming)
4. Rocky Mountain - In the fall (Colorado)
5. Glacier (Montana)
6. Yellowstone (Wyoming)
7. Olympic (Washington)
8. Hawaii Volcanoes (Hawaii)
9. Redwoods (California)
10. Virgin Islands (U.S. Virgin Islands)
11. Sequoia (California)
12. Great Smoky Mtns - In the fall (North Carolina and Tennessee)
13. Grand Canyon (Arizona)
14. Glacier Bay (Alaska)
15. Acadia (Maine)
16. Bryce (Utah)
17. Canyonlands (Utah)
18. Arches (Utah)
19. Haleakala (Hawaii)

20. Everglades (Florida)
21. Joshua Tree (California)
22. Kings Canyon (California)
23. Whitesands (New Mexico)
24. Carlsbad Caverns (New Mexico)
25. Shenandoah (Virginia)

How much does it currently cost?

- A single visit to a National Park can vary from $0 to $35 a vehicle entrance.
- A single-park annual pass ranges from $40 to $70.
- A yearly all-parks pass is $80 per vehicle.
- Senior all-parks pass (age 62+) is $20 annually or $80 for lifetime vehicle entrance.
- Current military, volunteers (250 hours), and 4th graders get free all parks annual passes.
- Permanently disabled, US Military Veterans, and Gold Star families get an all-parks lifetime pass for free.

Go for it! Simple start steps:

1. Learn about the National Parks online or with a book.
2. Plan to camp or stay at a hotel nearby.
3. Make reservations in advance (some parks get very busy and limit entrance).

Resources

1. List of all National Parks in the US by State link
2. Find Your Park link
3. The NPS app link
4. The 10 Most Visited US National Parks 2021 link

Books

1. Complete National Parks of the US by National Geographic link
2. Your Guide to the National Parks by Michael Oswald link
3. US National Parks by Becky Lomax link

Products

1. Hiking Backpack link
2. Waterproof Picnic Blanket link
3. Bear Spray link
4. National Parks Scratch Off Map link

Pairs well with: RV travel, photography, camping

You might also like: State parks, fishing, kayaking

* * *

E-biking

Get into nature, extend your range, and fear no hill

E-biking (electric-powered bikes) can change a retiree's everyday life for the better. It's an excellent choice for those looking to stay fit and healthy. The low-impact activity allows you to enjoy the outdoors, stimulate your mind, and contribute to a healthier environment. Plus, it's a fun and popular activity that can be tailored to any level of intensity. You can build up your stamina, strength, and aerobic fitness as you progress.

Sometimes, the terrain or your fitness level can make traditional biking a little too challenging. One big hill in your path can turn a fun ride into a physically demanding nightmare! Hills can limit your range, keep you boxed in around your house, or stop you from riding altogether out of fear of this discomfort or getting stuck somewhere.

Electric-powered bikes change everything! Now widely available and becoming more affordable, these normal-looking bikes with a battery pack and silent electric motor are your ticket to freedom. Depending on the model, they can help tackle steep hills and even provide assistance for a 35+ mile range. E-bikes can be peddled like regular bikes with no assistance on flat areas or when wanting a workout. On gradual inclines, you can choose the level of assistance to make things easier or use the throttle only and cruise without any effort!

E-bikes unlock your freedom to explore without fear, regardless of your level of fitness or mobility!

Health benefits of biking regularly[7]

- Improved cardiovascular fitness
- Decreased stress, anxiety, and depression
- Improved joint mobility
- Improved balance, posture, and coordination
- Decreased body fat
- Improved muscle strength and flexibility
- Reduces cardiovascular diseases such as heart attack, high blood pressure, and stroke

It had been a long time since I had ridden a bike when my father asked me to join him and his friend on his weekly e-bike ride. Every Wednesday morning, they choose one of their favorite routes around the city and along the coast. It's a chance to meet up, ride, socialize, and of course, stop for a donut and coffee along the way. I was a little skeptical of the higher-than-normal price tag ($1000+) for just a bike, so I wanted to see what it was all about.

Their chosen route was along the San Diego coast from Carlsbad to Torrey Pines and back. We rode south in the bike lane with fantastic ocean views from the cliffs, and it didn't take long before I started to remember how fun it was to be outside riding my bike as a kid. We stopped to watch some dolphins and pelicans in the distance before heading down the last steep hill. My father and his friend zoomed down the long hill at an incredible speed, and I tried to keep up as the wind blasted my face. It was thrilling as we coasted down the 200-foot descent to the beach.

I couldn't remember the last time I rode down a long hill because I'd have to suffer the climb back up when we eventually turned around! I was a little nervous to see how we were going to get home because this was a massive hill that I wouldn't be able to climb without walking, even though I was in decent shape. After some time at the beach, we headed back. To my amazement, we built up speed and actually went up faster than we raced down! When we finished, our bikes' odometer read 33 miles, and it was the most fun I've had in a long time. I was sold.

Did you know?

- 40% of work commuters in Amsterdam use bikes.
- E-bikes popularity is skyrocketing, with a 50% increase from 200 million in circulation in 2019 to 300 million by 2023.
- E-bikes can go up to 28 mph.
- E-bikes can save hundreds of dollars a year on gas. A vehicle that gets 20 mpg and $5 per gallon gas costs 25 cents per mile to drive. On one e-bike ride up to 35 miles, the gas saving would be $8.75 alone!
- E-bike stores typically sell very expensive bikes ($2,000-$5,000).
- Popular quality manufacturers such as Rad Power Bikes, Lectric, Ride 1 Up, and Aventon sell online and ship direct to your home for much less ($1200+).

Too old to ride?

Think again. Since their development in the 1800s, bicycles have remained essentially unchanged. Lightweight two-wheel designs for maximum human power efficiency reigned. Now, with electric power assistance, new designs are emerging since weight is no longer a primary consideration. Large cargo utility bikes can hold up to three children, additional large riders, the family pet, and even capacity for large loads such as groceries.

Concerned with your balance?

Don't be. Ride confidently on a stable 3-wheel electric trike such as the Rad Power Bikes, RadTrike. With a 415-pound payload capacity and a 55+ mile range, it's a clean energy machine that can handle all your neighborhood errands without the cost of gas. If mobility is an issue, e-bikes significantly extend your range beyond walking, giving you back the freedom to explore at your pace.

E-bikes and RVs are the perfect pair.

Several years ago, when our children were very little, we set off on a quest to see the United States by motorhome. They were at the age where after a few minutes of walking with their little legs, they'd want to be carried. Our range of exploring a new area on foot would be very short, and pushing a stroller everywhere would also be cumbersome and limiting. We decided to bring a pair of cargo-style e-bikes where the kids could ride with us, and we'd have more room to bring things like picnic baskets and extra jackets. Great decision.

The e-bikes became an unexpected highlight of our trip. Instead of things inevitably breaking down after short walks, we now had the freedom to explore a range of 35+ miles! We'd take off for the day from campgrounds or available parking far from the action and go anywhere we wanted in a new area. We'd stop at parks and attractions that we ran into and take things at our own pace without worrying about getting around or what hills we might run into. Scenic bike paths around National Parks like the Grand Tetons or city sightseeing in places like San Francisco were equally enjoyable because of the mobility provided by the e-bikes.

Many people choose to tow a vehicle behind their RV to go where big motorhomes can't. In many ways, e-bikes can replace these toads and give more options to get around, such as on trails or bike paths. For us, our RV and e-bikes were the perfect pair. If you travel in an RV with a pet, you may find that bringing an e-bike with you is a great way to take your furry friend along on your daily adventures.

It's easy to get started with e-biking.

Sometimes picking up a new hobby requires a lot of learning before you can start having fun. E-biking does not. Just get a bike and explore!

It's easy to get caught up in trying to learn all the technical performance details and options when shopping for an e-bike and become overwhelmed. Considerations like voltage (36 or 48), watts (500, 750, 1000), controller amps (peak and sustained), battery capacity (shown as either amp hours or watt hours), motor (hub or mid), torque (nm), class (1-3), price, style, size, weight, and more can make your head spin.

Sometimes it's just easier to ask a friend what they decided to go with and if they're happy with it. After lots of research and hundreds of hours of weekly riding, below is what my father went with (and he loves it). His decision was based on the best price and performance for an average rider but could help you as a baseline to go off of when evaluating other models.

Good Value Starter E-bike

Brand: Ride1UP

Model: Core-5

Price: $1,045 (current 2023 price)

Specs: 48 volts (v), 750 watts (w) sustained geared hub motor with 60-newton meters (nm) torque. 48 v/12.8 amp hour (ah) battery estimated at 25-45 miles range, depending on rider weight, terrain, incline, level of assistance, etc. 48 volt/ 22 amp class 3 controller with a potential peak output of 1000 watts. Mechanical disc brakes. 7 speed Shimano derailleur. 49 lbs with a 300 lbs weight capacity.

Website: www.ride1up.com

Note: Sold online and delivered (in North America only) for you to assemble or hire a local shop to assemble.

Another popular brand (the one I use) is Rad Power Bikes. They are highly rated and use a similar direct-to-consumer sales model to keep costs low. They are slightly more expensive, have higher performance, and even have a few showrooms in select west coast cities where you can test-ride all the models.

Tip: Whatever you choose, I'd recommend getting an e-bike with a powerful 750-watt motor. Although you can save a few hundred dollars by getting a smaller one, the peace of mind of knowing you can get over just about any hill you may come across is worth it.

Bike Rack

To go anywhere other than around your neighborhood, you'll need an e-bike rack (rated for the weight of your e-bike). Since my father rides every week at different starting locations, he keeps a two e-bike hitch rack on the back of his car. It folds up compactly when not being used and down to about two feet above the ground when needed for loading. An arm holds the bike tire and frame during transport. It's extremely easy to use, requiring only about 60 seconds and a short lift to load and unload. For infrequent use, the whole rack easily slips in and out of your car's hitch. Have U-haul or a similar business install one if you don't have a hitch on your vehicle. See the below resources section for the link to the model rack he uses, but you'll need one specific for your chosen bike and vehicle.

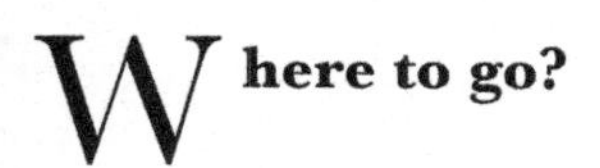

Where to go?

After buying an e-bike, your next question will be, where can you go? Aside from around your neighborhood, here's how you can find new routes.

- Google Maps cycle paths- Download the app on your phone or go to Google Maps on your computer, click on the "layers" square-looking icon in the corner, and choose the "biking" option under "map details." This reveals all available bike paths, lanes, and trails! Additionally, selecting the "cycling" option when getting Google Maps directions routes you on those bike paths, gives estimated time, and shows the vertical terrain along your ride.
- An online search of "top bike routes in [your city]" reveals many websites showing the best routes in your area, usually with points of interest and photos.
- Bikemap.net (free) has user-created bike route ideas around the world as well as in your neighborhood.
- Alltrails.com and Alltrails app (free) lets you find routes for all kinds of activities. Sort by "road biking" to see where to go next and even get turn-by-turn GPS navigation along the way!

Go for it! Simple start steps:

1. Learn a little about the features and available e-bike models online.
2. Google search for nearby e-bike stores. Visit a few to test-ride different types and ask questions to understand what features you really need.
3. Comparison shop online to decide on a bike. Purchase and enjoy!

Resources

1. E-bike facts and statistics link

2. Consumer reports e-bike buying guide link
3. Route ideas link

Products

1. Ride1UP, Core-5 e-bike (performance and value) link
2. Rad Power Bikes, RadTrike Electric Tricycle link
3. Rocky Mounts, Monorail 2 bike foldable hitch rack link

Books

1. Epic bike rides of the Americas by Lonely Planet link
2. Epic bike rides of Europe by Lonely Planet link
3. Ride: Cycle the World by DK link

Pairs well with: Travel, motorhomes, picnicking

You might also like: Motorcycle riding, mountain biking, road cycling

* * *

Photography

See the world through a different lens

If there is one hobby I'd recommend for someone to try, it is photography for many reasons.

7 Reasons to Start Photography

1. **It heightens our awareness of the beauty all around us.** After getting into photography, I started noticing beautiful things more because I was consciously looking for them to photograph. When I see unique buildings or sculptures while on travel, a beautiful sky, or a standout flower in a field, in the past I might have simply

just passed by without a second thought, but now I stop to appreciate it and think about how it would make a great photo. A photography mindset will pull you into the present moment and help you see the world differently.

2. **You're capturing memories to enjoy again later.** The older we get, things get a little fuzzy remembering the past. Photos remind us of those good times with the people and places we've been. Also, our digital memories will live on with our loved ones to remember us when our story has ended.
3. **It's active and body-strengthening.** There is only so much you can photograph around the house before you're ready to go out and explore to find the things you're interested in. You might not even notice the exercise you're getting as you walk around searching for the perfect picture.
4. **It's creative and mind-strengthening**. There are endless possibilities of what you can photograph, how to compose the shot in the frame, what technical parameters to set on your camera for effect (aperture/speed/exposure/depth of field), and creative ways to process and display your work.
5. **It's spirit-strengthening**. It's fulfilling to capture the things we love and are passionate about. Whether you're into travel, nature, sports, family, art, or people, photography will enhance the experience.
6. **It's a very low-cost hobby.** Remember when you needed to buy film and pay for print processing? Those days are gone, with digital photography costing nothing to snap away to your heart's content. Decent starter interchangeable lens cameras (DSLR and mirrorless) are inexpensive, and even the latest camera phones take amazing photos (you might not need to buy anything you don't already have).
7. **It's a gateway to a world of new possibilities.** There are many avenues to explore with a photography hobby. Some include sports photography, selling photos online, wedding or portraits, art exhibitions, HDR (high dynamic range) photography, tilt-shift, 360-degree,

stereoscopic (3D), aerial (drones), photo book creation, memory wall creation, lenticular, macro, architectural, landscape, wildlife, travel, photojournalism, videography, digital art, and social media.

While you could undoubtedly dive into learning (and possibly become overwhelmed by) all the gear choices, the technical and artistic side of taking photos, and how to process or display your images, you don't have to at the start. You could use the camera you already have, pick up a beginner's photography book, and get outside to see what you can find to photograph right now.

What camera do you need?

The best digital camera for you will depend on what or where you plan to shoot. Below is an overview of each significant camera style:

1. **Mirrorless**- The best. These interchangeable lens cameras are similar in style and quality to DSLR (digital single-lens reflex) cameras, but they have the advantage of being slightly more compact because they don't have a mirror in them as DSLRs do. Since you'll be able to change the lens to fit your application, interchangeable lens cameras will not fit in your pocket.
2. **DSLR**- Still great. When photography first went digital, this body style continued the mirrored film body mechanics. Camera manufacturers merely switched a digital sensor for where the film was. This older technology is slightly larger than mirrorless and less expensive but is similar in quality. It's a great, budget-friendly, interchangeable lens starter camera.
3. **Compact**- Travel-friendly. The advantage of compact cameras is that they are small and pocketable because the lens retracts into the body. Also, they can have a relatively decent optical zoom. The disadvantage is the image quality isn't as good as larger cameras, and some models don't allow

as many creative controls (aperture, speed, focus points, etc.).

4. **Camera phone**- Always there. A few years ago, camera phones were more of a novelty than a proper quality camera for photography. Things have changed. Despite their tiny size (usually bigger is better quality), phone manufacturers have leveraged the advantages of having a built-in minicomputer to process and improve the photos. This "computational photography" can now blur the background, analyze a scene, adjust the exposure for different areas, and make a photo look nearly as good as a big high-end camera. The convenience of always being with you, the big display to review your photos, and the ease of sharing are significant advantages. Unfortunately, the optical zoom and creative controls are limited, and fine landscape details are much softer than larger cameras.

If you're considering purchasing a new camera, it's worth doing a quick primer on basic photography to get a better feel for the technical intricacies that affect quality. Besides sensor size, other factors are pixel size, megapixel resolution, optical image stabilization (OIS), in-body image stabilization (IBIS), lens mounts, exposure, crop factor, shutter speed, f/stop aperture, depth of field, image noise, battery life, focus points, dynamic range, ISO, RAW, and print size.

Even if you're not interested in diving into photography as a hobby, chances are you snap a few pictures from time to time. Your everyday photos will be greatly enhanced if you take a few minutes to learn photography basics and shooting tips (rule of thirds, lighting, composition, focal length considerations, leading lines, colors interest, etc.).

Where will your hobby take you?

Sometimes hobbies can grow into something more. My wife and I decided to pick up photography after not being overly thrilled with our wedding photos. Despite working a full-time office job, learning photography unlocked a world of experiences I never imagined.

We started a portrait and wedding photography side business and captured memories for people on their special day. We had some fun with sports photography and were hired to take photos at marathon events around the world. We also turned a hobby of 360-degree photography into a business, creating "street view" photography tours for local businesses, including a small theme park in the area. I even decided to get my commercial remote pilot's license from the FAA when I considered moving into aerial drone photography. Besides new business opportunities, photography enhanced our travel experiences and family memories.

Go for it! Simple start steps:

1. Read about photography basics and tips for beginners.
2. Learn how to use the settings for your camera (owner's manual or online).
3. Go out and experiment (tweak some settings and see how your photo is affected).

Resources

1. Photography basics link
2. Photography tips for beginners link
3. Camera sensor size explained link
4. Detailed camera reviews and comparisons link

Products

1. One of the best professional cameras right now. Canon EOS R3 link
2. Great beginner to intermediate camera. Nikon D3500 link
3. A top affordable compact travel zoom camera. Panasonic Lumix ZS200 link

Books

1. The Digital Photography Book by Scott Kelby link
2. National Geographic Photo Basics by Joel Sartore link
3. Stunning Digital Photography by Tony Northrup link
4. Digital Photography Complete Course by David Taylor link

Pairs well with: Travel, hiking, social media, entrepreneurship

You might also like: Drawing, painting, videography, graphic design

Chapter 5

Explore the World

Being at home is fine and dandy for a small amount of time, but if you're like me, it doesn't take long before the desire to get out and explore starts screaming for freedom and new experiences. Stepping out into the unknown is where we're exposed to new people, places, food, cultures, ideas, and experiences that help us feel connected to the world and broaden our life experiences. It's the antidote to routine mindless boredom. It can be equally exciting and stimulating as it can be challenging and scary.

Travel is Life

For some, travel is life. Magnified. Enlarged. Expanded. Experienced. Lived. It's realizing there are so many possibilities. So many different ways and places people live their lives. It's constantly challenging what we think we know from what we have been taught and being thankful for the opportunity to do so. It's doing anything we want, anytime we want. It's a lifetime of new memories crammed into every moment.

. . .

Travel is More Accessible Than Ever

It's incredible that in all of history, only in the last century, humans can now be nearly anywhere in the world in a matter of hours. Instead of months at sea or difficult and perhaps dangerous overland journeys, we can be just about anywhere we choose in almost no time.

To me, that's amazing.

We're lucky to be living in this time in history. The world is smaller and more accessible than ever, especially to those of us who have been blessed to be born in a developed country with a favorable exchange rate.

Travel is Easier Than Ever

Not long ago, there were no cell phones with GPS guiding us to unfamiliar places, apps to beckon a driver in minutes no matter where we were, online travel planning sites and booking platforms, or vacation rental sites that make staying longer more affordable. These advancements have made travel more convenient, efficient, and accessible for people all over the world.

6 Reasons to Travel

1. **Personal growth-** Traveling exposes us to new cultures, ways of life, and perspectives, which can help us to expand our understanding of the world and ourselves.
2. **Education-** Learn about the history of the places you visit, natural wonders, and diverse traditions as you travel.
3. **Improved health-** Traveling can positively impact our physical and mental health. It can help us to reduce stress, improve our mood, and boost our immune system.

4. **Relaxation and stress relief-** It can help us to escape the daily routine, clear our minds, and recharge our batteries. Whether a beach vacation or a mountain hike, getting away from it all can be a great way to relax and unwind.
5. **Adventure and excitement-** Traveling allows us to step out of our comfort zones and experience new and exciting things. It can be a great way to try new foods, activities, and hobbies and to make memories that will last a lifetime.
6. **Building connections-** Traveling can be a great way to meet new people and connect with other cultures. It can be a way to make friends and learn about different ways of life.

Overall, traveling is an opportunity to learn, grow, and make meaningful connections. It can help us to gain a new perspective, appreciate what we have, and make the most of our time on this earth.

Chapter 5 Website Links

* * *

Take a Cruise

Effortlessly see the world without flying or hotels

There's a reason why cruising is so popular. It's awesome! Do yourself a favor, book a cruise, and just show up. That's it. The fun will follow. It's that easy.

. . .

10 reasons why cruising is wonderful

1. **It's super easy.** Travel planning can be a headache and intimidating, figuring out where to go, how to get there, what to do, where to stay, how to get around, what to eat, and a million other little details. Cruising takes care of everything, so you can worry about having a great time.
2. **It's a very comfortable way to travel.** Want to see many new places but aren't incredibly excited about airplanes or long bus rides to get there? When cruising, you put your head on a pillow, wake up, and you're there. Easy peasy.
3. **It's full of entertainment.** Modern cruise ships are floating resorts of fun by themselves. There is usually nightly entertainment, pools, spas, saunas, exercise areas, sports areas, yoga classes, dancing, games, waterslides, educational lectures, outdoor movies, art classes, special parties, events, and a lot more. You'd probably still have a good time if you never stepped off the ship to see new sights.
4. **Food.** Most cruises include your meals. You can sample a little of everything at the buffet, sit down for a formal dinner, or pay a little extra to dine at one of the other restaurants onboard, such as a steakhouse.
5. **Views.** Taking in the coastal or ocean views from a lounge chair on the upper deck or your private balcony is a relaxing and enjoyable experience.
6. **Social opportunities.** Cruising allows one to meet people from around the country and the world. You'll meet people at the dinner table, by the pool, at activities, or during social events.
7. **Visit exotic destinations.** Some cruises stop at port cities all around the world. Step off your floating oasis, and you could be immersed in a new foreign culture for the day and safely return to the familiarity of your ship that evening. Don't worry about not knowing the local language in Asia or

the Middle East's social customs to get around. Join a shore excursion tour, and you'll visit the best of an area without the stress.

8. **A mix of adventure and relaxation.** Depending on your preferred travel style and mood, you can fill your days with sightseeing, activities, and events or simply lounge by the pool with a frosty beverage. Cruises are the perfect place for both.
9. **Good value.** Cruising is a great deal when you add up the costs it would take to visit several cities or countries on a multi-day vacation independently. For one price, you get your hotel, transportation, entertainment, and all-you-can-eat food three times a day!
10. **A cure for boredom.** Without the daily workplace stimulation, it's easy to fall into the same daily routines and need something different now and again. A cruise is the perfect temporary escape, providing so many new experiences to take part in you'll have a tough time being bored. You'll return with new memories to share and most likely start dreaming about your next cruise destination!

There are three main considerations when getting started cruising.

1. Where to go?
2. What ship to go on?
3. What's my Budget?

1 - Where to go?

This might not be a surprise, but there are cruises that go...... everywhere (on water)! Oceans, rivers, lakes and even land (canals) are possible by ship. So start thinking about where you'd like to visit, and if there is water nearby, you can probably get there on a cruise. Here are some ideas to get your travel dreams flowing.

Ocean cruises:

Mediterranean, Caribbean, Alaska, Asia, Baltic, South Pacific, Mexico, UK, North America, Hawaiian Islands, Galapagos Islands, trans-Atlantic, trans-pacific, South America, Seychelles Islands, Philippines Islands, Micronesia, Arabian Gulf, North Africa, Panama Canal, Ha Long Bay Vietnam, Antarctica, and more.

River cruises:

Europe- Rhine River through Switzerland, France, Germany, and Holland. Danube River through Austria, Bulgaria, Croatia, Germany, Hungary, Romania, Slovakia, Serbia, and Ukraine. Volga River through Russia. Douro River through Spain and Portugal.

Asia- Mekong River through China, Burma, Laos, Vietnam, Cambodia, and Thailand. Yangtze River through China. Kerala Backwaters and Brahmaputra River through India.

South America- Amazon River through Brazil, Peru, and Colombia.

USA- Mississippi River.

Africa- Nile River through Egypt. Cuando River through Botswana, Namibia, Zimbabwe, and Zambia.

Lake cruises:

It's possible to take an overnight cruise along some of the larger lakes in the world, like North America's Great Lakes.

2 - What ship to go on?

Size Considerations:

There's truly something for everyone when it comes to cruise ship styles. The largest cruise ship in the world, Royal Caribbean's "Wonder of the Seas" holds nearly 7,000 passengers and offers oversized luxuries and the selections of a small floating city. You'll also find more intimate ships of all sizes going down to small river boats and even hired private yachts if you want to get away from everyone.

Company Considerations:

Certain cruise ships cater to different clientele, and the onboard entertainment and activities reflect that. For instance, Disney Cruises caters to Disney fans and families. Virgin Voyages, and many others, are adult-only. Princess caters to an older clientele, with an average passenger age of 57. Carnival targets family fun budget-conscious customers with onboard rollercoasters and sky rides. Doing a little homework on the companies to understand which might be the best fit for you will go a long way.

Specialty:

There are a variety of smaller location-specific cruise choices. "Expedition" cruise companies focus on a specific experience, such as traveling to more remote and hard-to-reach places like Antarctica, Galapagos Islands, and the Arctic. Several companies focus on river cruises, such as Viking. And finally, you'll run into local companies that only serve small markets like cruising on the Nile River.

Largest Fleets for North American Travelers (by passenger capacity)[8]

- Royal Caribbean: 25 ships; 88,307 berths.
- Carnival Cruise Line: 24 ships; 71,434 berths.
- MSC Cruises: 19 ships; 63,262 berths.
- Norwegian Cruise Line: 17 ships; 50,581 berths.
- Princess Cruises: 14 ships; 42,156 berths.
- Celebrity Cruises: 14 ships; 23,473 berths.
- Holland America: 11 ships; 22,810 berths.

Largest Cruise Companies in the World (by 2021 revenue)[8]

- Mediterranean Shipping Company: $28.2 billion, 1.4 million passengers (MSC Cruises, includes Shipping division)
- Carnival Corp: $1.9 billion, 5.8 million passengers (Carnival, Princess, Holland America, Windstar, Seabourn Cruise lines, and more)
- Royal Caribbean: $1.5 billion, 3.3 million passengers (Royal Caribbean, Celebrity Cruises, Silversea Cruises)
- NCLH: 17 ships; $.6 billion, 1.3 million passengers (Norwegian Cruise Lines, Oceania Cruises, Regent Seven Seas Cruises)

Luxury Cruise Companies

- Regent Seven Seas Cruises
- Silversea Cruises
- Seabourn
- Hapag-Lloyd Cruises
- Ritz-Carlton Yacht Collection

3 - What's my budget?

Duration:

Obviously, the longer the trip, the more expensive the total trip will usually cost. However, the per night price of longer cruises can be significantly less than on short cruises. When shopping for cruises online, consider sorting the results by per night cost, and you might find some unbeatable deals. One-way repositioning cruises, where a ship travels into a new area of the world for the season, can provide the best bang for your buck. Our first cruise was a budget change of port cruise crossing the Atlantic from Puerto Rico to Malaga, Spain, on Royal Caribbean. During the crossing, the extra time at sea allowed us to take advantage of the ship's amenities, and we were hooked. For those lucky few with more money than they know what to do with it, consider multi-month around-the-world cruises, or better yet, buy your own berth on a cruise ship. For less than an apartment in most places, you'll own a room on a cruise ship, enjoy all the perks of cruise ships (food, entertainment, gym), and travel the world simultaneously.

Class:

Ships usually fall into three categories- Mainstream, Premium, and Luxury. You might visit the same ports of call, but the cruise ship you get there on can cost significantly more or less than others.

Location:

Generally, "expedition" style cruises to remote locations are the most expensive, river cruises are less expensive, and ocean cruises are the least costly. This is not a hard-fast rule, however. Smaller local cruise companies booked directly can be very inexpensive. For instance, we found a wonderful budget river cruise on the Nile, booked a multi-day junk boat tour around Halong Bay through our hotel, and shopped around with local tour operators to get the best deal on an Amazon River cruise.

Reservations:

When planning your trip, there are strategies you can use to stretch your dollar and get the best deal to fit your budget.

How to get the most bang for your cruise buck

1. **Choose to sail off-season** (September, October, November, January, and February). Avoid high season and the periods around major holidays.
2. **Book super early.** Often when cruise lines first open departure bookings (sometimes 2-3 years out), they offer the lowest prices and then slowly raise the rates as the sail date nears.
3. **Look for last-minute deals.** If you're flexible and can travel on short notice, ships sometimes offer significantly discounted rates to fill berths just before departure. Don't

count on waiting for a specific cruise to go on sale, but if you sign up for deal alerts, you might score a deal and end up somewhere wonderfully unexpected.

4. **Sail on an older ship.** The older vessels won't come with all the amenities like newer, more in-demand ones, but they usually come with a discount.
5. **Comparison shop.** Sometimes the best deals come from cruise-focused travel agents with access to bulk rates. It's wise to consider all your options to avoid missing out on a great deal.
6. **Look for a repositioning cruise.** When cruise ships reposition from one part of the world to another because of the season, they offer some of the best deals you'll find anywhere. Look for sailings between the Caribbean and Europe in the spring and between Europe and the Caribbean in the fall. Other seasonal repositionings are between the Caribbean and Alaska, as well as the US west coast and Asia.

Go for it! Simple start steps:

1. Search online for cruise destinations you're interested in.
2. Learn about the available cruise ship styles and amenities.
3. Comparison shop to book the best deal.

Resources

1. Top Cruise Lines in the World link
2. 8 Most Popular Cruise Ships Compared link
3. Best Cruise Lines for the money link
4. Which Cruise Brand is Best for You link
5. Royal Caribbean World Destinations link
6. 11 Around the World Cruises link
7. Adult Only Cruise Lines link
8. 15 Largest Cruise Lines in the World link

Books

1. Mediterranean Cruise Ports by Rick Steves link
2. Caribbean Cruise Ports of Call by Fodor's link
3. Cruise Ports of European Rivers by Lonely Planet link
4. The Complete Guide to Alaska Cruises by Fodor's link

Products

1. Top Compact Travel Camera link
2. Travel Daypack Sling link
3. Compact Binoculars link

Pairs well with: Land tours, photography, foodies

You might also like: Rail journeys, around-the-world cruises, RV travel

* * *

Motorhome/ RV Travel

Explore the county at your pace and with the comforts of home

RVing is the ultimate in travel freedom! One of the first things every newly retired person should do is take advantage of their hard earned freedom and experience this amazingly diverse country. As a full-time RVer who's looped the country for two years on two separate adventures, the RVing experiences have been one of my life's highlights. And it can be for you, too! When it comes to slow, long-term travel, there is no better way to go.

11 Reasons Why You Might Love RVing

1. **Comfort-** Rather than living out of a suitcase in expensive or questionable hotels, you can bring a comfortable little apartment with you. Depending on the model, RV's can

have a refrigerator, freezer, toilet, shower, bed, table, multiple TVs, lots of storage for just about anything, appliances, stove, oven, heater, air conditioning, couches, recliners, and even washing machines. They can slide open on the sides to significantly increase the living space and some have elevated outside decks that swing down to hang out on.

2. **Convenience-** Did I mention you'll have just about anything you need within a few steps? Never worry about finding a restaurant, toilet, or hotel. Wherever you are, you can pull over in a parking lot to make lunch, use the restroom, or even take a nap!
3. **Access to nature-** Some campgrounds are unforgettable. We've woken up to see a family of deer going about their business just outside our window in the Grand Canyon and listened to the mating calls of elk at night while sitting around a campfire at the Rocky Mountain National Park. We've come close to wildlife like bison, moose, bears, bighorn sheep, armadillos, manatees, bald eagles, pronghorns, tortoises, and more.
4. **National Park and State Parks-** You could spend years exploring these treasures, and RV campgrounds take you right into the action for most. Stay for a week and hike, fish, bike, spot animals, see waterfalls, watch sunsets, capture photography, and truly get the feel of each park's uniqueness.
5. **Save money-** Within a few weeks of packing up our house and hitting the road full-time, we were surprised to find out that we were spending less and doing much more than at home. Fixed home expenses like rent/mortgage, electricity, gas, water, HOAs, property tax, home or renters insurance, television, second car insurance/registration, and internet are gone for long-term travel. Gas is a significant new expense, but if you spend a week or two in one spot, campgrounds are much less expensive than hotels, and there are no fuel expenses when you're not moving around. *See the actual costs

section below for a breakdown of our expenses for each RV trip.

6. **Unlock new experiences-** We've RV camped between the vines at a winery, enjoying the sunset with a bottle of wine we selected earlier that day during a wine tasting. We stayed on a farm near animals and went strawberry picking. We watched giant iguanas play and jump from trees into a lake next to our campsite. We've dry camped (no electric or water hookup) for free a few feet from the ocean and enjoyed complete silence surrounded by nature on BLM (Bureau of Land Management) public lands miles from other people. We stayed in the snowy Colorado mountains (Tiger Run Resort, Breckenridge) and enjoyed a season pass to the nearby ski resorts.
7. **Enjoy complete freedom-** Go anywhere you want, do anything you like, and stay as long as you enjoy yourself. Really. The first time we hit the road, all we had planned was a rough direction of travel (a counter-clockwise loop) around the US. We figured out the rest along the way by stopping at visitors centers, dry-camping (free overnight parking) when needed, and adjusting our route and length of stay with almost no advance reservations.
8. **It's social-** There is a subculture of fun-loving retired RV travelers who have been roaming for years and love to share travel stories. Some RV resorts are for ages 55+ only and have regular social activities. Check out the calendar of events and show up at the clubhouse for a game of pool volleyball, pickleball, shuffleboard, music nights, BBQs, outdoor movie nights, wine tastings, or local hikes. Most RVers are a social bunch, and it's customary to get to know your neighbor. They frequently sit outside to enjoy the sunset with a relaxing beverage, and it's not uncommon to be invited to an informal meet-up around someone's bonfire to share a few drinks.
9. **It's active-** Living is a verb, an action. The best part of life is experiencing all we can while we're able to. RVing isn't a sedentary lifestyle. You'll be out actively exploring new

places and doing new things. The rest of the time, you'll be strengthening your mind while planning where to go, how to get there, and what to do next. You'll enjoy your favorite outdoor activities (hiking, fishing, golf, kayaking, biking, etc.) in the best locations with a mobile RV lifestyle.

10. **It's a minimalist lifestyle-** Living with only the essentials (for the most part) is very freeing. Gone are the clutter, maintenance, additional costs, and time drain on things that don't really matter. What is left is less stress, more time, more independence, fewer distractions, and ultimately a happier existence while focusing on doing what you love rather than what you have.
11. **It's an adventure-** Most RVers love to travel and explore. They have the confidence to overcome challenges and live an unconventional lifestyle to experience new adventures. They'll escape the monotony of daily routines and eventually return with fond memories and grand stories to tell.

How much does it cost?

Like most things in life, RVing can be made to fit a tight budget, or you can go crazy, and it can cost a fortune.

Vehicle ($8,000-$2,500,000): Seriously. There are multimillion-dollar coaches and inexpensive van conversions. Our first RV was a $9,000 14-year-old fixer-upper that needed a new roof. It took us through 37 states and 20,000 miles around the US just fine. Get out there with whatever you can afford now, and don't wait for life to pass you by!

Registration & insurance (varies): It will depend on your state, driving record, and your RV's cost. However, it's similar to what you can expect to pay for a typical vehicle at home.

Additional Vehicle Costs (varies): Other potential RV costs include a pre-purchase inspection ($300-500), new tires ($400 each), maintenance, or necessary fixes to get on the road. RV dealers and most RV repair shops think RVers are all millionaires and charge unbelievable rates to fix anything. Plan to do a little YouTube DIY research, get handy where possible, and you'll save hundreds.

Our full-time RV living expenses: We kept a detailed spreadsheet of everything we spent traveling around the US. This should help you get an idea of what to expect if you hit the road full-time. However, your travel style will be different, so it is a good idea to do your own budgeting estimates and track your spending as you go.

Van Life Style Daily Averages:

$100 Total Per Day ($3,000 per month)

$36 Fuel (7 mpg, 34' Class-A RV, 20,000 miles, $3.56/gal ave)

$30 Food (2 adults)

$9 Fun Activities

$6 RV Expenses (propane, water, sewer, maintenance, etc.)

$5 Sleep (mostly free dry-camping)

$8 Shopping

$3 Communications (phone, internet, etc.)

$3 Dog stuff

The above breakdown is our average daily cost for two people and a dog from roughly a year on the road. The nightly rate was very low because we rarely paid for campgrounds or RV parks. Except for a little time in the mountains, we chose to stealth camp (quietly find an overnight parking space somewhere) wherever we ended up after a day of exploring. We were younger and moved around a lot, taking advantage of what is now considered "van life" to save money and keep flexible. Since our 34' Fleetwood Southwind was relatively self-contained with solar panels for electricity, a generator for microwave, gas stove, oven, heater, water, and holding tank capacity for 7-10 days, we didn't see the point of paying $30+ a night for a place to park at a campground. This fast-paced, move-everyday style is draining after a while and misses some of the best parts of RVing. Slowing down and taking in a good campground for a few days to a week will recharge your spirits and is well worth the nightly rate.

Family Fun Daily Averages:

$123 Total Per Day ($3,690 per month)

$51 Food (2 adults and 2 small children)

$28 Fuel (7.6 mpg, 33' Class-A RV, 17,000 miles, $3.68/gal ave)

$20 Shopping

$11 Sleep (campgrounds, RV parks, membership discounts, etc.)

$7 RV Expenses (propane, water, sewer, maintenance, etc.)

$4 Fun Activities

$2 Communications (phone, internet, etc.)

The above breakdown is our second full-time RV trip around the US, but we now had two small children with us including a dog. The averages are for four people traveling for roughly a year. With kids, we choose a much slower pace, staying at campgrounds and RV parks. We kept the nightly rate lower than you might expect with a year membership to Thousand Trails (TT) (see resources below for the website). It allowed us to stay free for up to two weeks at almost any of their 200+ properties around the US. Factoring the yearly membership cost and the nights we stayed free, it worked out to $8 per night. We used TT as little rest stops to recharge while passing through but found that the locations are slightly out of the way of most points of interest. We also had a year membership to Harvest Host (HH), where we stayed on a business's property (farm, vineyard, brewery, golf course, restaurant, etc.) for free with a recommended purchase of something. This made for some incredible experiences and, usually, last-minute stops when we needed a place to stay. Factoring in the HH membership and our purchases at the business, it worked out to $36 per night.

. . .

Budgeting Note:

Our above totals are for traveling thrifty, occasionally splurging when we felt it was worth it. Break down the major spending categories to get a more accurate estimate specific to your situation and lifestyle.

1. **Food-** Track your average spending on food before leaving and add a little bit because you'll find yourself wanting to eat out more than usual. Sampling the local cuisine is half the fun of travel!
2. **Fuel-** Step 1- Look up the average MPG of your RV or one you're considering buying. Step 2- Get your estimated mileage using Google Maps for the general route you're considering. Step 3- Google search for the average gas price in the US, state, or city. It's usually updated daily. Or use the GasBuddy app to get current prices along your route. Step 4- Calculate your estimated distance divided by your vehicle's MPG and multiply it by the average gas price to get a reasonably close fuel estimate.
3. **Sleep-** Decide where you'd like to spend most of your nights. BLM (designated public lands usually in the middle of nowhere), stealth camping in neighborhoods, some casinos, and other business parking lots are free. State and county campgrounds are generally the least expensive ($15-$35+). Basic campgrounds are ($25-$50+). National Parks and better campgrounds vary widely depending on the season and location, but if you're looking for a ballpark, say ($35-$75+). RV "resorts" differ widely based on amenities ($35-$150+). Weekly or monthly rates can lower your average, but try to estimate how many nights in a month you'll be in each accommodation class. Then add the total, divide by 30, and multiply by the length of your trip. *Tip: Seniors can receive a 50% discount on campsites at National Parks.

4. **Highlights-** Think about what you'll be doing and visiting. Price out the bigger stuff like local attractions, tours, museums, and weekly equipment rentals, then add a cushion for the unexpected.

Types of RVs

There are pros and cons to each RV style, so ultimately, the best RV is the one that fits what you plan on doing. Remember that RVing is about the experiences it unlocks, not the vehicle itself.

Class A- RVs with a distinctive big front windshield and flat bus-like rectangle shape. It's the most common style for all-around and full-time travel. Great for storage and usually big enough to be quite comfortable on the road or when camping. The high front seating and panoramic windshield are absolutely wonderful for seeing everything when driving. It's the favorite part of our Class A. The larger size makes it less ideal for city driving, parking, and like a Class C, the MPG may not be the best.

Class B- Small motorhomes or van conversions. Great for fuel efficiency, ease of driving and parking, stealth camping, and getting around a city. Their small size can also work against it. With less space, it's less comfortable, especially for longer trips, and can limit what you can bring. Note: Don't confuse their small size with a small price, however. Class B's can be as expensive or more than larger Class A or C motorhomes.

Class C- RVs that are usually built on a van-style chassis with a distinctive sleeping area above the front windshield. Great for those wanting extra sleeping space for a grandchild, and some people feel more comfortable driving them because the seating is low. This RV style ranges from compact to large, and the best deals can be found on these older-looking RVs. The overhead sleeping area protruding in front of the driver's windshield can limit visibility slightly.

Travel Trailer- Variations of these towed recreational vehicles range from compact pop-up styles to larger, more comfortable sizes. Some lightweight models can be towed by a car, and without a motor, they can be less expensive and have lower maintenance costs. An advantage is disconnecting the trailer and using the pulling vehicle to get around. When towing, all passengers ride in the towing vehicle and cannot take advantage of the comforts of the trailer. Opting to maximize living space, dedicated storage is usually limited. Extra items are typically stored in the towing vehicle or piled in the living space when in transit. Driving and parking the trailer is more difficult. It also takes more time to level the trailer and set up for camping, so there are better styles for those looking to do stealth camping.

Fifth Wheel- These are usually big and incredibly comfortable trailers that require a powerful truck to pull. They typically have multiple rooms, lots of storage and are great for staying stationary for extended periods. The detached towing truck can be used to get around easily near the campsite. The downside is the high cost of the fifth wheel and expensive towing truck. Difficulty towing, parking, setting up, lack of amenities when in transit, high fuel costs, and lack of stealth camping options are some downsides to this style.

Buying Tips

There is no substitute for going inside as many RVs as possible to get a feel for the incredible diversity of floorplans. RV expos like the Florida RV Supershow (Tampa every January) and others are the best. You'll be able to go inside many different models and have no salesperson pressure. Dealer lots are the next best place to get an idea of what you're looking for, to ask questions, and even see how you feel driving a few. New models are significantly more expensive than picking up a 5+ years old RV. Private sellers will save you even more, and it's a good idea to get it inspected so you can factor into the price any possible maintenance issues that may be necessary.

Below are some of the features that I recommend if deciding to buy a Class A or Class C style:

1. **Solar panels-** Having one or more solar panels with sufficient batteries allows you to power just about everything you need (lights, heater, TVs, computers/ electronics with a power inverter, etc.) without needing to pay for a campground power hookup or run a loud generator.
2. **Automatic levelers-** RV refrigerators need to be pretty level, or they can become damaged. Most campgrounds and overnight parking spots are not flat. Without mechanical leveling jacks, you'll need to spend 5-10+ minutes setting up a stack of blocks to drive onto, hoping to get level. At night, in bad weather, or when stealth camping, you'll especially appreciate simply pressing a button inside the coach to level.
3. **Slideouts-** These amazing inventions add a ton of room to the inside of your coach. At the press of a button, the sides of your RV can slide out and make a big difference in livable inside space.
4. **Electric bikes-** Forget towing a vehicle to get around better. Bring some e-bikes, and you'll have up to 35 miles range to go where you want and a new activity to enjoy along the way.

Fuel Saving Tips

One of the most significant expenses while RVing is fuel. Here are three simple things you can do to save hundreds.

1. Use a credit card with 3% back on gas. This works to about 13 cents off a $4.50 gallon or $10 off each fill-up.
2. Gass Buddy, the free app. This super helpful app shows all current gas prices along a chosen route and even factors in the best rates considering the distance off your original course. Planning a fill-up along our route at the half-tank mark gives us a lot of flexibility to get the best price.
3. COSTCO membership. Usually the cheapest gas around.

. . .

Top Apps for RVers

You may be exploring unfamiliar areas, but you'll never be lost with the right tools. Here are a few apps that help you find what you'll need while on the road.

- **Google Maps-** Navigation, trip planning, traffic, points of interest, food, terrain maps, it's our most used app. The ability to get points of interest ideas on Google Travel with a laptop, then automatically save it to show up on the Google maps app as a pin, is an advantage over other navigation apps like Apple Maps and Waze. Keep an eye out for low bridge clearances because it won't consider your rig height when navigating.
- **InRoute-** Plan your route with RV height, elevation, weather, and other considerations factored in.
- **Campendium-** A map with thousands of campgrounds, BLM spots, and RV parks, with user reviews, photos, pricing, cell service reports, and more. It makes it easy to find a place to stay along your route, nearby for the night, or save favorites in advance to plan your route.
- **Roadtrippers-** A route planning app (and website) with user-suggested routes highlighting attractions you might be interested in.
- **RV Trip Wizard-** A trip planning app and website.
- **Allstays-** 34,000 campgrounds to sort through.
- **Recreation.gov** - Find campsites and experiences at National Parks, Forests, and other Federal Recreation sites.
- **iOverlander-** Find a place to stay for the night. A good selection of users created free camping spots for those looking to quietly park for the night.
- **FreeRoam-** Highlights free "boondocking" spots on the Bureau of Land Management (BLM), US Forest Service (USFS), and more.

- **Harvest Host-** Find and navigate to businesses that allow members to stay overnight for free.
- **GasBuddy-** Find the cheapest gas near you.
- **Windy-** Great app for showing wind conditions for high-profile vehicles.
- **Weatherbug-** Set the app permissions to always use your location to get severe weather alerts in unfamiliar areas.

Go for it! Simple start steps:

1. Pick up some travel books, or go online to decide what you'd like to see and do.
2. Plan a general route that includes your chosen locations.
3. Visit an RV Expo or dealers to decide on an RV type that fits your potential travel style.
4. Estimate trip duration and costs with your selected RV.
5. Search for the best deal that fits your budget (RV Trader, Craigslist, RVT, Facebook marketplace, etc.) online.
6. Purchase your RV and fix it up to your wants and needs. Learn how to use it.
7. Decide on a start date; ideally, 3+ months in the future that considers weather and events (warmer winter conditions in the south, avoid extreme weather locations). Start making reservations to popular campgrounds (National Parks, etc.) as soon as possible. With seasonal winter snowbirds (retirees escaping the cold northern areas) flocking to warmer southern climates, last-minute campsite bookings for winter in Florida can be challenging but not impossible.
8. Store or sell possessions you're not bringing.
9. Sell, rent, or move out of your home or apartment.
10. Leave for an RV adventure of a lifetime!

Resources

1. 99 tips after 7+ years of full-time RV travel link

2. How to find the right RV for you link
3. Florida RV Supershow link
4. Thousand Trails campground membership link
5. Harvest Host camping membership link

Products

1. RV Into the Unknown Gear link
2. Rad Power Bikes (e-bike) link
3. Phone Holder for GPS Navigation link

Books

1. The RV Camping bible by Zack Bergman link
2. 100 Parks, 5000 ideas by National Geographic link
3. Bucket list USA by Fodors link
4. USA by Lonely Planet link

Pairs well with: Photography, e-bikes, hiking, foodies

You might also like: Cruise travel, camping, world travel

* * *

Visit the Seven New Wonders of the World

See a Wonder of the World

Travel can be about visiting those exotic bucket list type places you've always dreamed of seeing but never had the time before retirement. If you're looking for travel inspiration, consider starting at the top and seeing a wonder of the world with your own eyes! Spread around the globe, each location is also an exotic cultural experience that can enrich us and grow our understanding of the world.

Only one of the original "Seven Wonders of the World" from 225 BC remains; The Great Pyramid of Giza. So, in 2000, a campaign to choose the New Seven Wonders of the World was launched, and 100 million people worldwide voted. The list was announced in 2007.

Below is my "favorite" ranking of these seven new (human-made) wonders. They are absolutely worth a visit!

7 Wonders of The World Ranked

1. **Taj Mahal, India-** By far the most beautiful building I've ever seen. The scale and symmetry of the ivory-white marble complex are breathtaking. Add the exoticness of the Islamic style architecture with India's cultural experience, and you have a trip of a lifetime when visiting this wonder! **Tip:** Consider a hotel nearby with a rooftop lounge view of the Taj. Relaxing with a beverage while watching rooftop monkeys and the sunset's interplay of colors on the structure makes the perfect ending to this bucket list adventure.
2. **Petra, Jordan-** You can't help but feel like you're in an Indiana Jones movie as you walk through the desert canyon and view these ancient carvings. **Tip:** Be prepared for a long day of hiking (or hire donkeys/camels), and make sure to make it up to The Monastery in the back, which is larger and more impressive than the famous Treasury carving you'll run into first. Also, don't miss the popular "Petra by Night" candlelit two-hour tour held a few days a week. Due to its proximity, add a visit to Israel and Egypt to round out this trip of a lifetime!
3. **Machu Picchu, Peru-** It's a very photogenic little mysterious mountain top with stacked rock wall ruins. **Tip:** While the adventurous (and in shape) can choose the gorgeous 4-day high-altitude hike along the Inca trail to reach Machu Picchu, there is a much easier (and more popular) way that requires little strenuous effort. Take one of two trains (Inca or Peru rail) to the base town of Aguas Caliente and transfer to a shuttle bus that goes right up to the entrance. A limited number of entrance tickets are available each day, so book ahead as far as possible. Spend some time exploring the towns (and fantastic markets) of the nearby Sacred Valley, and be aware that the gateway city of

Cusco is one of the highest in the world at 11,152 feet. A quick stop at the local pharmacy for altitude sickness pills (Acetazolamide) or passing through quickly to a lower town near Machu Picchu (7,972 feet) helps acclimate.

4. **Chichen Itza, Mexico-** Impressive Mayan pyramids and archeological complexes of a great ancient civilization. **Tip:** Remotely located in the center of the Yucatan Peninsula, roughly 2 hours 30 minutes by toll road from the typical gateway airport of Cancun. After you visit the ruins, continue on another 1 hour 30 minutes to enjoy a night or two in the vibrant colonial city of Merida. Most Sundays hold a festival in the central plaza with local music, food, crafts, and dancing in traditional dress. You may want to have a margarita and join in with the locals to celebrate your recent wonder of the world experience!
5. **Colosseum, Italy-** This historic stadium in the heart of Rome is probably the most accessible Wonder. **Tip:** Tour the inside on foot or consider seeing it along with the nearby archeological and city sites with a Segway tour. These self-balancing scooters are a great way to zip around to the highlights of any new location without the effort of walking.
6. **Great Wall of China-** An impressively long and tall meandering stone wall. **Tip:** Most people visit the restored sections of this 6000 km wall by (1.5 to 2.5 hour) bus from Beijing. While in this large city, you won't want to miss the Chinese cultural highlights of the Forbidden City, Summer Palace, Temple of Heaven, and Tiananmen Square!
7. ***Not ranked* Christ the Redeemer, Brazil-** I haven't visited (and therefore can't officially rank) this famous 125-foot concrete and soapstone statue. Its arms stretch wide open on a local mountain 2,300 feet above Rio de Janeiro. Completed in 1931, it's by far the most modern wonder of the world at less than 100 years old.

Original Seven Wonders of the Ancient World

Below are the original Seven Wonders of the Ancient World created by a Byzantine Scholar based in Alexandria, Egypt, in 225 BC.

1. **Great Pyramid of Giza (near Cairo, Egypt)-** The only surviving Ancient Wonder built over 4,500 years ago in 2560 BC! For about 4,000 years, it reigned as the tallest building in the world. Built by Pharos as burial complexes, it's still somewhat of a mystery how the massive stone structure was built without modern tools.
2. **Hanging Gardens of Babylon (near Euphrates river in what is now present-day Iraq)-** Around 600 BC, Babylonian King Nebacannezer II planted the towering gardens (perhaps 75 feet) on stone terraces to console his wife who missed the greenery of her homeland. Modern scholars debate the details of this Wonder, even to the point of questioning its actual existence.
3. **Statue of Zeus at Olympia (Greece)-** A 40-foot ivory and gold-plated Greek Mythology statue of the King of all Gods stood where the Olympics games (held to honor him) took place for over 800 years.
4. **Temple of Artemis at Ephesus (Greek port city in modern-day Turkey)-** Marble temples built around 550 BC for the Greek goddess of the hunt. According to legend, it was first burned down the same night Alexander the Great was born in 356 BC by a citizen who wanted his name to be known in history.
5. **Mausoleum at Halicarnassus (present-day Turkey)-** A 135 feet tall white marble architecturally intricate tomb with Lycian, Greek, and Egyptian influences. Built in 353 BC by Artemisia for her husband and also brother Mausolus, King of Carnia in Asia Minor. An earthquake in the 13th century destroyed it. Pieces were later found and are now in the British Museum.

6. **Colossus of Rhodes (Greece)-** The largest statue ever built in 280 BC stood for 60 years at the harbor entrance to this trading port city. The massive bronze god of the sun, Helios, was toppled by an earthquake, and its broken pieces cluttered the docks for 1000 years before being melted down and sold as scrap metal.
7. **Lighthouse of Alexandria (Egypt)-** The lighthouse was the second tallest human-made structure (380 feet) when it was built in 270 BC. It stood for 1,500 years, illuminating on a small island for ships coming in and out of the Nile river at the busy harbor of Alexandria.

Where to start?

If you're interested in visiting a wonder, you have two options. Book a tour that will take care of all or most logistics (transportation, hotel, experience, etc.), or you can plan it all yourself. There are certainly benefits and drawbacks to both. If the high cost of a tour is outside your budget, fear not! Planning the trip yourself will save hundreds and sometimes thousands of dollars, give you more flexibility, strengthen your mind, and provide a sense of accomplishment. Bonus!

Go for it! Simple start steps:

1. Search for tours to your chosen destination to get ideas (prices, highlights, itinerary).
2. Book a tour or start piecing your visit together (highlights, hotels, ground transport, air transport).
3. Go and enjoy making memories that will last a lifetime!

Resources

1. 7 New Wonders of the World link
2. 200 Wonders of the World link

3. Great Wall of China Insider Guide link

Products

1. Convertible rolling backpack luggage link
2. Portable luggage scale link
3. Compression packing cubes link
4. Electronics travel cube link

Books

1. Wonders of the World by Lonely Planet link
2. Destinations of a lifetime by National Geographic link
3. Man Made Wonders of the World by DK link

Pairs well with: Travel journaling, videography, photography, social media

You might also like: Rail journeys, cruising, RV travel

* * *

Plan a Trip Around the World

Go on a trip of a lifetime

Newly retired and need help deciding what to do first? After a healthy helping of relaxation, why not start planning the trip of a lifetime? Go big. Plan a trip around the world. I'm serious. You can do it. It's just like planning a short vacation to one location, but instead of taking an expensive flight back home, you move on to your next location somewhere nearby. Intercountry transportation is much cheaper than long flights, so it's actually more affordable than you'd think. You'll never be more mobile and energized than right now. It will take a couple of months of planning while you put your travel dreams into motion, but it is a very enjoyable process.

I'll walk you through the process we used and give you some resources that will go more in-depth. Hopefully, it will give you the confidence to dream big and see that this is possible. If money is no object, some travel companies also specialize in planning these long-term trips.

8-Step Process to Planning a Trip Around the World

1. **Dream with intention-** This is one of the most fun steps in the planning process, so enjoy it! Here, you get ideas on where you'd like to visit and what you'd like to do. You're creating a travel bucket list with the intention of actually experiencing it in the near future. How exciting is this! Make a list of everything and everywhere you're interested in, from reading travel websites, best-of travel books from your library or bookstores, picking up tour brochures, asking friends/family for recommendations and watching YouTube travel idea videos.
2. **Organize ideas-** Organize your lists by location, events, and experiences. This will give you an idea of where you're most interested in visiting.
3. **Put together a general route of travel-** From your organized list, you'll have an idea of where you're most interested in visiting. Prioritize those areas and the bucket list things you're most excited about. Then connect those locations in a logical order with the least backtracking. Short hops are preferable, and look through tour brochures for ideas on how they link up popular highlights in an area. Around the world travel books also give good suggestions on popular slow travel routes. Slow travel is the best for absorbing your surroundings.
4. **Do a best season/ event check-** Give yourself a "best time to visit" framework by researching the weather and events where you're planning on visiting. It's as simple as searching for the best time to visit [your chosen] country. Unfamiliar parts of the world can have strange seasonal weather like monsoons or exceptionally busy times of the

year to avoid. Know that you will save money and it'll be less crowded when you travel shoulder seasons.

5. **Research longer flights and estimate hotel/ hostel/ rental costs-** With a rough idea of your route, now do a budget analysis by looking up the costs of the most expensive parts of the trip. Go to Google Travel, then the flights section, and search for flight prices for the longer flight legs during the months you're estimating flying. Get an idea of hotel/ hostel/rental prices in the countries you'll visit so you can estimate an average nightly cost. Add up other significant expenses you're considering, such as cruises, local events or tours.
6. **Fine-tune your plan and route to fit your budget and any time constraints-** After analyzing the major expenses, fine-tune the route or adjust the length of stay to fit your budget.
7. **Lock in the trip start date at least 3-6 months in advance-** Purchase airfare or other transportation, such as a one-way repositioning cruise, for the first leg of your journey. This is a big deal. It's where you commit to the trip and get the ball rolling on making reservations. It will motivate you to grind out the reservations and logistics details in the next step.
8. **Work out logistics in sequence**- Starting at the landing location and date of your first flight, work out the logistics in the following order:

   a. *Estimate stay length at the location based on how many things there are in the area that you want to see and do. It should be a minimum of three nights because of lost time due to afternoon check-in and mid-day checkout.*
   b. *Keep notes on the points of interest you'd like to do at that location. You'll use those notes as a guide to plan your days when you're there.*
   c. *Research transport options and make a note of how to book. For instance, when you land, how will*

you get to the hotel/hostel (taxi, shuttle van, rideshare, or train)?

d. Book hotel and transport in advance to lock in travel plans or keep the notes to book later if you want flexible travel plans.

e. Decide on the next location.

f. Repeat a-e above.

Locked-in reservations vs. flexible travel plans

When planning independent long-term travel, you can either book as much as possible in advance, which makes it easier when you're traveling, but it takes away the flexibility to stay longer, shorter, or change your route if you learn about somewhere new you'd like to visit. Or you can stay flexible and book your travel a little bit at a time as you go. There are tradeoffs to both. On our trip, we booked everything at the start for three months during the high season. Then after we got comfortable on the road, we stayed flexible by booking in small chunks as we went along. If you book in advance, make sure to add a day of rest into your plans at least every week. We didn't do this, and the constant moving wore us down, and by the end of the third month, we had to stay put for a week to recharge. On the other hand, being flexible and booking as you go eats into your travels as you have to hole up for a day or so to make plans and reservations for the next leg.

Connectivity

Research and have a plan in advance to stay connected while you travel. You can either get a phone plan with international data, buy a local sim card where needed and get an inexpensive prepaid mobile phone plan, or use wifi at your hotel or restaurants. I'd recommend buying a local sim and having a mobile phone plan because you'll be able to use the data for navigation to points of interest or for calling rideshare companies with your app.

. . .

Organization

Staying organized by putting notes and plans into a cloud-based document such as Google Docs or a spreadsheet such as Google Sheets is extremely helpful. You'll be able to access the information from any computer at home or on travel, easily collaborate with others, and easily share important contact info such as emergency details. Another advantage is knowing that the information is backed up securely on the cloud in case a laptop is damaged or stolen on travel.

Finally, beware of analysis paralysis. You can easily get swept up in the information-gathering process, creating neverending notes and spreadsheets. It can become overwhelming and burdensome to sift through everything and make sense of it all. Be ok with not knowing everything. Make a point to just get enough info to feel comfortable and don't overdo it. In reality, it's just procrastination from making concrete actionable plans because of the fear of uncertainty. Tackle one micro-step at a time and use its completion to motivate you to move on to the next step. You'll feel yourself getting closer to living out the amazing experiences you're dreaming of. The fear of missing out should push you forward when it's easier to do nothing or give up.

> *"Twenty years from now you will be more disappointed by the things that you didn't do than by the ones you did do. So throw off the bowlines. Sail away from the safe harbor. Catch the trade winds in your sails. Explore. Dream. Discover." -Mark Twain*[9]

Hopefully, with the above info, you'll have a better idea of how to plan your trip around the world. Grab an informative travel book about long-term travel to help you feel more confident, then take the first steps to plan your trip. I can wholeheartedly say that the effort is well worth it. The trip will change you and could be the highlight of your life.

Resources

1. How to Design An Around The World Itinerary link
2. Planning A Trip Around The World link
3. How to Plan An Around The World Trip link

Books

1. The Rough Guide to First-Time Around the World by Rough Guides link
2. Destinations of a Lifetime: 225 of the World's Most Amazing Places by National Geographic link
3. How to Travel the World on $50 a Day: Third Edition: Travel Cheaper, Longer, Smarter by Matt Kepnes link
4. The Bucket List: 1000 Adventures Big & Small by Kath Stathers link
5. Lonely Planet Lonely Planet's Ultimate Travel List 2: The Best Places on the Planet ...Ranked by Lonely Planet link
6. Where to Go When by Lonely Planet link
7. The Rough Guide to the 100 Best Places on Earth by Rough Guides link
8. Lonely Planet Lonely Planet's Ultimate Eats by Lonely Planet Food link

Pairs well with: Events, cruises, museums, volunteering, free walking tours

You might also like: Around the world cruise, visiting new seven wonders of the world, RV travel, moving overseas

* * *

Travel to Famous Places

Experience iconic locations

Mary was a retired schoolteacher with a passion for history and a deep appreciation for the beauty of the Taj Mahal. She had always dreamed of visiting the iconic monument, but life had always gotten in the way. Finally, she decided it was time to make the trip and see the Taj Mahal in person.

The journey was filled with excitement and adventure as she explored the vibrant culture of India and its rich history. When she finally reached the Taj Mahal, she was struck by its beauty and grandeur. The stunning monument was even more magnificent in person, and Mary was filled with a sense of awe and wonder. The experience was truly life-changing, and Mary will always cherish the memories of her visit. Now every time she sees a photo of the monument, she is transported back to that magical moment and the adventures she had in India.

Famous landmarks like the Eiffel Tower, Statue of Liberty, and the Great Pyramids are just some icons we've seen a thousand times in travel brochures or on TV. They are exotic and full of wonder. Traveling to see them with our own eyes is extremely exciting. A photo of a breathtakingly scenic lake is one thing, but swimming in that lake is better. Below is a list of some famous landmarks. You've most likely seen them before, now consider seeing them for real!

30 Famous Travel Locations

1. **Sydney Opera House-** A world-renowned architectural masterpiece located in Sydney, Australia. Visitors come from around the world to admire its unique design, catch a performance at one of its many venues, and take in fantastic views of Sydney Harbour.
2. **Petra-** Located in Jordan, Petra was an ancient city carved into sandstone cliffs. It is now a popular tourist destination for its well-preserved ruins, including temples, tombs, and other structures, offering a glimpse into the rich history and culture of the Nabataean people.
3. **Forbidden City-** The Forbidden City, also known as the Palace Museum, is located in the heart of Beijing, China. It was the imperial palace for 24 emperors during the Ming and Qing dynasties. Today, it is a museum showcasing

ancient Chinese architecture and impressive cultural heritage, attracting tourists worldwide.

4. **Leaning Tower of Pisa-** The Leaning Tower of Pisa is an iconic, freestanding bell tower in the Italian city of Pisa. It is famous for its unintended tilt, which began during construction in the 12th century, making it a popular tourist destination for its unique architecture and as a backdrop for humorous photographs.
5. **Great Pyramids of Giza-** Located near Cairo, Egypt, the Great Pyramids are among the world's most famous and iconic ancient structures. They were built as tombs for the Pharaohs and their consorts over 4,500 years ago and remain an exciting tourist destination for their historical and architectural significance, as well as the mysterious allure of their purpose and construction.
6. **Machu Picchu-** Machu Picchu is an ancient Incan city located high in the Andes Mountains of Peru. It is one of South America's most well-known and popular tourist destinations, attracting visitors with its stunning mountain setting, sophisticated architectural and engineering feats, and status as one of the world's most important archaeological sites.
7. **Statue of Liberty-** The Statue of Liberty is a colossal statue located on Liberty Island in New York Harbor, USA. It is a symbol of freedom and democracy, attracting millions of visitors annually who come to see this iconic symbol of American history and climb to the crown for panoramic views of New York City and the harbor.
8. **Eiffel Tower-** The Eiffel Tower is an iron lattice tower in Paris, France. It is one of the most recognizable structures in the world. It was built as the entrance arch to the 1889 World's Fair and is now a major tourist destination. It offers stunning views of Paris and serves as a symbol of French innovation and culture.
9. **Great Wall of China-** The Great Wall of China is a series of fortifications made of brick, tamped earth, stone, and other materials, stretching over 21,000 km through

China. It is the longest wall in the world and a popular tourist destination, showcasing the ancient Chinese engineering marvel and offering breathtaking views from its highest points.

10. **Taj Mahal-** The Taj Mahal is a stunning mausoleum in Agra, India. Built by the Mughal Emperor Shah Jahan in memory of his wife Mumtaz Mahal, it is widely considered one of the most beautiful buildings in the world, attracting millions of visitors each year to admire its intricate marble work, stunning gardens, and rich history.
11. **Angkor Wat-** Angkor Wat is a temple complex located in Siem Reap, Cambodia, and is the largest religious monument in the world. It was initially built as a Hindu temple in the 12th century and later converted to a Buddhist temple, attracting tourists with its stunning Khmer architecture, extensive relief carvings, and its status as a symbol of Cambodia's cultural heritage.
12. **Burj Khalifa-** The Burj Khalifa is the tallest building in the world, located in Dubai, United Arab Emirates. It attracts tourists with its height and modern architectural design and offers breathtaking views of the city from its observation deck. Visitors come from all over the world to admire this engineering marvel and to experience the unique blend of tradition and innovation that defines Dubai.
13. **Mount Rushmore National Memorial-** Mount Rushmore is a massive sculpture in the Black Hills region of South Dakota, USA. It features the carved faces of four US Presidents: George Washington, Thomas Jefferson, Theodore Roosevelt, and Abraham Lincoln. Tourists visit for its historical significance, stunning natural setting, and its status as a symbol of American democracy.
14. **Mont Saint-Michel-** Mont Saint-Michel is a fairytale-like castle on an island off the coast of Normandy, France. It is famous for its medieval Benedictine abbey and castle-like town, built on top of a rocky islet and surrounded by vast

tidal flats. Visitors admire the island's stunning architecture, medieval history, and unique coastal setting.

15. **The Acropolis-** The Acropolis is a citadel located on a hill in Athens, Greece, featuring well-preserved ancient Greek buildings, including the Parthenon temple, the Erechtheion temple, and the Propylaea gateway. It is a well-known tourist destination for its historical and architectural significance, offering visitors a glimpse into ancient Greek culture and the birth of Western civilization.
16. **Uluru-** Uluru, also known as Ayers Rock, is a 1,141-foot tall red sandstone rock towering alone among a flat landscape in the southern part of the Northern Territory, Australia. It is an important religious site for the Anangu, the traditional owners of Uluru. It is a popular tourist destination for its unique natural beauty, aboriginal heritage, and its status as a symbol of Australian identity.
17. **Great Barrier Reef-** The Great Barrier Reef is the largest coral reef system in the world, located off the coast of Queensland, Australia. It is home to a diverse array of marine life, attracting snorkelers, divers, and marine biologists from all over the world to explore its vibrant coral formations and crystal-clear waters.
18. **Easter Island-** Easter Island, also known as Rapa Nui, is a remote volcanic island located in the southeastern Pacific Ocean. It is famous for its massive stone statues, known as Moai, which have captivated visitors for centuries with their mysterious origins and cultural significance. Easter Island is one of the most remote inhabited islands in the world.
19. **Golden Gate Bridge-** The Golden Gate Bridge is a suspension bridge spanning the Golden Gate Strait, connecting San Francisco to Marin County in California, USA. It is an iconic landmark known for its stunning orange color, Art Deco style, and its status as an engineering marvel, attracting tourists from all over the world to walk or bike across its 1.7-mile-long main span and admire the views of the bay and the city.

20. **Neuschwanstein Castle-** Neuschwanstein Castle is an enchanting 19th-century Romanesque Revival palace located in the Bavarian Alps in Germany. It is famous for its status as the inspiration for the castle in the Disney movie "Sleeping Beauty," attracting tourists from all over the world to admire its beautiful interiors, sweeping views, and its role in shaping the fairy tale castle archetype.
21. **Victoria Falls-** Victoria Falls is a massive waterfall located on the Zambezi River between Zambia and Zimbabwe in southern Africa. It is one of the largest waterfalls in the world, attracting tourists with its exquisite natural beauty, adventurous activities such as bungee jumping, whitewater rafting, and scenic helicopter rides, and its status as a UNESCO World Heritage Site.
22. **The Western Wall-** The Western Wall, also known as the Wailing Wall, is a retaining wall of the Temple Mount in Jerusalem, Israel. It is one of the holiest sites in Judaism and a popular destination for Jewish pilgrims, who come to pray and place written prayers into the cracks between the stones. The Western Wall also holds great historical and cultural significance, attracting visitors worldwide to admire its ancient history and cultural heritage.
23. **Buckingham Palace-** Buckingham Palace is the official London residence of the British monarch. The palace in the City of Westminster features 775 rooms, including 19 staterooms, 52 royal and guest bedrooms, and 92 offices. Visitors come to watch the famous Changing of the Guard ceremony held at the palace gates to admire the architecture and because of its role as a symbol of the British monarchy.
24. **La Sagrada Familia-** La Sagrada Familia is a large Roman Catholic church in Barcelona, Spain, designed by the famous Catalan architect Antoni Gaudí. It is an iconic landmark of the city, famous for its distinctive, undulating stone spires and its status as an unfinished masterpiece, attracting tourists from all over the world to admire its unique architecture and learn about Gaudi's distinctive vision for the church.

25. **Christ the Redeemer-** Christ the Redeemer is a massive statue of Jesus Christ located atop Mount Corcovado in Rio de Janeiro, Brazil. It is one of the most famous landmarks in South America, attracting tourists with its sweeping views of Rio, its iconic status as a symbol of the city and of Brazilian culture, and its religious significance as a pilgrimage site for Catholics.
26. **Blue Mosque-** The Blue Mosque, also known as the Sultan Ahmed Mosque, is a historic mosque in Istanbul, Turkey. It is known for its captivating architecture, intricate tile work, and its six minarets, attracting tourists from all over the world to admire its beauty and learn about its history and cultural significance.
27. **The Colosseum-** The Colosseum is a massive amphitheater located in Rome, Italy, and was used for gladiatorial contests, animal hunts, and public spectacles. Visitors come to learn about Roman history and imagine the excitement of the gladiatorial games once held there.
28. **The Grand Palace-** The Grand Palace in Bangkok, Thailand, is a complex of buildings that served as the official residence of the Thai King from 1782 to 1925. The palace, located in the heart of Bangkok, is famous for its architecture, intricate details, and status as a Thai culture and history symbol.
29. **Stonehenge-** Stonehenge is a prehistoric monument in Wiltshire, England, composed of massive standing stones arranged in a circular formation. It is iconic for its mystery, cultural significance, and role as a symbol of ancient England.
30. **Blue Domes of Oia-** The Blue Domes of Oia are a picturesque group of buildings in the village of Oia on the island of Santorini in Greece. The buildings are famous for their brilliant blue domed roofs, gorgeous views of the Aegean Sea, and their status as a Greek culture and history symbol. Visitors come to admire their beauty, enjoy the scenic views, and to experience the unique charm of Oia and the island of Santorini.

Resources

1. 32 of The Most Famous Landmarks In The World link
2. Top 10 Most Famous Landmarks In The World link
3. These are the top 25 landmarks in the world, according to TripAdvisor link

* * *

Travel for Nature and Beauty

Experience the most beautiful areas

Traveling to experience nature's beauty is an incredible and life-changing journey. When we venture out into the great outdoors, we are surrounded by a natural wonderland that never fails to leave us in awe. From the breathtaking views of majestic mountains and cascading waterfalls to the tranquil sounds of birds chirping in a lush forest - there's something truly magical about being one with nature.

Nature's sights, sounds, and smells can be incredibly calming and rejuvenating for our minds and souls. Our spirit is filled with joy as we take in the beautiful scenery all around us. We feel connected to something greater than ourselves; it's like stepping into another world where everything is peaceful and serene. You realize how seemingly insignificant you and your problems are when you step outside your bubble.

Exploring new places also gives us a sense of adventure that can't be found anywhere else. We get lost in our thoughts as we wander through winding trails or paddle along rivers, soaking up every moment of this magical experience. Whether hiking through a National Park or camping under the stars, being outside helps us unplug from everyday life so we can focus on connecting with nature and appreciating its beauty. You feel alive!

. . .

20 Eye Opening Nature and Beauty Experiences

1. **Angkor Wat Cambodian Temple at sunrise-** At the crack of dawn, the sky slowly begins to lighten, shifting from inky blackness to a deep navy blue that hints at a beautiful sunrise. In the distance, you can make out the shape of Angkor Wat, its spires and towers silhouetted against the horizon. As you approach this grand ancient temple complex, your eyes feast upon its intricate carvings and bas-reliefs that have survived centuries of time and weathering. The sun's rays gradually begin to break through the darkness as they creep up from behind Angkor Wat's towers. You are mesmerized by the delicate pink hues that dance across its sandstone walls until, finally, they are bathed in orange and gold sunlight. This incredible sight is a reminder of how vast and powerful nature can be - one that will stay with you long after your visit ends.
2. **See a total solar eclipse-** The beauty of a total solar eclipse is like nothing else on earth. As the sky darkens and the sun goes out, you are left with an awe-inspiring moment of pure wonder. The sky turns to night, and the stars appear while a deep red hue radiates across the horizon. You can almost feel time slowing down as you take in the moment. With no light pollution to interfere, you can gaze up at the stars in all their glory while watching as they are framed by a glowing ring of color around the dark disc that was once our sun. A total solar eclipse is breathtakingly beautiful and humbling, a reminder of how small we really are compared to the grandeur of nature's power.
3. **Netherlands biking-** From the moment you arrive in the Netherlands, you can feel the air of adventure that awaits. With its flat terrain and numerous bike paths, it's no surprise that biking is a favorite pastime here. As you pedal your way through this stunning landscape, you'll be rewarded with spectacular views of rolling fields lined by beautiful canals, charming Dutch villages full of traditional architecture, and lush forests and parks that offer plenty of

opportunities to stop and explore. Along your journey, take time to appreciate all the natural beauty that surrounds you —from vibrant wildflowers blooming in meadows to majestic windmills standing tall against a bright blue sky. Whether it's a leisurely ride or an adrenaline-filled trek, biking in the Netherlands will surely be an unforgettable experience!

4. **Grand Canyon helicopter ride-** Experience the breathtaking beauty of the Grand Canyon from a whole new perspective. Take a thrilling helicopter ride and soar high above the canyon's dramatic walls and scenic buttes, taking in its ever-changing landscape of deep reds and oranges as you go. Gaze down upon miles of winding canyons, rivers, forests, and mountain ranges in all their majestic glory as you take your time to marvel at this natural wonder of the world. The view is a memorable experience that no amount of photos or words could ever do justice to.
5. **Fall foliage in Smoky Mountain National Park-** A visit to Smoky Mountain National Park in the fall is an awe-inspiring experience. The vibrant colors of the falling leaves set against the majestic backdrop of the Appalachian Mountains create a dazzling landscape. As you hike along, you will be surrounded by a colorful tapestry in shades of orange, yellow, and red that seem to stretch on forever. With each step, you can feel your stress melting away as you crackle through the leaves and take in the beauty of nature's artwork.
6. **Scenic train around Switzerland-** From the lush green meadows to the captivating snow-capped mountain peaks, a scenic train ride around Switzerland offers an extraordinary experience. As you pass through historic villages, you'll be enchanted by the stunning vistas of wildflower fields and rolling hills. You'll also be enthralled by sensational views of majestic glacier-fed lakes and pristine rivers that wind through dense forests full of enchanting wildlife. An incredible journey awaits as you

discover Switzerland's spectacular natural beauty from your window seat on this unforgettable train ride.

7. **Ride a scooter around Southeast Asia-** Traveling around Southeast Asia on a scooter is an experience like no other. The vibrant colors of the local markets, the salty ocean breeze blowing through your hair, and the sound of exotic birds singing in the distance make for a truly unique journey. As you move from place to place, you'll be amazed by the magnificent temples and ancient ruins that line the roads. Every turn will bring a new surprise as you explore this incredible region on two wheels.
8. **Feel small among the giant trees in the Avenue of the Giants-** Witnessing the towering redwoods of California's Avenue of the Giants is a humbling experience. Standing beneath their immense boughs, you feel like an ant in comparison to their grandeur. Dappled sunlight cascades through the leaves, and a cool mist clings to the bark. The ancient trees have stood for centuries, and it's easy to get lost in their beauty as you wander down this magnificent avenue.
9. **Snowmobiling through fresh powder-** The thrill of snowmobiling through untouched powder is unbeatable. The crisp air, the smell of the trees, and the pristine white landscape all combine to create an amazing experience. With each twist and turn, you'll be mesmerized by the untouched beauty of your surroundings – from rolling hills covered in snow blankets to crystal-clear rivers reflecting back a million shades of white. Snowmobiling through fresh powder is a breathtaking adventure that will leave lasting memories for years.
10. **Visit the Royal Palace in the UK-** The Royal Palace in the UK is a sight to behold. Its sprawling grounds, lush green gardens, and glittering gold facade will leave you awestruck. Inside, intricate tapestries and artwork adorn the walls while massive chandeliers hang from the ceilings, illuminating the ornate detailing of every room. Stroll

through this grand palace's halls and be transported to a world of regal beauty.

11. **Dip toes in Moraine Lake-** The tranquil beauty of Moraine Lake in the Canadian Rockies is something to behold. The emerald-green waters and surrounding snow-capped peaks will take your breath away. When you dip your toes in its icy waters, you'll feel like you're in a dream—the perfect place to replenish your spirit and find peace. With every glance, you'll be reminded of just how beautiful nature can be.
12. **Walking among temples of Thailand-** Thailand's temples are an awe-inspiring sight, with their intricate designs and colorful decorations. Walking among them is like stepping into another world, with the peaceful atmosphere allowing you to take in every detail. Everywhere you look, there is something new to marvel at, from detailed sculptures of gods and goddesses to magnificent murals depicting stories from ancient times. The beauty of these temples is sure to leave an indelible impression on anyone who visits them.
13. **Black sand beach-** Punaluu Beach is a breathtaking black sand beach in Hawaii with its dramatic lava-covered coastline. Its unique black sands are created from the cooled lava that flows from Kilauea, one of the world's most active volcanoes. The shoreline is often filled with giant sea turtles basking in the sun and playing in the waters - an amazing sight to behold! The dark sands contrast perfectly with bright blue waves crashing against them, creating an image of natural beauty that will stay with you evermore.
14. **Yellowstone geothermal features-** Experience the raw power of nature at Yellowstone National Park, home to an array of geothermal features. From the thunderous roar of Old Faithful to the pink and orange hues of Grand Prismatic Spring, you'll be in awe of the beauty and grandeur of God's creations. Marvel at dazzling hot springs and bubbling mud pots as you explore this natural

wonderland, a kaleidoscope of color unlike any other on earth.

15. **Aspen Skiing-** Soar down the powdery slopes of Aspen Skiing and take in the breathtaking beauty of its alpine landscape. Feel the rush of gliding over freshly fallen snow as you explore every corner of this glorious mountain range. Capture a glimpse of rare wildlife, such as elk and ptarmigan, or take in the majestic views atop one of its many scenic overlooks. Find yourself surrounded by nature's wonders at one of the most enchanting ski resorts on earth.
16. **Batu Cave-** Batu Cave is a majestic and awe-inspiring natural wonder in Malaysia. The cave entrance is adorned with a 140-foot golden statue of Lord Murugan, and inside, you will discover an enchanting rainforest filled with exotic wildlife and lush foliage. Climb the 272 steps that lead to the top of the cave, where you can take in breathtaking panoramic views of Kuala Lumpur's skyline or enjoy a tranquil sunset from underneath its massive limestone formations. Whether admiring its stunning architecture or exploring its vibrant natural beauty, Batu Cave will undoubtedly leave you spellbound.
17. **Santorini, Greece-** Santorini, Greece, is one of the most beautiful places on Earth. From the iconic white-washed buildings and blue domed roofs to the postcard-perfect views, you will be mesmerized by its beauty. The crystal clear Aegean Sea glistens against the bright white cliffs, while the gorgeous sunsets paint a picture of paradise. As you stroll along the cobblestone alleys and explore Santorini's hidden gems, you'll be captivated by its stunning landscape and Mediterranean charm.
18. **Cogwheel train in Switzerland-** The Jungfraubahnen cogwheel train ride is a journey like no other. You'll be transported up into the Swiss Alps, passing through snow-capped mountains and verdant meadows with vibrant wildflowers as far as the eye can see. At the top, you'll be rewarded with breathtaking views of the glacier and a panorama of the surrounding valley that will leave you

speechless. The crisp alpine air and awe-inspiring landscape will remain in your memory forever.

19. **Krabi, Thailand-** Krabi, Thailand, is a tropical paradise that will take your breath away. From the stunning limestone cliffs of Railay Beach to the crystal-clear waters of Maya Bay, you'll be surrounded by breathtaking beauty. The atmosphere here is peaceful and calming, allowing you to relax and forget your worries. Take in the sunsets as they turn the sky into a vibrant display of oranges, pinks, and purples - it's sure to be an unforgettable experience.
20. **Iguazu falls Brazil-** Iguazu Falls is an awe-inspiring natural wonder. The thunderous roar of the cascading falls can be heard from miles away, and their majestic beauty is spectacular. Standing at the edge of the precipice overlooking the powerful waterfall, you feel like you are standing on top of the world. A dip in its fresh, clear waters will refresh your soul and rejuvenate your spirit.

Resources

1. 55 of the World's Most Beautiful Destinations link
2. The 51 Most Beautiful Places in the World link
3. The Most Beautiful Place in Each US State link

Books

1. The World's Most Beautiful Places by The Editors of National Geographic link
2. The Rough Guide to the 100 Best Places on Earth by Rough Guides link
3. Amazing Places to See in North America by Publications International Ltd. link

* * *

Travel for Adventure

Go for a daring journey into the unknown

Adventure is a daring journey into the unknown, with a willingness to take risks, embrace the unfamiliar and explore thrilling possibilities. It is an opportunity to discover something new and to push the boundaries of your comfort zone. Adventure can be a physical journey, an intellectual quest, or an emotional rollercoaster. It is a chance to step away from the mundane, to seek out excitement, to challenge yourself, and to grow. Adventure is a way to break free, to find yourself, and to experience the extraordinary.

Carl had been retired for a few years now and was starting to feel restless. He'd always been an adventurous person, but lately, he found himself feeling bored and unfulfilled. He'd tried taking up new hobbies and spending more time with friends, but nothing seemed to give him the excitement he was looking for.

One day, Carl was flipping through travel magazines and came across a beautiful picture of a remote mountain village in South America. It was just the kind of adventure he was craving! He booked a flight, packed his bags, and embarked on his journey.

As he explored the quaint, cobbled streets of the village and hiked through the stunning mountain scenery, Carl felt a sense of joy and excitement that he hadn't felt in years. He tried new foods, met interesting people, and even learned a few words of the local language.

At the end of his trip, Carl returned home feeling rejuvenated and grateful for the chance to have this incredible experience. He realized that he didn't need to wait for an invitation to live life to the fullest and decided to plan more trips and seek out new adventures whenever he had the chance.

Travel is Adventure

You don't necessarily have to seek out bucket list adventures when you travel because, in many ways, travel itself is an adventure.

Navigating to unfamiliar places, trying unique foods, understanding foreign cultures, and even attempting to communicate in a different language is an adventure in itself! There will undoubtedly be difficulties and challenging moments, but these moments make for great memories in hindsight. If you're still looking for more adventure to write home about, take a look at some ideas below and buckle up, life's about to get very exciting!

33 Adventure Ideas

1. Spend a night in the Sahara Desert- Erg Chebbi, Morocco
2. Climb Sydney Harbor Bridge- Sydney, Australia
3. Ride the longest zipline in the world (1.76 miles long)- Ras Al Khaimah, United Arab Emirates
4. Hike to the top edge of Half Dome (5,000' cliff)- Yosemite National Park, California
5. Travel overseas solo
6. Campervan around the Outback- New South Wales, Australia
7. Trek to Everest base camp- Lukla, Nepal
8. Take the Ring Road self-drive tour of Iceland- Reykjavik, Iceland
9. Learn Kung Fu at a Shaolin Temple- Beijing Shaolin Wushu School, China
10. Go inside a pyramid- Cairo, Egypt
11. Ride an ice explorer on a glacier- Alberta, Canada
12. Climb Mount Kilimanjaro- Tanzania, Africa
13. Shark cage snorkel- Oahu, Hawaii
14. Storm chasing tour in tornado alley- Oklahoma City, Oklahoma
15. Snorkel the Great Barrier Reef- Queensland, Australia
16. Run with the bulls- Pamplona, Spain
17. Kayak among icebergs- Kenai Fjords National Park, Alaska
18. Safari in Africa with Glamping- Masi Mara, Kenya
19. Sandboard in a desert oasis- Huacachina, Peru
20. The Rickshaw Run- India

21. Bioluminescent kayaking- Mosquito Bay, Vieques Island, Puerto Rico
22. Hike Patagonia- Torres del Paine National Park, Chile
23. Take a dogsled tour- Lapland region of Finland
24. Spend the night hanging on the side of a cliff in a transparent dome- Skylodge Adventure Suites, Peru
25. Watch the sunrise from the top of a Myanmar temple- Bagan, Myanmar
26. Night hike in the Amazon jungle- Leticia, Colombia
27. Visit Burning Man Festival- Black Rock Desert, Nevada
28. Multi-Day whitewater rafting tour in Grand Canyon- Peach Springs, Arizona
29. Hot air balloon ride- Cappadocia, Turkey
30. Skydive- Oahu, Hawaii
31. Multi-day motorcycle tour- Sturgis, South Dakota
32. Climb a volcano- Mount Rinjani on the island of Lombok, Indonesia
33. Scuba dive with whale sharks- Isla Mujeres, Mexico

Resources

1. 21 Adventures for Thrill-Seeking Senior Travelers link
2. 22 Awesome Outdoor Adventures for Seniors link
3. The Best Senior Adventures To Experience link
4. 7 Day Iceland Self Drive Tour link

Books

1. Epic Journeys: 245 Life-Changing Adventures by National Geographic link
2. 100 Hikes of a Lifetime: The World's Ultimate Scenic Trails by Kate Siber link
3. World's Best Travel Experiences: 400 Extraordinary Places by National Geographic link

* * *

Travel for New Experiences

Try things different

Traveling for new and different experiences can be an incredibly exciting reason to explore the world. Think about it – you could take a thrilling ride on a cable car in San Francisco with its iconic views of the Golden Gate Bridge, live like a monk in a Japanese monastery, experience a magical mermaid show in Florida, or witness the awe-inspiring haka war dance in New Zealand. Each experience is unique and filled with potential adventure!

26 New or Different Experiences to Travel For

1. Christmas markets in Europe
2. Candlelit jungle waterfall dinner at Sai Rung Waterfall, Thailand
3. Picnic on the lawn of the Eiffel Tower
4. Paddleboard yoga
5. San Francisco cable car ride
6. Tokyo subway
7. Cable car ride in Medellin, Colombia
8. Tuk Tuk ride in Thailand
9. Hong Kong gondola ride
10. Silverton Durango train ride
11. Hike the narrows in Zion National Park
12. Havana, Cuba
13. Get out of your element in Marrakech Morocco Market
14. Firefly boat tour in Malaysia
15. Mermaid show at Weeki Wachee Springs, Florida
16. Big wave surfing in Hawaii
17. Below Zero Ice Bar in Queenstown, New Zealand
18. Ride on the London Eye observation wheel
19. Go to the top of the Eiffel Tower
20. India Yogi Ceremony
21. Tibet monk temple stay
22. Budapest thermal bath

23. Learn to flamenco dance in Barcelona
24. Helicopter over Tokyo
25. New Zealand haka dance
26. Irish Bars in Dublin

Resources

1. 10 Best Christmas Markets in Europe link
2. Candlelit Jungle Waterfall Experience link
3. 14 Unique, Once In A Lifetime Travel Experiences Worth Having link

Books

1. Fodor's Bucket List USA: From the Epic to the Eccentric, 500+ Ultimate Experiences by Fodor's Travel Guides link
2. 1,000 Perfect Weekends: Great Getaways Around the Globe by George Stone link
3. Lonely Planet Lonely Planet's Ultimate Travel List 2: The Best Places on the Planet. Ranked by Lonely Planet link

* * *

Travel for Food

Explore with your mouth

Trying new foods is a wonderful way to experience the culture and traditions of different places around the world. It opens your taste buds to an array of flavors, spices, and ingredients that you might never have encountered before. Food is the heart and soul of a culture, and it's a unique way to connect with the local community.

There are almost endless options for sampling new foods while traveling, but some popular foodie destinations you might consider visiting include Tokyo, Japan; Paris, France; and Bangkok, Thailand. These cities offer a vibrant and diverse food scene, with street food vendors, traditional restaurants, and innovative fusion cuisine that will tantalize your taste buds and leave you with unforgettable culinary memories. If you're ready to pack your bags, here are some mouthwatering foods worth traveling for.

51 Foods to Travel For (and one to stay away from☺)

1. Pizza in Naples, Italy
2. Sashimi in Tokyo, Japan
3. Tacos in Mexico City, Mexico
4. Pad Thai in Bangkok, Thailand
5. Curry in Mumbai, India
6. Barbecue in Kansas City, Missouri, USA
7. Croissants in Paris, France
8. Pho in Hanoi, Vietnam
9. Pasta in Rome, Italy
10. Biryani in Hyderabad, India
11. Lobster rolls in Maine
12. Cuy (guinea pig) in Peru
13. Tex Mex in San Antonio, Texas
14. Hawaiian shaved ice in Big Island, Hawaii
15. Key lime pie in Key West, Florida
16. BBQ in Kansas City, Missouri
17. Fish and chips in London, England
18. Sausages in Munich, Germany
19. Croissants in Paris, France
20. Kimchi in Seoul, Korea
21. Putin in Canada
22. Ouzo in Greece
23. Gelato in Italy
24. Cheese and chocolate Fondue in Switzerland
25. Hot pot in Taiwan
26. Peking Duck in China
27. Kalua Pork in Hawaii
28. Paella in Spain
29. Pierogi in Poland
30. Trappist beer in Belgium

31. Baklava in Turkey
32. Falafel in Israel
33. Tanjin in Morocco
34. Port wine in Port, Spain
35. Smoked Salmon in Alaska
36. Papaya salad in Thailand
37. Chili crab in Singapore
38. Afternoon Tea in the UK
39. BBQ in Argentina
40. Carne Asada Burrito in San Diego, California
41. Guinness beer in Dublin, Ireland
42. Chocolate-dipped churros in Canary Islands, Spain
43. Jewish Deli in New York City, New York
44. Okonomiyaki in Japan
45. Coca tea in Peru
46. Dim Sum in Hong Kong
47. Kava Tea in Fiji
48. Curry in India
49. Scotch in Edinburg, Scotland
50. Escargot in Paris, France
51. Shepards pie in Ireland
52. Ambergris (whale barf) beer in New Zealand

Food tours

Sometimes food can be intimidating in a new city. One of the best ways to find your favorite new dishes is to take a food tour. These half or full-day tours, given by passionate locals, will walk you in a small group to sample some of the best foods around. You'll leave with a full stomach and a bunch of new favorite foods to order later.

Cooking classes

Another exciting way to experience a new city's cuisine is to learn to cook it. Cooking classes are a popular way of learning a new cooking style right from the source. Imagine discovering the secrets to delicious Thai food at a day class, then getting a relaxing Thai massage on your chopping arm that evening.

Books

1. 1,000 Foods To Eat Before You Die: A Food Lover's Life List by Mimi Sheraton link
2. Best Places to Eat in Every Country by Lonely Planet Food link
3. The Food Lover's Guide to Paris by Helen Massy-Beresford link

* * *

Travel for Culture

See a different way of life

Traveling to experience different cultures is a truly transformative experience. It opens your eyes to new perspectives, exposes you to diverse ways of living, and helps you broaden your horizons.

Why travel for culture?

1. **It boosts your empathy-** When you immerse yourself in a new culture, you have the opportunity to see the world through someone else's eyes. This can help you develop a deeper understanding and empathy for others, even when you come from vastly different backgrounds.
2. **It's a confidence booster-** Navigating a new country or culture can be intimidating, but pushing yourself out of your comfort zone and trying new things can help you build confidence. You'll return home feeling more self-assured and capable of handling new challenges.
3. **It broadens your perspectives-** Seeing the world from different angles can help you reexamine your own

beliefs and values. By encountering different perspectives and ways of life, you may realize that there are multiple ways to live a happy and fulfilling life.

4. **It provides unique memories and experiences-** Traveling and experiencing new cultures gives you stories and memories that you'll treasure for a lifetime. You'll have a wealth of experiences to look back on and share with others.

10 Locations for a Unique Cultural Experience

1. **Japan-** With its ancient traditions, fascinating culture, and high-tech cities, Japan offers a unique blend of the old and the new. Whether exploring Tokyo's neon-lit streets or visiting a traditional tea ceremony, you will surely be captivated by this fascinating country.
2. **Morocco-** From the bustling markets of Marrakech to the stunning architecture of Fes, Morocco is a sensory overload. You'll be surrounded by vibrant colors, exotic aromas, and the sounds of traditional music and chanting.
3. **Peru-** With Machu Picchu as its centerpiece, Peru offers a rich history and diverse cultural experience. Its celebrated traditions blend indigenous beliefs with Spanish Catholicism. Whether you're exploring the Amazon jungle or discovering the ancient ruins of the Inca Empire, you'll be mesmerized by the beauty and diversity of this country.
4. **India-** With its complex history, vibrant culture, and diverse landscapes, India offers a truly unique cultural experience. From the bustling streets where sacred animals like cows roam free in Delhi to the serene backwaters of Kerala, there's something for everyone in this fascinating country.
5. **Bhutan-** With its majestic scenery, fascinating culture, and commitment to Gross National Happiness, Bhutan is unlike any other country in the world. Whether exploring the ancient monasteries of Paro or discovering the unique

way of life in Thimphu, you're sure to be captivated by this intriguing country.

6. **Indonesia-** Indonesia is a melting pot of cultures and traditions. Whether you're exploring the lush rainforests of Bali or discovering the unique culture of Jakarta, you'll be amazed by the beauty and diversity of this country.
7. **Brazil-** With its sensational beaches, vibrant culture, and varied landscapes, Brazil offers a truly unique cultural experience. Explore the bustling streets of Rio de Janeiro or discover the beauty of the Amazon rainforest and be captivated by this colorful country.
8. **Mexico-** From the bustling streets of Mexico City to the tranquil beauty of the Yucatan Peninsula, there's something for everyone in this fascinating country.
9. **Egypt-** Egypt offers a glimpse into an impressive ancient civilization. Whether you're exploring the pyramids of Giza or discovering the mysteries of ancient Egyptian history, you'll be captivated by this fascinating country.
10. **Italy-** Explore the canals of Venice or discover the art and architecture of Florence, Italy's culture is worth experiencing.

Resources

1. These Countries Have The Most Cultural Attractions link
2. Top 10: world's best destinations for culture link
3. 17 Cultural Tourism Destinations in the World Culture-Buffs Must Visit link

Books

1. International Travel Secrets: Take Shorter Trips, More Often, for Less by Michael Wedaa link
2. How to Travel the World and Live with No Regrets.: Learn How to Travel for Free, Find Cheap Places to Travel, and Discover Life-Changing Travel Destinations by Dr. Ernesto Martinez link

3. Travel the World Without Worries: An Inspirational Guide to Budget and Adventure Travel by Marek Bron link

* * *

Travel for Unique Stays

Sleep somewhere unusual

Staying in a unique property can be an incredibly exciting vacation destination all its own. Whether it's a castle, ice hotel, treehouse, jail cell, or underwater lodge - you're sure to find yourself surrounded by incredible ambiance and one-of-a-kind experiences.

Nothing beats the thrill of waking up in an actual castle each morning! You'll get to explore hidden corners and secret passageways deep within the walls while admiring views of stunning landscapes from atop parapets or ancient towers. And at night? Sleep under towering ceilings surrounded by centuries-old art and artifacts that are sure to bring some magical dreams.

Venturing up into the treetops for a stay in a treehouse can offer breathtaking vistas with fresh air that encourage a connection with nature. Imagine having your coffee on a wrap-around porch looking out over peaceful valleys below, or listening to birdsong as you read your favorite book beneath lush foliage. Plus, there will likely be plenty of adventure opportunities such as zip lines and other aerial activities - not to mention the chance for genuinely unforgettable star gazing come nightfall.

How to find unique properties?

With vacation rental sites like Airbnb that have allowed people worldwide to list their sometimes very unique properties, staying in a boring hotel room is a thing of the past. In fact, on Airbnb, you can search by the accommodation type no matter where it is in the world. Consider making a special trip just to experience a night in an unusual property.

. . .

40 Unique Stay Airbnb Categories

1. Castle
2. Treehouse
3. Cabin
4. Dome
5. Tiny Home
6. Oh My Gosh! (Very Weird Places)
7. Amazing Views
8. Lakefront
9. Beachfront
10. Cycladic Homes
11. Ski in/ Ski out
12. Dessert
13. Mansions
14. Earth Homes
15. Islands
16. Chef's kitchens
17. National Parks
18. Farms
19. Camping
20. Caves
21. Yurts
22. Ryokans
23. Hanoks
24. Arctic
25. Vineyards
26. Top of The World
27. Golfing
28. Historic Homes
29. Minsu
30. Shepherds Huts
31. Boats
32. Barns
33. Houseboats

34. Windmills
35. Campers
36. Towers
37. Containers
38. Trulia
39. Grand Pianos
40. Riads

For more inspiration, take a look at some of the unique places listed on the sites in the resource section below.

Resources

1. Airbnb (airbnb.com)- link
2. Vrbo (vrbo.com)- link
3. 19 Most Unique Places to Stay Around the World link
4. The most unusual places to stay around the world link
5. 27 Most Unique Hotels in the World – Amazing and Unusual Stays link
6. 25 Most Unusual and Unique Hotels In The World link
7. 15 Mind-Blowingly Unique Places to Stay in the US link
8. 22 Most Unique Places to Stay in California link

* * *

Volunteer Travel

Travel for good

Traveling to help others can be a truly life-changing and fulfilling experience. It's a chance to give back, make a difference, and feel like you're making a positive impact in the world. Plus, you'll experience new cultures, make new friends, and see the world in a new light.

Whether you're interested in volunteering your time, skills, or resources, there are many opportunities out there for you to help others outside of your local community.

Travel volunteer programs bring travelers and local organizations together, allowing you to work on projects that make a real difference in the lives of those in need. Some popular examples of these programs include building homes with Habitat for Humanity, teaching English to children in developing countries, or providing medical care to underserved communities.

For example, if you're passionate about education, consider volunteering at a school in a rural community. Here, you'll have the chance to share your knowledge and experience with young students and help lay the foundation for their future success. And if you have a background in healthcare, you could volunteer in a clinic or hospital, where you can use your skills to improve the lives of people in need.

No matter your interests or skills, there's a travel volunteer opportunity out there that aligns with your values and interests. Pack your bags. You're off for good!

10 Popular Travel Volunteer Ideas

1. **Working with children-** Many retired individuals are passionate about helping future generations, and traveling to help with child-centered volunteer projects is a great way to do so. There are opportunities to work with orphanages, schools, and community programs. Notable organizations that present chances to help include UNICEF, Save the Children, and Habitat for Humanity. Cambodia, Peru, and Kenya are countries with a high demand for child-centered volunteer projects.
2. **Building communities-** For those who love to get their hands dirty and build communities, there are many travel volunteer opportunities to help communities in need. Projects can range from building schools, homes, and infrastructure to providing access to clean water and basic healthcare. Organizations such as Build Abroad, Habitat for Humanity, Community Builders, and All Hands and Hearts provide community-building volunteer programs in

countries with great need, such as Haiti, Indonesia, and Nepal.

3. **Environmental conservation-** Traveling to help with environmental conservation efforts is a great way to preserve the planet. Popular organizations such as World Wildlife Fund, The Nature Trust, and Sierra Club offer opportunities for wildlife preservation, reforestation, and beach clean-up projects. Costa Rica, Thailand, and South Africa are countries in high demand for environmental conservation volunteers.
4. **Education-** For those passionate about education, why not explore the opportunity to make a difference by traveling to volunteer on education projects? There are many ways to contribute, from teaching English as a foreign language to providing tutoring or even setting up libraries. Organizations such as Volunteer South Africa, ProWorld, and International Volunteer HQ are just a few that offer such opportunities. Immerse yourself in a different culture and make a real impact in countries like Guatemala, Ethiopia, or India, where the demand for educational volunteers is exceptionally high.
5. **Healthcare-** Volunteering in healthcare projects can make a significant impact. Organizations like Doctors Without Borders, Health Volunteers Overseas, and Project Hope offer opportunities for basic healthcare and medical missions in countries such as Haiti, Guatemala, and the Philippines that need volunteers.
6. **Wildlife conservation-** Individuals passionate about wildlife can travel to help with conservation efforts. Projects include wildlife rehabilitation, monitoring, and research. Organizations like the World Wildlife Fund, Wildlife Trust, and African Wildlife Foundation offer them. Popular destinations include South Africa, Kenya, and Tanzania.
7. **Agriculture-** Volunteer projects from sustainable farming to local markets are offered by WWOOF, Farm Africa, and the Agroecology Fund. High-demand countries include Peru, India, and the Philippines.

8. **Disaster relief-** Those concerned with disaster relief can make a difference by traveling to help in response or long-term efforts with organizations such as Red Cross, World Vision, and Samaritan's Purse, especially in countries like Haiti, Indonesia, and the Philippines.
9. **Cultural preservation-** Retirees interested in preserving cultural heritage and supporting traditional ways of life can volunteer with organizations such as the National Trust for Historic Preservation, UNESCO, and the Society for the Preservation of Arts and Culture. Volunteer opportunities range from festivals, museums, and cultural centers to arts and crafts. Popular destinations for cultural preservation volunteers include Peru, India, and Italy.
10. **Sports and recreation-** Organizations such as Right to Play, Special Olympics, and Play for Peace provide opportunities to coach youth sports, assist with community events and sports clinics, and build/maintain sports facilities. High-demand countries for volunteers include Kenya, Brazil, and the Philippines.

Go for it! Simple start steps:

1. Search for volunteer opportunities you might be interested in.
2. Consider the work you'll be doing, the organization's credibility, costs (volunteering is by and large a paid expense), and who'll benefit most.
3. Contact your top choices and get more information before deciding on one and moving forward.

Resources

1. Volunteer Abroad Opportunities for Seniors and Retirees link
2. Volunteer Abroad Opportunities link

3. Best Adult Volunteer Abroad Programs link

Books

1. Volunteer Vacations: Short-Term Adventures That Will Benefit You and Others by Bill McMillon link
2. Travel with Purpose: A Field Guide to Voluntourism by Jeff Blumenfeld link
3. Learning Service: The essential guide to volunteering abroad by Claire Bennett link

Chapter 6

New Experiences to Try

Sometimes we need a little push to experience things outside our comfort zone or just different than we're used to. Maybe we'll love it, and it will unlock something inside us we'll want to explore further, or perhaps we'll realize it's not for us and once was enough. Either way, having a mindset open to trying as many new experiences as possible will lead to excitement and a fully experienced life.

Try it all

Think of trying new experiences that will broaden your life experiences. Don't be a one-trick pony, so to speak. If you're only interested in sports, try your hand at something outside of your element, like art. If you've always played it safe, do something that might make you pee your pants. Become obsessed with doing new things, and consider each a personal life experience accomplishment until you run out. I'll bet even if you live to 120, you'll never run out and will have a lifetime of unforgettable memories.

. . .

The New Experience Age Game

A friend turned 60 and decided to challenge herself with a game of trying 60 new things that year. What a great idea to keep from getting stagnant in our everyday routines. Give it a try on your next birthday, and try to match new experiences with your age. Keep a record of your progress and try to select the broadest range of new things (not just 60 new foods, for instance). It might motivate you to soak up life and have your best year yet.

Chapter 6 Website Links

* * *

New Year's Eve Countdown in Times Square New York

Celebrate at the crossroad of the world

A bucket list item for some, once you experience ringing in a New Year in Times Square, you'll never view it on television the same again. Millions of people from around the world converge on the streets of New York early in the day to get the best spot for the ball drop celebration. Most of the time is spent self-entertaining and socializing with the people squished around you. As the night progresses, those lucky enough to be within viewing range of a stage or giant screen have some entertainment before the highly anticipated crystal ball drops at midnight. I braved the crowds and the Y2K fears for the Millenium celebration in Times Square with friends and have since recommended it to family members who also had a great time. It's a once in a lifetime experience you'll always remember and possibly never want to repeat!

Did you know?

- The NYE crystal ball is 12 feet in diameter and 11,875 pounds.
- Times Square NYE celebrations began in 1904.
- The first NYE ball was made of iron and wood.
- The first "ball drop" was in 1833 atop England's Royal Observatory to allow viewing boat captains to precisely set their chronometers (sensitive navigational instruments).

Pairs well with: Festive hats, champagne, lots of snacks

You might also like: Macy's Thanksgiving Day Parade, Germany Oktoberfest, New Orleans Mardi Gras

* * *

Attend the World's Largest Hot-Air Balloon Festival

Walk among giant enchanting colorful balloons

Imagine walking among hundreds of giant colorful hot-air balloons as they glow in the setting sun before fireworks and a synchronized drone light show. The 9-day Albuquerque International Balloon Fiesta brings as many as 500 hot-air balloons of all shapes, colors, and cartoon characters from around the world, as well as over 750,000 spectators to be enchanted by these balloons taken to the sky. It's truly a magical sight and a bucket-list event for many!

What happens?

Each day has different events that usually start before the sun comes up when the winds are most likely calm, and the balloons can fill the dark sky with their glow. Some days they all take off together in the morning. Spectators are allowed to walk among these giant balloons while they inflate and sometimes chaotically lift off together. During the day, there are car shows, chainsaw carving demos, skydivers, balloon target drop competitions, remote-controlled balloons, photo booths, a concert, and more. In the evenings, there are night glows, fireworks, and drone light shows on some days.

Inside Scoop

Plan to get your entrance tickets and accommodations as early as possible. If you have an RV, this is the best way to visit. Several fields closeby to the event turn into RV camping spots for hundreds of RVs. There are free shuttles to the fiesta and back which is very convenient for morning events that start before 6 am. Give yourself at least 3 days because weather, such as wind, can call off an event. You wouldn't want to miss the day all balloons go up together, called mass ascension. Bring your camera, some good walking shoes, and perhaps a picnic blanket or lawn chair. Usually, people show up for the early morning events, go back to rest or sightsee in Albuquerque during the day, and come back again to watch the evening events. For a small fortune, some balloons will take up spectators during the event if booked in advance. Don't miss the free hot-air balloon museum right outside the event.

Go for it! Simple start steps:

1. Visit the Balloon Fiesta website and view the upcoming schedule of events.
2. Secure accommodations for your chosen dates.
3. Purchase tickets.

Resources

1. Albuquerque International Balloon Fiesta link
2. Balloon Rides link

3. Visit Albuquerque link

Products

1. Compact Waterproof Picnic Blanket link
2. Compact 30X Zoom Camera link
3. Sling Day Bag link

Books

1. Frommer's Easy Guide to Santa Fe, Taos, Albuquerque by Barbara Laine link
2. Lonely Planet Southwest USA by Hugh McNaughtan link
3. Balloons over Albuquerque by Steve Larese link

Pairs well with: RV travel, photography, New Mexican food

You might also like: Oshkosh Air Show, Yi Peng Lantern Festival, Walt Disney World

* * *

Go Skinny Dipping

Get your chunky dunk on ☺

Now we're getting to the good stuff here. When the clothes come off, and you hit the water baring it all, you're either skinny dipping or chunky dunking. You know who you are. Either way, you'll be adding a little thrill back into your life and affirming you're still the same fun-loving free-spirited person you were as a kid. If you're the serious type or never had the chance as a youth, this is your moment to shine. Let down your guard and pants and hit the water completely free. Free of what others think (but I'd recommend finding somewhere private to keep from scaring children), free of what you're supposed to do as an adult, and free to do something as wild and crazy as you think this is. Retirement is freedom. What will you do with it? Get naked.

. . .

Favorite shirts to wear before skinny dipping

- "It's weird being the same age as old people"
- "I don't know how to act my age. I've never been this old before"
- "Don't forget my discount"
- "I see no good reason to act my age"
- "Normal people scare me"
- "Do not mess with old people. We didn't get to this age by being stupid"
- "I may be old, but I.... What was I saying?
- "I never dreamed that one day I'd be a grumpy old man, but here I am killing it"

Pairs well with: A few drinks, a spouse or someone special, darkness

You might also like: Nude beaches, nudist colony, Seinfeld

* * *

Run a Marathon

Go the distance

Your body may be getting old, but your mind says you've got a lot of life left in the tank. Marathons are the place to prove it to yourself and let everyone else know you're not slowing down yet.

Marathons worldwide draw up to tens of thousands of people of all ages together for the chance to test themselves and make it to the finish line.

Did you know?

- A half marathon is 13.1 miles. A full marathon is 26.2 miles.

- A marathon can take just over 2 hours for world-class athletes to 8 hours or more for walkers. The average time is 4:30 for males and 4:56 for females.
- There are over 1,100 marathons in the US every year.
- The Boston Marathon is the world's oldest annual marathon, established in 1897.
- The first modern Olympic marathon race in 1896 was 25 miles, inspired by a legend of a Greek messenger who ran from Marathon to Athens with word of a significant Greek victory over the Persians.
- In 1908 at the London Olympics, the length of the Olympic marathon was extended to 26.2 miles because Queen Alexandria wanted to start at the lawn of Windsor Castle (so little royals could watch from the nursery windows) and finish at their Olympic Stadium.
- Most races give prizes and sort results by gender and age categories (generally in 5-year blocks) from under 15 to 90+.
- Walt Disney World Marathon runs through all 4 Florida Disney theme parks for an unforgettable experience.

What to expect

Runners gather at the starting line before the sun rises, with the fastest runners at the front. A race starts with a gun, or sometimes fireworks signal the beginning. Roads are closed, and runners are given the rare opportunity to run down the middle of the street, uniquely seeing the city or town. Water stations, snack areas, port-o-potties, bands, first aid stations, runtime checkpoints, spectators, and volunteers are spread along the route. Some marathons have a minimum finishing time, but others, such as the Honolulu Marathon, allow runners to take as long as they need to complete the marathon.

How to do it

Running a marathon is not easy at any age. Still, it can be accomplished by almost anyone with proper training and determination. Prospective finishers typically follow a training routine of 3 to 4 days a week, several months (typically 16 weeks) in advance while slowly building up distance and endurance. Running clubs and training groups can be joined to help with conditioning and keep them motivated. Proper shoes, hydration, and good running form are essential, as well as the mental determination to keep going forward when things get tough.

Fight against growing old

My first marathon was unexpected. I wasn't a big fan of running (and rarely did it), but I do enjoy challenges. Planning to move, I mentioned to a friend that I regretted not doing the famous marathon in my city before leaving. It turned out our moving plans got postponed, and I semi-unenthusiastically found myself having to live up to my words. I read running articles, bought shoes, and started running with my wife as a support coach, biking alongside me with a water bottle.

Weeks into training, my body hurt, and I had "hit the wall" (ran out of energy) a few times and questioned if I could finish. I worked on changing my stride to a less bouncy shuffle to protect my knees and brought some energy gel packets to keep from hitting the wall. I signed up for a half marathon about a month before the full marathon, hoping it would give me confidence. It did not. In fact, quite the opposite. Barely surviving the half, I now questioned if I'd even finish the full. I doubled down on training and knew I'd be in for a battle on the big day.

When it arrived, I was amazed by the 30,000+ runners of all ages and abilities. For 26.2 miles, the mob of runners, volunteers, and excitement propelled me forward. Sure, I was passed by women pushing strollers, grandparents, and even a guy from Japan wearing traditional wooden sandals, but hey, I finished. I vowed never to do that again, but as time passed, the painful memories faded, and the glory of the moment grew in my mind until a few years later, I was running again to beat my previous time. I'm now at five marathons and half marathons. I still don't like to run, but I love trying to beat my previous times as I fight against growing old.

Insider Tips

- Purchase and train in high-quality shoes. Acquire light and comfortable running gear. For monitoring pace and distance, consider buying a GPS running watch or using a similar phone app. Lastly, a lightweight music setup such as an iPod shuffle clip-on MP3 player and wired headphones can enhance your running experience.
- Drink water every 15 minutes, thirsty or not.
- Bring a small running belt with several energy gels for when you need a boost.
- During training, stretch before and after without exceptions.
- Perfect a soft stride to avoid repetitive impact injury on joints and back.
- On longer run days, practice along areas of the actual route (if possible) to gain confidence on race day.
- When things get difficult, just keep moving forward without long breaks, and you'll eventually make it.

7 Stages of Marathon Running

1. Let's do this!
2. This is fun!
3. Why am I doing this?
4. I'm going to die.
5. I wish I was dead.
6. I'm dead.
7. I can't wait to race again!

. . .

Go for it! Simple start steps:

1. Ask your doctor before considering running a marathon.
2. Search for runs near you and register.
3. Download a suggested training schedule, join a marathon training program, and buy gear.
4. Stick to your training program and never give up!

Resources

1. 15 Fun Marathons for Beginners link
2. How long does it take to run a marathon? link
3. Marathon Training Plans link

Products

1. Body Glide Anti-Chafe Balm link
2. Compact Running belt link
3. Large Running Belt link
4. GPS Running Smartwatch with Music link

Books

1. Marathon: The Ultimate Training Guide by Hal Higdon link
2. Never Too Late: Inspiration From 7 Later-in-Life Athletes by Kate Champion link
3. The Runner Kitchen: 100 Stamina-Building Recipes by Emma Coburn link

Pairs well with: Travel, massages, Gatorade

You might also like: Dash and Splash (run and swim races), outrigger paddling clubs, cycling races

* * *

Eat at a Michelin Star Restaurant

Savor your fancy food

A Michelin Star is the ultimate hallmark of culinary excellence. Think fancy food, elegantly presented, in thoughtful miniature portions, on oversized plates. Ok, maybe that's not entirely true for all Michelin-rated restaurants, but the exclusive rating means it's going to be an experience you'll remember. How many meals can you say that about?

The Michelin Guide was initially published in 1900 in France by the Michelin Tire Company to encourage drivers to travel more. With fewer than 3,000 cars on the roads in France, the free guide contained maps, gas stations, hotels, and car mechanics throughout the region. In 1926 the first star rating system was revealed, and the travel guides covered only some regions of the world. It wasn't until 2005 when a guide for the United States came out that allowed US restaurants to be eligible for Michelin Stars.

Facts about the Michelin Guide and Stars[10]

- A rated restaurant can receive 0-3 stars. 1- "a very good restaurant," 2- "excellent cooking that is worth a detour," 3- "exceptional cuisine, worth a special journey."
- Anonymous inspectors judge the restaurant with rigorous secret criteria over several visits.
- Currently, there are only about 140 three-star Michelin Rated restaurants worldwide and under 3,000 total restaurants with stars.
- The countries with the most Michelin Star restaurants are currently: France 632, Japan 413, Italy 363, Germany 305, Spain 212, and the US 193 (89 in California).
- The "Bib Gourmand" award for "good food at moderate prices" was created in 1955.

- There are between 80 and 120 full-time inspectors who each evaluate an average of 240 restaurants a year.
- In 2016 a street-food vendor in Singapore called Hawker Chan won a Michelin Star, making it the least expensive star restaurant in the world (it lost its star in 2021).

Go for it! Simple start steps:

1. Search online for Michelin Star restaurants near you or where you intend to vacation.
2. Attempt to get a reservation (some require booking months in advance).
3. Get dressed up and enjoy.

Resources

1. Top 16 Michelin Rated Restaurants Around the World link
2. 50 Best Restaurants in the World link
3. Michelin Starred Restaurants You Should Visit At Least Once link

Books

1. Best Places To Eat In Every Country by Lonely Planet link
2. Food Journeys of a Lifetime by National Geographic link
3. The Mere Mortals Guide To Fine Dining by Colleen Rush link

Pairs well with: Wine, special occasions, significant other

* * *

Volunteer

Do good

In a world where we've learned to think and act with a "what's in it for me" mentality, volunteering can break the norm by focusing on benefiting others. Giving our time to those in need is a wonderful way to connect with people in a positive way. Also, when we give, it makes us feel good. That's why it's been said that if you want to make yourself feel better, start by doing something nice for someone.

12 Reasons to Volunteer

1. **Provides you with a sense of purpose-** Helping others can give your life new meaning and keep you mentally stimulated.
2. **Provides a sense of community-** Feel connected to those you're helping in your neighborhood.
3. **Meet new friends-** Connect with other caring volunteers who have similar interests.
4. **Do good-** Good people do good things. Volunteering is one way to positively affect the world.
5. **Increases your social skills-** A chance to talk to many new people and sharpen your social skills.
6. **Improves self-esteem-** Doing something that you feel is worthwhile and good for the community gives you a sense of accomplishment that can make you feel more fulfilled and confident.
7. **Learn valuable new skills-** The training and hands-on experience you gain while volunteering could benefit your future endeavors.
8. **Can bring fun into your life-** If you choose to volunteer in an area of your interests or hobbies, you'll be doing something you enjoy and making a difference.

9. **Can make you happier-** Doing something meaningful for others can make you feel good. It can lower stress, anger, or anxiety levels in your life.
10. **Strengthens your mind-** Actively overcoming challenges and dealing with social situations will keep your mind sharp.
11. **Strengthens your body-** Many volunteer activities may require physical effort to achieve, which will strengthen your body.
12. **Strengthen your soul-** Being a part of something greater than yourself, positively contributing to society, and connecting with others, leads to a feeling of fulfillment and well-being.

Areas to Volunteer

There are many ways to volunteer other than helping assemble meals for the homeless on Thanksgiving or serving in your place of worship. Here are some areas with volunteer opportunities; human rights, animals, arts and culture, children and youth, community, computers and technology, education and literacy, health and medicine, seniors, crisis support, disaster relief, employment, environment, faith-based, homeless and housing, hunger, immigrants and refugees, international causes, justice and legal, LGBTQ+, media and broadcasting, people with disabilities, politics, race and ethnicity, sports and recreation, women, veterans and military families.

Go for it! Simple start steps:

1. Google "volunteer opportunities" or try the VolunteerMatch website in the resources section below.
2. Decide how to help.
3. Contact a volunteer organization.

Resources

1. VolunteerMatch (www.volunteermatch.org) link
2. How to Find The Ideal Place To Volunteer link
3. A Reference Guide: 20 Top Volunteer Websites To Help You With Your Search link

Books

1. How to Be An Everyday Philanthropist by Nicole Boles link
2. Chicken Soup For The Soul: Volunteering and Giving Back by Amy Newmark link
3. Learning Service: The Essential Guide To Volunteering Abroad by Claire Bennett link

* * *

Attend a Symphony Orchestra

Feel music being created

Onstage in front of you, the conductor begins by waving his hands. Behind him, up to 100 musicians with all types of instruments take their cue and softly start playing. You open yourself up to the music and focus on how the instruments combine to create a musical story, from periods of calm delicateness played by violins to moments of excitement with powerful percussion crashes—the music dances in your ear. You feel the rhythms of the music, and it triggers emotions inside you.

10 Extraordinary Benefits of Listening to Classical Music[11]

Studies have shown mental and physical benefits to listening to classical music.

1. Lowers blood pressure
2. Boosts memory
3. Sparks creativity
4. Reduces stress levels
5. Fights depression
6. Relieves pain
7. Improves sleep quality
8. Increases dopamine levels which makes you happy
9. Improves productivity
10. Improves test performance

10 Greatest Symphonies of All-Time[12]

Here's a great place to start if you're sold on the impressive list of benefits of listening to classical music and need help figuring out where to begin. Unwind to these ten greatest symphonies of all-time and find your favorite.

1. Beethoven - Symphony No. 3 (1803)
2. Beethoven – Symphony No. 9 (1824)
3. Mozart – Symphony No. 41 (1788)
4. Mahler – Symphony No. 9 (1909)
5. Mahler – Symphony No. 2 (1894 rev. 1903)
6. Brahms – Symphony No. 4 (1885)
7. Berlioz – *Symphonie Fantastique* (1830)
8. Brahms – Symphony No. 1 (1876)
9. Tchaikovsky – Symphony No. 6 (1893)
10. Mahler- Symphony No. 3 (1896)

Resources

1. 10 Things That Happen To Your Body When You Listen To Classical Music link
2. Tips For First Time Visit To A Symphony link
3. 20 Greatest Symphonies of All Time link

4. Research Has Great News For Those Who Love Classical Music link

You might also like: Opera, learning an instrument, history

* * *

Houseboat on a Lake

Take a house on the water

It's a house. It's a boat. No, it's a houseboat! How fun are these little floating motorhomes? Unlike most compact feeling ocean-going boats, these lake-bound vessels are like spacious open apartments. Grab a few friends or extended family and spend a few days together on a lake having fun. Houseboats are comfortable floating platforms of up to two levels with everything you need to sleep, eat, relax, and play. Adults can socialize or fish for dinner, while the grandkids can play in the water or waterslide. Bring kayaks, or tow a watercraft for more excitement waterskiing, wakeboarding, or inner tubing. Or pick up anchor and explore the lake to find secluded coves of peaceful quiet serenity. Take in the sunset relaxing on the top deck, and wake up to calm mirror glass water surrounding your bed. What a wonderful way to spend quality time with the people you love or to recharge as you enjoy the beauty of nature all around this summer.

Top 10 Best Houseboating Lakes in the US

- **Shasta Lake, California-** Dubbed "houseboat capital of the world." Take in the views of 14,180-foot Mount Shasta and the 165 miles of breathtaking shoreline in California's largest artificial lake.
- **Crane Lake and Voyageurs National Park, Minnesota-** Explore the only water-based National Park in America and see bald eagles, black bears, white-tailed deer, moose, and aquatic birds.

- **Lake Powel, Utah, and Arizona-** A major boating destination in America with 2,000 miles of shoreline to explore.
- **Lake Cumberland, Kentucky-** One of the best fishing lakes in America, also claimed to be the "houseboat capital of the world," with over 1,500 houseboats.
- **Raystown Lake, Pennsylvania-** A beautiful piece of nature three hours from Washington, DC.
- **Lake Billy Chinook, Oregon**
- **Table Rock Lake, Missouri**
- **St. Johns River, Florida**
- **Sutton Lake, West Virginia**
- **Lake Mead, Nevada, and Arizona**

Hooked on houseboats? It's common to find places around the world where people actually live on a boat.

10 Best Spots in the US to Live on a Houseboat

1. Miami, Florida
2. Lake Havasu, Arizona
3. Sausalito, California
4. Fort Washington, Maryland
5. Seattle, Washington
6. Portland, Oregon
7. Hot Springs, Arkansas
8. Shasta Lake, California
9. Lake Cumberland, Kentucky
10. Fort Worth, Texas

Resources

1. Houseboating Lakes Map And Info link
2. Best Houseboat Lakes By State link
3. Best Places To Live On A Boat In The US link

Books

1. Designing and Building A Houseboat by M.E. Huebbe link
2. Rock The Boat: Boats, Cabins, and Homes on the Water by Gestalten link
3. The Houseboat Book by Barbara Flanagan link

Pairs well with: Summer, fishing, kayaking

You might also like: RV motorhome travel, sailing, unique Airbnb rentals

* * *

Take a Brewery Tour

Go behind-the-scenes of one of the world's most popular drinks

From a low of 50 brewing companies in 1978 to over 9,000 operational breweries in the US, the world's most popular alcoholic beverage is exploding with new talent and new flavor choices. Getting a behind-the-scenes look at the big shiny stainless steel tanks and all the industrial equipment can be almost as fun as sampling the beers afterward. Most breweries of all sizes have tours. An enthusiastic guide will give you the company's history, tell you a little about how beer is made, and walk you around the equipment used to brew beer. A brewery tour is an interesting look at economies of scale and efficiency from the big brewing companies and, in contrast, a painstaking labor of love for the small local craft brewers. Both sizes of brewery tours are equally fascinating. Some even give free beer samples at the end of the big breweries or a chance to chat with the brewer owners at the small ones.

Production Brewery or Brewpub?

When looking for a local brewery to visit (California alone has over 1000 to choose from), look for a production brewery instead of a brew pub. Production breweries are usually in industrial areas and have small tasting areas. Their primary purpose is to supply great-tasting beer to other establishments in kegs or bottles and cans for retail sales. These places have a lot to see and a relaxed European beer hall style. Generally, they produce higher quality beer than brewpubs, whose primary purpose is a restaurant. Also, brewpubs usually don't have tours.

Vacation stop

After you've enjoyed a few brewery tours in your area, it's always fun while traveling to stop in at your favorite beer company or try an unknown local favorite. Things magically taste better on vacation, and that's doubly true for fresh out-of-town beer straight from the source. He's a few popular states, breweries, and beers to try on your next vacation.

Top 5 Beer States

1. **Vermont-** With the most breweries per capita, at 15 breweries per 100,000, Vermonters are a thirsty bunch. Top-rated breweries are The Alchemist, Lawson's Finest Liquids, and Fiddlehead Brewing Co.
2. **Colorado-** Hosting the nation's largest ticketed beer festival, the Great American Beer Festival, where over 40,000 attendees can sample over 2,000 different beers, Colorado knows how to get that Rocky Mountain high. Sit on the lawn at New Belgium with a VooDoo Ranger IPA, or try WeldWerks Brewing Co.'s Medianoche-Coconut, a Beer Advocate top 100 rated beer.
3. **California-** California has the most breweries and craft beer produced in the country. West coast style India Pale Ale (IPA's) are a favorite here, with style icons like Pliny the Elder (and Younger) from Russian River Brewing Co is worth a try (if you can find it). Stone Brewing Co, Lagunitas,

and Sierra Nevada are big IPA makers. One of my favorites is The Bruery in Los Angeles for barrel-aged and sour beers.

4. **Oregon-** 300+ breweries and stalwarts like Deschutes and Rogue make Oregon a top beer destination.
5. **Pennsylvania-** Over a billion beers a year are cracked open thanks to this 2nd overall beer-producing state. It is home to the oldest operating brewery in the country, Yuengling, with its decadent Hershey's Chocolate Porter. Other favorite breweries here are Troegs and Victory.

10 Best Beer Tours In the US

1. Magic Hat Brewing Company, South Burlington, Vermont
2. Samuel Adams Brewery, Boston, Massachusetts
3. Dogfish Head Craft Brewed Ales, Milton, Delaware
4. Brooklyn Brewery, New York City, New York
5. Stone Brewing, Escondido, California
6. New Belgium Brewing Company, Fort Collins, Colorado
7. Deschutes Brewery, Bend, Oregon
8. Troegs Brewing Company, Hershey, Pennsylvania
9. Sierra Nevada Brewing Company, Chico, California
10. Maui Brewing Co, Kihei, Hawaii

Capital of Craft Beer

With 150+ local breweries in San Diego, you won't have far to go to find a great brewery tour. If you're on a "beer journey" exploring the diverse range of beer styles and would like to calibrate your pallet to appreciate the best, here are the San Diego winners of the 2022 World Beer Cup. This international competition judges over 10,000 beers from 2,500 breweries from 57 countries to award medals to the best of the best. Here are the 13 San Diego breweries' winning beers from "the most prestigious beer competition in the world." Many of these small breweries' beers can only be found locally, so go explore the crafty libations.

Gold Medals

- North Park Beer Co. | Hop-Fu! | American-style IPA
- AleSmith Brewing Co. | Wee Heavy | Scotch-style ale
- Pizza Port Bressi Ranch | Dieguito | American-style pilsener
- Ballast Point Brewing: Little Italy | Schlenkerla | Smoked beer

Silver Medals

- SouthNorte Beer Co. | Agavemente | Specialty beer | Chula Vista
- Kilowatt Brewing | OB Bubble Dubbel | Belgian-style Abbey ale | Kearny Mesa
- Burgeon Beer Co. | Invita | International light lager | Carlsbad
- Pure Project Brewing | Houblon Deluxe | Hazy or juicy imperial IPA | Vista

Bronze Medals

- Karl Strauss Brewing Company | Aurora Hoppyalis IPA | American-style IPA | Pacific Beach
- Craft Coast Beer & Tacos | Oscura | International pilsner or lager | Oceanside
- The Lost Abbey | King of Tyre | Old ale or strong ale | San Marcos
- Craft Coast Beer & Tacos | Shootz Mahalo | Juicy or hazy strong pale ale | Oceanside
- Kings & Convicts Brewing | Haze in the Park | Juicy or hazy pale ale | Miramar
- Attitude Brewing Co. | Pils Bitte | Kellerbier or zwickelbier | Barrio Logan

Beer Shirts to wear on your visit

- IPA lot when I drink
- I like crafts
- In the pursuit of hoppiness
- I'd give up beer, but I'm no quitter
- That's cute, now bring your Grandpa a beer

Resources

1. Best States For Beer Lovers link
2. Beer Production Statistics By State link
3. Best Beer Tours in the US link
4. San Diego Breweries link
5. 31 Essential Craft Breweries to Try In San Diego link

Books

1. Craft Beer Brewery Guide To All 50 States by Mark Donovan link
2. United States of Craft Beer by Jess Lebow link
3. National Geographic Atlas of Beer by Nancy Hoalst-Pullen link

Pairs well with: Food trucks, music, beer samplers

You might also like: Wine tours, international brewery tours, vehicle manufacturing tours (Ford, Tesla, etc.)

* * *

Live in a Foreign Country for at Least a Month

Sample the expat life with slow travel

Have you ever wondered what it would be like to live in a foreign country as an expat (a foreigner who lives abroad)? Instead of a typical touristy visit somewhere where there is rushing from one place to the next, seeing everything in a day or two, you'll be able to relax and live like a local. You'll get to know the local people, shop at the local grocery stores, and explore the neighborhood coffee shops or sidewalk cafes at an easygoing pace. Stumble upon local events, and get the scoop on the best places to visit from neighbors. If you're interested in immersing yourself in a new culture, slow travel might be just up your alley. It's never been easier or more affordable than it is now.

Vacation Rental Websites

With the rise of private rental sites like Airbnb and VRBO, one of the most expensive aspects of long-term travel, where you stay, is significantly reduced. In countries with a favorable exchange rate, you can find weekly and monthly discounts that will put you into fully furnished apartments in the heart of the action or even in luxury homes in quiet neighborhoods for much cheaper than you'd expect in the United States. After your flight, taking things slow abroad isn't much more money than a brief visit staying only at hotels. With monthly and weekly discounts, I stayed in a lovely furnished apartment in Ecuador for $570/ month ($19/day), Medellin, Columbia, $182/ week ($26/day), and $36/ night in the Sacred Valley of Peru near Machu Picchu.

The rentals have kitchens, so after you wander the local markets and pick out the best produce, you can bring it home and cook it. No eating out every day, hotel travel fatigue. Also, your host is always there to ask for assistance whenever you need suggestions on what to do, how to get around like a local, or the best places to eat. They can have laundry, office space, wonderful private balconies, internet, full TV and streaming video choices, and more for all the comforts of being at home, just in an exciting new location.

Pair With Rideshare Apps

Taking public transportation on travel can be an experience in and of itself. Rideshare apps like Uber and Lyft are incredibly freeing when you're not feeling like an adventure. With a few taps on your phone, you'll have a tracked car pull up and take you directly to where you need to go. No cash is required (payment is electronic through the app), no haggling over price, no language barriers, no directions need to be exchanged, and it's usually highly affordable compared to other forms of transportation like taxis.

Popular Vacation Rental Websites

- **Airbnb** (www.airbnb.com)- Originally, Airbed and Breakfast when it was founded in 2008. The company's original concept involved offering air mattresses and breakfast to attendees of an annual design conference in San Francisco who had difficulty finding affordable accommodation. Now, the most well-known vacation rental company with 6 million listings in over 220 countries. They have a great website to sort listings by map location or accommodation type (castles, tiny homes, treehouses, cabins, amazing views, lakefront, skiing, National Parks, farms, vineyards, etc.). Be sure to look for locations with heavy monthly discounts for 28+ days. The fantastic app allows you to message hosts, get directions, and more.
- **Vrbo** (www.vrbo.com)- Vacation Rentals By Owner. Owned by Expedia, with over 2 million listed properties in 180 countries and a heavy concentration in Europe and the US.
- **Agoda Homes** (www.agoda.com)- Over 700,000 apartments, vacation homes, guest houses, and private rooms in 50 countries, with the largest number in Asian countries.
- **Plum Guide** (www.plumguide.com)- A London-based company with over 10,000 properties and a significant concentration near international cities like Paris, London, Rome, and Los Angeles.
- **Booking.com** (www.booking.com)- Besides hotels and hostels, vacation rentals are available worldwide in 200

countries. There are 6 million locations, including many apartments in Europe, Australia, North America, Asia, South Africa, and northern Africa.

- **Homestay** (www.homestay.com)- 150 countries with properties with a larger concentration in Europe and major cities worldwide.

Tips for Longer Stays

Unless you're looking to get away from it all, look for locations with enough to do and see to keep you from getting bored for the length of your stay. A month feels very long when you're not thrilled with the location. Consider taking little getaways to nearby areas and leave the bulk of your bags in your long-term stay location. Use Google Maps "Street View" to look around the neighborhood to see if you'll feel comfortable there before you book. Many places have local inexpensive food delivery service apps, like Rappi, that can bring food to you when you don't feel like walking around searching for new restaurants. Look for delivery company names on motorcycles with bags on the back.

In some places like South East Asia, the hotels may already be inexpensive and in great locations. You may not need to look for affordable vacation rentals to have more budget-friendly long-term stays. A VPN will allow you to watch your home country streaming content (Netflix, Amazon Prime, etc.) without restrictions because you're out of the country. Buy a local mobile phone company sim card and monthly prepaid plan that includes some data for the internet. It's very helpful to have data on your phone while exploring, to use Google maps directions, rideshare apps, and WhatsApp to call locally or internationally.

Resources

1. Airbnb (airbnb.com) link
2. The best Apartment Booking Websites link
3. Becoming an Airbnb host link

Books

1. Create Your Escape: A Practical Guide for Planning Long-Term Travel by Mike Shubbuck link
2. How To Move Abroad and Why It's The Best Thing You'll Do by Jessica Drucker link
3. The Rough Guide to First Time Around The World by Rough Guides link

Pairs well with: Big festivals, photography, foodies

You might also like: Moving overseas permanently, cruising, RV travel

* * *

Visit a Japanese Onsen

Feel how the Japanese relax

Sometimes called the ultimate bathing experience, Japanese mineral-rich hot springs known as onsens can relieve tense muscles, and the tranquil surroundings can clear your mind. Over centuries of development, onsens have become the preferred method of relaxation. They can be found throughout the country, in hotels, or the most beautiful natural outdoor settings. Many older Japanese come to their local onsen weekly. Once you experience it, you'll want to visit again and again as well.

In Japan's land of cherry blossoms bright,
Where hot springs flow both day and night,
A retiree came for some respite,
To soothe their bones and feel alright.

Into the water they did slide,
Their cares and worries cast aside,
The heat and tranquility they did bide,
And felt their aches and pains subside.

As time did pass, the person knew,
That in this place they felt anew,
Refreshed and rested, their spirit grew,
Ready for more adventures, brand new.
-Onsen Love

Resources

1. Japanese Etiquette 101- How to Onsen link
2. 10 Best Onsens And Onsen Towns In Japan link
3. 10 Best Onsen Destinations in Japan link

Books

1. Japanese Inns and Hot Springs: A Guide to Japan's Best Ryokan & Onsen by Rob Goss link
2. Onsen of Japan: Japan's Best Hot Springs and Bath Houses by Steven Wide link
3. Japan - Culture Smart!: The Essential Guide to Customs & Culture by Culture Smart! link
4. Fodor's Essential Japan (Full-color Travel Guide) by Fodor's Travel Guides link
5. Lonely Planet Japan by Rebecca Millner link

Pairs well with: Visit to a temple, sake, ryokan

You might also like: Mt. Fuji hike, Shinkansen (bullet train), Nikko

* * *

Earn a Certificate or License Just for Fun

Stay sharp and prove it

After years of working and dedicating your time to a career, getting a new certificate or license just for the fun of it can be a rewarding and fulfilling experience. It can provide a sense of accomplishment, challenge your mind, and keep you engaged and active.

For some retirees, the desire to learn and try something new is a natural part of aging. Getting a new certificate or license can provide a sense of purpose, stimulate your mind, and bring excitement and joy back into your life. Whether you're interested in learning a new skill, or even flying a plane, getting a certificate or license can give you the confidence and recognition to take on a new challenge.

Learning something new can improve your mental and physical well-being, and the social aspect of taking a class or meeting other people with similar interests can help you feel connected and part of a community. When you enroll in a class or training program, you'll be surrounded by people who are all there to learn and grow. Whether you're sharing a love for a new hobby or connecting over a shared passion for a particular subject, making new connections is a valuable benefit of returning to a school setting.

Another reason you might want to get a new certificate or license is that it opens up new career opportunities. Whether for personal fulfillment or a source of additional income, a new certificate or license can help a retiree find new work opportunities that align with their interests and skills. For instance, someone who has always been fascinated by cooking might get a certificate in culinary arts and turn their passion into a part-time job as a private chef.

Getting a new certificate or license is a great way to keep your mind and body active, try something new, and meet new people. Whether it's for personal growth, to pursue a new hobby, or simply for the fun of it, getting a certificate or license can bring excitement, satisfaction, and a renewed sense of purpose to your life. So, go ahead and embrace the possibilities, and let the fun begin!

28 Certificates or License Ideas for Fun or Curiosity

1. **Pet psychology certification-** Pet psychology certification is for those who have a passion for animals and

want to understand them on a deeper level. Whether you're a pet owner or just love spending time with furry friends, this certification can help you communicate with your pet and improve their behavior.

2. **Pet grooming certification-** A fun and rewarding way to show your love for animals. Whether you want to start your own grooming business or help friends and family with their pets, this certification will give you the necessary skills and knowledge.
3. **Life coach certification-** A life coach is a professional who helps people identify and achieve personal goals. A life coach works with clients to create an action plan to help them reach their desired outcomes and develop skills and strategies to help them succeed. Life coaches can help people become more successful personally or professionally by providing support, guidance, and insight.
4. **Nutritionist certification-** A nutritionist certification is perfect for those who have a love for healthy living and want to educate others on the importance of good nutrition. Whether you're a fitness enthusiast or just enjoy cooking and experimenting with different foods, this certification can help you share your knowledge with others and positively impact their health.
5. **Wine sommelier certification-** A wine sommelier certification is a surefire way to elevate your appreciation for one of life's greatest pleasures: wine. Whether you're a seasoned connoisseur or just enjoy a good glass of red or white, this certification will give you the knowledge and skills to confidently navigate a wine list and impress your friends with your newfound expertise.
6. **BJCP beer judge certification-** Being a beer judge is a delicious way to indulge in your love of beer and a great way to expand your knowledge and appreciation of this beloved beverage. Whether you're a seasoned brewer or a beer lover, this certification will give you the skills and expertise to judge beer like a pro.

7. **Bartending certification-** For those who love the nightlife and want to learn the art of mixology. Whether you're a retiree who wants to bartend for a social part-time job or love making unique drinks, this certification can help you perfect your skills and bring joy to others. It's a fun way to be creative, socialize, and learn something new.
8. **Sailing certificate-** Ahoy, matey! Get certified in sailing and set sail on the high seas for adventure and relaxation. The wind in your hair and the salt on your skin will create ocean filled memories for years to come.
9. **Ski Patrol certification-** Love to hit the slopes? A ski patrol certification will teach you how to keep skiers and snowboarders safe on the mountain, so you can help make winter sports even more fun for everyone.
10. **First aid certification-** A practical and valuable skill that can be a great addition to your repertoire. Not only will you be prepared in an emergency, but you'll also have peace of mind knowing you're equipped to help others in need. Whether you're helping a friend or family member or simply want to be prepared for any situation, first aid certification is a fun and practical way to do so.
11. **CPR Certificate-** Want to be the hero of any situation? A CPR certificate gives you the skills to save someone's life in a medical emergency, and you'll feel like a pro. Plus, you never know when those skills might come in handy.
12. **Yoga instruction certification-** A perfect way for a person to dive into a new hobby and bring a touch of peace and mindfulness into their life. Not only will you learn the art of yoga, but you will also be able to share your newfound knowledge with friends and family. Whether you want to take your practice to the next level or share your passion for yoga, this certification will allow you to do so in a fun and rewarding way.
13. **Certified personal trainer-** Getting certified as a personal trainer is a fun way to challenge yourself physically and mentally. Whether you're a retired athlete or just someone who loves to stay active, this certification will

give you the skills and knowledge to help others achieve their fitness goals while also helping you stay fit and healthy.

14. **Fitness class instructor certification-** Get fit and your heart pumping by becoming a certified fitness class instructor. You'll have the inside scoop on all the latest workout trends and inspire others to live healthier lives.
15. **Solo skydiving certification-** Getting a solo skydiving certification is a daring and thrilling way to experience the thrill of flight. Whether you're an adrenaline seeker or want to experience the freedom of jumping out of a plane alone, this certification will give you the skills and knowledge to soar through the sky safely.
16. **Scuba diving certification-** An exciting and adventurous hobby that will allow you to explore the world beneath the waves. Not only will you see amazing sea life and breathtaking coral formations, but you'll also get a new perspective on the world.
17. **Commercial drone license-** A commercial drone license, aka remote pilot certification, is a must-have for anyone who loves technology and photography. Whether you're a retired pilot or just love flying cameras, this license allows you to operate drones legally for commercial purposes and capture breathtaking aerial footage. Not only is it fun to fly and take pictures, but it also opens up new opportunities for work and travel.
18. **Pilot's license-** Soar high in the sky and live the dream of being a pilot. A pilot's license opens up a new world of possibilities, from scenic flights to quick trips to exotic destinations.
19. **Motorcycle license-** A fun and exciting way to experience two-wheel freedom on the open road. If you're ready for adventure and want to try something new, this license will give you the skills and knowledge to safely enjoy the wind in your hair and the unobstructed open road ahead.
20. **Commercial Drivers License (CDL)-** Ever dreamt of hitting the open road and seeing the sights? A commercial

driver's license allows you to drive big rigs, buses, and other commercial vehicles to make your big-wheel dreams a reality.

21. **Floral design certification-** Getting a floral design certification is a creative way to bring beauty and joy into your life and the lives of others. This certification will give you the skills and knowledge to create stunning floral arrangements for all occasions.
22. **Massage therapist-** Love to pamper others? A massage therapist certification gives you the skills to soothe tired bodies and relieve stress so that you can make a difference in people's lives every day.
23. **Personal stylist certification-** A personal stylist certification is for those who have a passion for fashion and love helping others find their style. Whether you're a retiree who wants to keep up with the latest trends or just love shopping and putting outfits together, this certification can help you turn your hobby into a career. It's a fun way to stay stylish and make others feel confident and beautiful.
24. **Gemologist certification-** Unleash your inner gemstone aficionado and become a certified gemologist. You'll impress everyone with your knowledge of diamonds, rubies, and sapphires and maybe even find a few treasures of your own.
25. **Real estate license-** Getting a real estate license can be a fun and exciting way to explore a new career path. You will have the opportunity to help others find their dream home and gain a wealth of knowledge about the real estate industry. Whether you're looking to buy or sell property for yourself or explore a new career, getting a real estate license is a fun way to do so.
26. **Travel agent certification-** Imagine being the ultimate travel guru and planning unforgettable trips for friends and family. Get certified, and you'll be the one everyone turns to for the best recommendations and insider tips. As a bonus, you'll enjoy the perks and discounts of being a part of the travel industry.

27. **Art and photography certification-** Unleash your creative side with an art and photography certification. From capturing breathtaking landscapes to painting portraits, the possibilities are endless. Get ready to fall in love with art all over again.
28. **Animation certification-** Want to bring your imagination to life? An animation certification will teach you the skills you need to create animations, and you'll have a blast bringing your characters to life on the screen.

* * *

Try Everything Once

Never get bored

This is the catchall suggestion in this "new experiences to try" chapter. It's a chance to look inward and think, "what haven't I done yet?" Make a list, and start doing them and checking them off your "try once" list. Your initial reaction will be, "I've done it all." But as you really start thinking about it, there will be a lot of things that you've dismissed for one reason or another. Start with the easy ones and give them a try. You may find that the things you thought you wouldn't like aren't as bad or difficult as you thought. You might even actually enjoy it! At the very least, you'll enjoy broadening your life experience and the feeling of accomplishment after each new experience. If you keep an eye open for new experiences, you'll find many more chances to stay active and engaged in life.

Here's a broad list of ideas to consider if you've ever done them.

- Attend a major professional sporting event.
- Attend every professional sporting event- baseball, basketball, football, hockey, soccer, motocross, golf, horse racing, formula one, tennis, rugby, NASCAR, etc.
- Visit every state.

- Go to a parade.
- Go to a concert.
- Go to a convention.
- Taste every type of food- Mexican, Japanese, Mediterranean, Korean, BBQ, African, Pakistan, Indian, etc.
- Learn to play an instrument. Try every instrument!
- Create a work of art- Paint, sketch, photograph, sculpt, etc.
- Learn a dance.
- Memorize a poem.
- Go on a boat. Try everything that floats- kayak, sailboat, motorboat, river raft, stand-up paddle board, inner tube, boogie board, surfboard, outrigger canoe, jet ski, waterski, cruise ship, ferry, houseboat, etc.
- Learn a language. Learn a few words in many languages.
- Try every vegetable. Try every fruit.
- Try every cereal.
- Light fireworks.
- Take a train.
- Hike a mountain.
- Visit every National Park.
- Go camping.
- Learn about religions.
- Eat at a rooftop restaurant.
- Stay up all night.
- See an eclipse.
- Care for a pet.
- Visit another country. Visit every country.
- Ride an animal. Ride every rideable animal- horse, dogsled, camel, donkey, etc.
- Tour a factory.
- Visit a circus.
- Get a massage. Try every style of massage.
- Join a gym.
- Go to a supper club.

Chapter 7

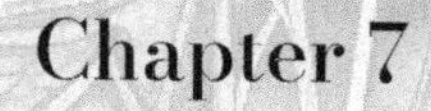

At Home Fun

Retirement is a time of leisure, a chance to pursue the passions that have been put aside in the hustle and bustle of life. The thought of being home all day might seem daunting, but it is a goldmine of opportunities waiting to be explored. A retired person's home is a castle of endless joys, a place where creativity blooms and the heart sings with happiness.

A world of adventure awaits as you delve into your creative pursuits. Whether painting, writing or crafting, you can finally indulge in the art of expression and bring your imagination to life. If music is your calling, strum your guitar or tickle the ivories and let the notes fill the air with melody.

Never stop learning, for knowledge is the key to a rich and fulfilling life. Delve into history, geography, or science, and be amazed at how much there is to discover. Pick up a new language and be able to communicate with people from all over the world.

Hobbies are a great way to stay active, both mentally and physically. Plant a garden and watch your flowers bloom, bake a cake and savor the sweet taste, or build a model and marvel at your creation. The opportunities are endless.

Home improvement projects are a great way to add value to your home and also keep you active. Grab some power tools, lumber, and paint. What will you create? Remodel your home for comfort or aesthetics.

For the tech-savvy, the computer opens up a world of gaming, socializing, and entertainment. Play games with friends, connect with family and friends via video calls or explore the vast world of the internet.

Animals and plants bring joy and beauty to our lives, and caring for them can be a source of comfort, companionship and relaxation. Adopt a furry friend or plant a garden and watch it flourish.

With so many exciting activities to do at home, a retired person's life is far from dull. Embrace this time, explore your interests, and create memories to cherish. Let's jump into this chapter and discover how adventure awaits in your very own home.

Chapter 7 Website Links

* * *

Home Improvement Projects

Do it for the house

Engaging in home improvement projects is a great way to breathe freshness and life into your home. Not only will you have the opportunity to add unique elements to your home, but you'll also be able to enjoy the reward of a job well done and watch with pride as your home transforms into something truly special. Remodeling is one of the first projects retired people undertake after retiring.

If you're feeling creative, home improvement projects can be wonderfully rewarding. You can express yourself through your home décor by adding pieces that reflect your personality. You can choose colors and fabrics that speak to you and bring life to a room with lively furniture and wall hangings.

Home improvement projects don't have to be expensive, either. You can find great deals on second-hand furniture, paint, and pieces that can be easily upcycled. If you're handy, you can make some pieces yourself that will be truly unique.

Home improvement projects are also a great way to add value to your home. Whether you want to increase your home's value before selling, make sure it looks its best, or is the most suitable for your golden years, a few simple improvements can go a long way.

Home improvement projects are fun, creative, and rewarding. With a little effort, you can transform your home into something extraordinary and watch with pride as your space reflects your style. So get creative and get to work!

A recent survey[13] found that 89% of homeowners were currently working on or planning to do a home improvement project within the year.

Most Common Home Improvement Projects

- 84% planning a heating-related project
- Calking/ weather striping drafty doors and windows
- Adding a smart thermostat to save money
- Adding insulation
- Adding storm windows/doors
- Upgrading HVAC system
- 14% planning kitchen projects
- 14% living room projects
- 12% home exterior

- 11% bathrooms
- 10% outdoor landscaping

Top Home Improvement Project Motivations

- 47% fixing existing issues
- 43% increase home value
- 39% improve aesthetics
- 33% simplify maintenance
- 31% add smart home features

8 Home Improvement Project Ideas

1. **Redecorate-** If you're looking to spruce up your space, redecorating is a perfect way. Adding a fresh coat of paint to your walls, changing your furniture or rug, or even switching up the lighting fixtures can create a whole new look you'll love. For a bold statement, consider introducing a bright accent wall with unique wallpaper. Or, you can keep it subtle and switch up the cushions on your sofa with a few new patterns. A few well-placed plants or curtains can also make a big difference. Redecorating can be the perfect way to give your home the makeover it needs.
2. **Remodel for mobility-** Installing ramps, widening door frames, or using adjustable shower heads can all help us remain independent in our later years. Adding handrails in the bathroom or installing sturdier flooring with better grip and traction can help ensure safety and peace of mind. Not to mention, these modifications can add a touch of style and flair to any home. With a few simple changes, remodeling for mobility can make any house a safe and stylish place to enjoy our golden years.

3. **Go ECO-** Going green and making home improvements that are good for the environment is becoming increasingly popular. Not only is it better for the planet, but making eco-friendly changes can save you money on utilities and provide long-term financial benefits. For example, solar panels can dramatically reduce energy costs, while low-flow toilets and faucets can reduce water bills. For those looking to reduce their waste, consider composting, recycling, and repurposing items like furniture and kitchen utensils. You can help the environment and your wallet by being ECO-friendly with your home improvements.
4. **Feng shui-** Feng shui is a great way to bring some energy and life into your home. It's all about using the power of the five elements - wood, fire, earth, metal, and water - to create balance in your house. You can make small changes, like rearranging furniture or adding plants to bring in a bit of nature, to larger projects like changing the color of your walls or painting a mural on a wall. All these changes will make your home look better and feel better to be in. In addition, you'll be able to tap into the power of the elements and use it to maximize the potential of your home.
5. **Outdoor landscaping for minimum maintenance-** Focus on transforming the outdoors into a beautiful, low-maintenance landscaping space that adds to the home's value. Installing artificial grass is an excellent option for a low-maintenance yard, and an outdoor kitchen or dining area is sure to make a statement. Plus, adding a hot tub or a patio or deck area can make the backyard the perfect place to relax and entertain. With a little bit of creativity and know-how, anyone can create a stunning outdoor oasis that stays green year-round without the need for constant upkeep.
6. **Install a meditation trail-** Installing a meditation trail in your backyard will help bring some peace and tranquility to your life. Imagine walking along a path, surrounded by nature and beauty, while feeling the day's stress and worries melt away. A meditation trail is perfect for honing your

mindful awareness and is a great way to create a calming oasis in your own backyard. For ideas on how to get started, you could use solar lighting to illuminate your path and create a magical atmosphere, line the path with natural elements like stones, driftwood, and plants, and even set up a small seating area at the end of the trail with comfortable pillows and a fire pit as a finishing touch. You'll be amazed at how much your mental health will improve with this simple and peaceful addition to your home.

7. **Minimalism-** Minimalism is a popular home improvement trend taking the world by storm. It's all about paring down your living space and decluttering your home so that it's easier to keep clean and organized. Going minimalistic has many benefits, like reducing stress, saving time, and creating more space. Some specific ideas include removing anything you don't absolutely need, investing in multi-functional furniture and storage, and adding some plants to your home. Going minimalistic will help you create a clean, peaceful, and beautiful home.
8. **Smart home-** Smart home technology is the perfect way to take your home to the next level. It has many benefits, no matter your lifestyle, from increased safety and convenience to energy efficiency and cost-effectiveness. With innovative home technology, you can control your home's lights, locks, temperature, security cameras, and more from your phone, tablet, or AI voice assistant such as Alexa. You can even set up automatic routines, like turning your lights off when you go to bed or having your thermostat adjust to an optimal temperature when you come home or wake up. Smart home technology is the future of home improvement and is an incredibly smart investment in your home.

10 Aging in Place Home Renovations

1. Convert to an open floor plan

2. Add a first-floor primary suite
3. Replace flooring according to needs
4. Widen doorways and hallways
5. Update with smart home tech
6. Install a walk-in shower
7. Paint in contrasting colors
8. Increase kitchen accessibility
9. Eliminate thresholds wherever possible
10. Build housing for a caregiver

26 DIY Building Project Ideas

1. **Bench-** Give your outdoor space a cozy seating area by building a custom bench- it's a great way to add a touch of charm and a perfect spot to relax. You can craft a bench with angled sides, back support, and built-in storage with the right materials and tools.
2. **Outdoor pergola-** Transform your outdoor space into a tranquil oasis with a pergola. It is a great way to provide shade and shelter and adds a touch of style to your backyard. Consider adding string lights to create a romantic atmosphere and comfortable furniture to make it the perfect spot for entertaining.
3. **Dog house-** Keep your pup warm, dry, and happy with a custom-built dog house. It's easy to assemble and gives your four-legged friend their very own little space to rest and relax. Plus, it makes a great conversation when having friends over.
4. **Umbrella table-** Add a bit of pizzazz to your deck or patio with a creative umbrella table. Not only does it provide much-needed shade and protection from the elements, but it also gives your outdoor space a unique touch. Consider adding a fun pattern or color to make this a standout piece.

5. **Outdoor fireplace-** Create a cozy spot to gather around with an outdoor fireplace. It's a great way to bring friends and family together for conversation and smores. Plus, you can customize it to suit your style with colorful fire bricks, stone, and accent pieces.
6. **Outdoor lighting-** Outdoor lighting will give your home an inviting ambiance so you can enjoy relaxing outside at night. Get creative with it and install accent lighting such as string, pathway, and colored spotlights.
7. **Cat claw pole-** Climb to new heights with a cat claw pole for your furry friend! Choose from various materials, sizes, and colors to ensure your cat has a blast climbing.
8. **Birdhouse-** Invite some feathered friends to your backyard by building a birdhouse. A great way to show off your carpentry skills and your love of nature, pick out a stylish design you can proudly display in your garden.
9. **Porch or deck-** Enjoy the outdoors in style with a new porch or deck. Pick a spot in your garden and get creative with materials, textures, and colors to create a unique outdoor oasis.
10. **Bird feeder-** A bird feeder is a perfect way to entice wildlife and watch them in their natural habitats. Pick an easy-to-clean design and decorate it with vibrant colors to make it truly stand out.
11. **Guest cabin, she-shed or man-cave-** Design and build a guest cabin to give your guests a home away from home. Create a getaway space that's all your own with your she-shed or man-cave.
12. **Arbor-** Transform your yard into a shaded paradise with a beautiful arbor, perfect for outdoor entertaining and dining. With a few simple tools and some elbow grease, you can bring your dream arbor to life with a custom design that fits your space, style, and budget.
13. **Polished concrete tabletop or coffee table-** Create a unique, modern, and industrial look in your living room with a DIY polished concrete table top or coffee table. Not only will you be able to customize the dining, coffee, or

accent table to fit your needs, but you'll also get to show off your creative skills and hard work.

14. **Flower retaining wall-** Showcase your favorite flowers and add a touch of rustic charm to your garden with a retaining wall. With a few basic materials, easy instructions, and a touch of imagination, you can create a landscape feature that will make your garden look like a million bucks.
15. **Outdoor brick walkway-** Put your DIY skills to the test and create a stunning outdoor brick walkway for your garden or patio. The classic design and timeless brick look will add charm and elegance to any outdoor space, perfect for entertaining guests or enjoying peaceful moments in nature.
16. **Adirondack chair and loveseat-** Add comfort and style to your outdoor space with a handmade Adirondack chair and loveseat. With the right supplies and easy-to-follow instructions, you can create a cozy seating area that will be the highlight of your garden or patio.
17. **Garden hutch-** Create a storage oasis with a unique and practical garden hutch. With a few simple steps, you can build a hutch that provides space to store garden tools, outdoor accessories, and other items while giving your garden a pop of color and personality.
18. **Coat and mitten rack-** Create an inviting entryway with a coat and mitten rack, perfect for getting organized and ready for whatever the day brings.
19. **Shoe storage booster stool-** Create extra space with a shoe storage booster stool, freeing up floor space and creating a neat and orderly look.
20. **Hanging wall bookcase-** Bring style and organization to your wall with a hanging wall bookcase, perfect for displaying your favorite books in an eye-catching way.
21. **Suspended bookshelves-** Upgrade your home office with suspended bookshelves, perfect for giving your valuable books an elegant home.

22. **Floating bookshelves-** Make a statement with floating bookshelves, ideal for creating a unique and sophisticated look for your walls.
23. **Wall bed bookcase combo-** Make the most of your space with a wall bed bookcase combo, perfect for a multi-functional bedroom.
24. **Showcase wall-** Showcase your favorite pieces with a showcase wall, ideal for making your décor stand out in any room.
25. **Hidden bookcase storage-** This DIY project is a great way to turn a forgotten corner of your home into a dreamy storage spot. It will add a touch of character to your space and provide extra space to organize your belongings without taking up any additional floor space.
26. **Wallpaper accent wall-** Create a bold statement in your home by giving a single wall a new life with some wallpaper. With a few simple steps, you can transform an otherwise bland wall into a masterpiece, adding color and texture to any room.

Resources

1. Aging in Place: Growing Older at Home link
2. 50 Incredible DIY Home Projects link
3. 50 DIY Home Improvement Projects Under $50 link

Books

1. Feng Shui that Makes Sense - Easy Ways to Create a Home that FEELS as Good as it Looks by Cathleen McCandless link
2. 100 Weekend Projects Anyone Can Do: Easy, practical projects using basic tools and standard materials by Editors at The Family Handyman link
3. Great Book of Woodworking Projects: 50 Projects for Indoor Improvements and Outdoor Living from the Experts

at American Woodworker (Fox Chapel Publishing) Plans & Instructions to Improve Every Room by Randy Johnson link

* * *

Move and Downsize

Live somewhere new with less

If things have gotten a little too routine and stale, consider moving. Moving changes everything. New sights, sounds, tastes, and experiences are right outside your door because you moved somewhere new. Retirement is the perfect time to reevaluate your living situation and perhaps move somewhere you've always wanted. Moving is one of the most popular things to do upon retirement, whether to a different area of your town or a foreign country.

Downsizing

Moving into a smaller place and stashing some cash might make a lot of sense with children all grown up and all the rooms in your house no longer needed. Larger homes, and yards, typically require more maintenance effort and costs. Something smaller may be freeing from those burdens, especially the older we get. Less space means less stuff needed to fill it with. It could be a perfect excuse to declutter and enjoy the benefits of a freeing minimalist lifestyle.

Where to go?

Ask 100 people something, and you might get 100 different opinions, but below are some ideas about where you might enjoy moving to. WalletHub recently ranked 182 US cities to retire to based on 1) affordability, 2) quality of life, 3) activities, and 4) health care.

. . .

Top 10 US Cities to Retire[14]

1. Orlando, Florida
2. Charleston, South Carolina
3. Scottsdale, Arizona
4. Tampa, Florida
5. Minneapolis, Minnesota
6. Denver, Colorado
7. Cincinnati, Ohio
8. Fort Lauderdale, Florida
9. Miami, Florida
10. Atlanta, Georgia

12 US States that don't tax social security and pensions

1. Alaska
2. Florida
3. Illinois
4. Mississippi
5. Nevada
6. New Hampshire
7. Pennsylvania
8. South Dakota
9. Tennessee
10. Texas
11. Washington
12. Wyoming

10 US Cities with the Most Retirees

US Census Bureau data showing cities with the highest percentage of their population 65 and older.

1. North Port, Florida (32% of the population is 65+)
2. Palm Coast, Florida (30%)
3. Tamarac, Florida (28%)
4. Walnut Creek, CA (27%)
5. Port Charlotte, Florida (27%)
6. Scottsdale, Arizona (27%)
7. Georgetown, Texas (27%)
8. Delray Beach, Florida (26%)
9. Boca Raton, Florida (25%)
10. Deerfield Beach, Florida (24%)

Where is the best place to retire outside the US?

Below are the top 10 countries for international retirement from the Expatra Global Retirement Index 2022.

1. Portugal
2. Spain
3. Costa Rica
4. Italy
5. Greece
6. France
7. Cyprus
8. North Cyprus
9. Turkey
10. Malta

Top 9 Tax-free Retirement Countries for Americans[15]

List of top tax-free retirement counties, according to Greenback Expat Tax Services.

1. Panama

2. Costa Rica
3. Portugal
4. Ecuador
5. Greece
6. Belize
7. Nicaragua
8. The Philippines
9. Malta

Live like a local before you move.

Before selling everything and rushing off somewhere around the country or the world, spend some time there as a local. We recently spent six weeks in a highly rated overseas retirement area in South America. The inexpensive, fully furnished Airbnb was wonderful and gave us a real sense of the city. However, it didn't take long before the cold, high altitude weather, constant rains (outside the rainy season), relatively high prices for South America, and our limited Spanish language struggles were enough to make it clear this place wasn't for us.

Go for it! Simple start steps:

1. Research online for potential new locations you might be interested in moving to.
2. Rent and AirBnB or similar for a month in your top 3-6 locations.
3. Return home and make a plan to move or not.

Resources

1. Best Places to Retire on Earth link
2. 20 Best Countries to Retire Abroad link
3. 9 Tax-free Retirement Countries for Americans link

Products

1. Moving Labels link
2. Foam Pouches link
3. Heavy Duty Packaging Tape link

Books

1. Right Place, Right Time by Ryan Frederick link
2. Keep the memories, lose the stuff by Matt Paxton link
3. America's 100 Best Places to Retire by Annette Fuller link

Pairs well with: Wine, Airbnb stays, foodies

You might also like: Living on a cruise ship, full-time RV travel

* * *

Unlock the Computer and Internet

Use one of the greatest tools we have

A recent US census report showed that 93% of Americans use the internet. Most Americans had a computer with the internet in their homes by the early 2000s. Why? Because computers and the internet are one of the greatest inventions ever. Gone are the new technology fears that had us thinking that only predators were online waiting to get us. It's now used by nearly everyone, good and bad. It's an incredibly powerful resource that everyone should learn to use and take advantage of.

A home computer is a marvelous tool for humanity, allowing us to access and explore a world of knowledge, creativity, and connections. It is the ultimate tool for creativity, communication, and productivity, making it an invaluable asset to our lives.

The computer is a powerful tool for learning, allowing us to access a seemingly endless array of educational resources, from textbooks and lectures to online tutorials. It is a great way to expand our knowledge, stay connected with the world, and stay ahead of the curve in terms of technological advancements. The computer can provide access to important information, such as current events and news, which can help us stay informed and make better decisions.

It is also an invaluable tool for creativity. With the right software and hardware, we can create art, music, and videos and develop our own websites and online stores. We can share our creations with the world, allowing us to reach a much wider audience. We can also use the computer to explore our interests, whether it's writing, programming, or designing.

A computer is also an essential tool for communication. We can use it to keep in touch with family and friends, as well as to connect with new people and build relationships. We can use it to share our thoughts, ideas, and experiences with others and to stay up to date in the lives of the people we care about.

Finally, the computer is an incredibly powerful tool for productivity. We can use it to stay organized, to manage our finances, and to keep track of our daily tasks.

Get ready to unleash your inner tech guru and discover all the wondrous and wild things your home computer has to offer. With all the fun computers provide, try not to forget the world beyond.

As I sit with bated breath,
Awaiting the unleashing of its digital depth,
My computer hums with potential and power,
Ready to entertain me every hour.

With every click and every clack,
My fingers dance upon the track,
On this digital playground I'm the boss,
My computer is my albatross.

And as I surf through cyberspace,
My imagination starts to race,
My dreams and ideas begin to soar,

With the endless possibilities at my core.

But in my mind, I take flight,
And fly above this digital sight,
For while my computer may bring joy,
It's the world beyond that's my true toy.
- Ancient Chinese Proverb ☺ -

7 Popular Ways People Use the Computer

1. **Communication-** Email, social media, chat, and video calls.
2. **Work-** Word processing, spreadsheets, databases, programming, and graphic design.
3. **Entertainment-** Gaming, streaming video, music, and web browsing.
4. **Education-** Online courses, research, and virtual field trips.
5. **Shopping-** Online stores, auctions, and comparison shopping.
6. **Banking-** Online banking, paying bills, and money transfers.
7. **Health-** Telemedicine, tracking health stats, and managing medical records.

10 Most Beneficial Uses of the Computer for a Retiree

1. **Staying connected-** Email, Skype, and social media.
2. **Learning new skills-** Online courses, tutorials, YouTube, and webinars.

3. **Staying physically active-** Exercise apps and online fitness classes.
4. **Keeping up with current events-** Online news sources.
5. **Enjoying entertainment-** Streaming services, online games, and digital music.
6. **Managing finances-** Banking, investing, and budgeting applications.
7. **Researching health information-** Medical reference sites and online pharmacies.
8. **Volunteering-** Online communities and virtual opportunities.
9. **Shopping-** Online marketplaces and comparison shopping.
10. **Staying Organized-** Productivity tools and calendar applications.

Top 10 Fun Things to Do on a Computer for Retirees

1. Online gaming
2. Virtual travel and sightseeing
3. Online shopping and auctions
4. Video conferencing and catching up with friends and family
5. Learning new skills or hobbies through online courses
6. Online reading and book clubs
7. Digital photo and video management
8. Creative expression through music, art, and writing
9. Online investing and managing personal finances
10. Online volunteering or community engagement

89 Ideas for Fun and Helpful Things to Do on the Computer

COMMUNICATE

- **Email-** Email is a convenient and easy way to communicate with people around the world. Popular email providers include Gmail, Yahoo, and Outlook.
- **Video conference-** Video conferencing has changed the way people communicate, allowing for virtual face-to-face conversations. Popular providers include Zoom, Microsoft Teams, and Google Meet.
- **Social networks-** Social networks are a great way to stay connected with friends, family and follow interests. Popular social networks include Facebook, Instagram, Snapchat, and Twitter.
- **Audio conferencing-** Audio conferencing allows users to connect with others in real-time using their computers, phones, or other devices.
- **Messaging-** One of the best ways to keep up with one person or groups is with text messaging, video chats, photo and video sharing, audio calls, and even real-time location sharing. Try WhatsApp, Facebook Messenger, WeChat, Line or Google Hangouts.
- **Chat rooms-** Whether you're looking to make new friends, discuss your interests, or pass the time, chat rooms provide an exciting and dynamic virtual environment to connect with others. Try Discord, Yahoo! Chat, or a site dedicated to your interest.
- **Forums-** The most popular forums include Reddit, Quora, and Yahoo Answers, where people can join communities, ask questions, and participate in interesting conversations with people from around the world.
- **Friendships and dating sites-** Friendship and dating sites are a fun way to connect with new people, share common interests, and find potential romantic partners. Popular websites such as SilverSingles, SeniorFriendFinder,

OkCupid, and OurTime offer a variety of features such as personality quizzes, chat rooms, and virtual gifts to enhance the user experience.

- **Telehealth-** Telehealth is the use of digital technologies to access health care services remotely and is growing in popularity as a convenient and accessible way to connect with health care professionals from the comfort of your home. Some of the most popular telehealth websites include Teladoc, Doctor on Demand, and Amwell, offering virtual consultations, diagnoses, and treatment plans.

ENTERTAINMENT

- **Electronic newspapers-** Electronic newspapers provide a convenient and up-to-date way for anyone to stay informed about the world, with popular websites like The New York Times and The Guardian offering an array of articles, videos, and interactive features that bring the news to life. Whether it's to stay informed about current events, to delve deeper into topics of interest, or to pass the time, electronic newspapers offer endless opportunities for learning and entertainment.
- **Electronic magazines-** A fun and engaging way to explore the latest news and trends in your favorite interests. From fashion and lifestyle to cooking and travel, you can find many digital magazines on popular websites like Zinio, Apple News+, and Amazon Kindle.
- **Websites-** A fun way to entertain oneself on a computer, providing endless content and resources.
- **Electronic books-** Reading electronic books is an entertaining way to enjoy your favorite books without carrying heavy physical copies. Major places to find e-books include Amazon's Kindle store, Apple Books, and Google Play Books, with millions of titles available at the touch of a button.
- **Audiobooks-** Audiobooks bring books to life with narration, providing a more immersive and engaging

experience than just reading. You can find a wide range of audiobooks, from classic literature to modern bestsellers, on popular websites such as Audible, Amazon, and iTunes. Great while exercising or driving long distances.

- **Games-** Playing games on the computer can be an exciting way to pass the time, and there are numerous websites and platforms to choose from, such as Steam, Epic Games Store, and Big Fish Games, offering an array of options from action-packed adventures to chess to mind-bending puzzles.
- **Competitive online games-** Get ready to unleash your competitive spirit with the exciting world of competitive online PC games, where players from all over the world come together to battle it out in thrilling matches. Whether you're a fan of strategy games, first-person shooters, or sports games, popular platforms such as Steam, Origin, and Blizzard Battle.net offer a vast selection of the latest and greatest games, so you're sure to find something that suits your interests.
- **Open-world games-** Open-world PC games provide an immersive and captivating experience, allowing players to freely explore vast virtual worlds and engage in various activities and quests rather than simply making it to the end like other games. Popular titles in this genre include Grand Theft Auto, The Witcher, and Skyrim, which can be found on popular gaming platforms like Steam, Epic Games Store, and GOG.
- **Listen to music-** Listening to music on the computer is a fun and entertaining way to enjoy your favorite tunes and discover new ones. Some popular websites to find and listen to music include Spotify, Apple Music, Amazon Music, Soundcloud, and Pandora.
- **Stream movies and TV shows-** Streaming movies and TV shows on the computer is a great way to enjoy your favorite shows and movies from the comfort of your home. Popular websites for streaming movies and TV shows include Netflix, Amazon Prime Video, Hulu, and Disney+.

- **Watch live TV-** A flexible and convenient viewing experience, with major streaming platforms such as Hulu, Sling TV, YouTube TV, and DirecTV Now offering access to a variety of live television channels.
- **Watch YouTube videos-** An entertaining way to pass the time and explore a wide range of interests, from hilarious comedic sketches to informative, educational content, making it a popular choice among people of all ages. With an endless library of user-generated content, it's easy to find something that piques your curiosity, and the ability to subscribe to your favorite channels ensures you never miss a new video.
- **Podcasts-** A great way to stay informed and entertained on a variety of topics, from current events to hobbies and interests. Some of the most popular places to find podcasts include Apple Podcasts, Spotify, and Google Podcasts, where you can browse and subscribe to your favorite shows for free.
- **Access your local library online-** A convenient way to browse and check out digital books, audiobooks, magazines, and more. Significant platforms for accessing local libraries online include OverDrive, Libby, and Hoopla.
- **View maps of the world-** Exploring the world from the comfort of your home has never been easier. With a simple search, you can access interactive maps that allow you to zoom in and out of countries, cities, and even streets, making it a fun and engaging way to discover new places and broaden your knowledge of geography. Major places to find it include online map services like Google Maps, Google Earth, and Bing Maps.
- **Take 360-degree tours of almost anywhere-** Explore iconic landmarks, natural wonders, famous museums, and even remote locations through virtual 360-degree tours available on various websites and platforms such as Google Maps and Street View.

FIND INFORMATION

- **Current events-** Staying informed and up-to-date on current events is crucial for staying in the loop with the world. You can find news and current events on websites such as CNN, BBC, or Fox News or through news aggregators like Google News or Flipboard. You can have your online newsfeed learn your topics of interest.
- **Politics-** Following politics online allows you to stay in the know on the latest developments, debates, and decisions being made at the local, national, and international levels. Some places to find it include news websites, social media, and dedicated political platforms like Politico, The Hill, and BBC News.
- **Finding local events-** Discovering local events is simple with the vast online platforms on the computer. From community calendars to event-specific websites, the digital world provides a convenient way to find exciting activities in your area.
- **Weather-** Plan your day and stay aware of severe weather. You can find accurate and up-to-date weather information on Weather.com, Weather Underground, AccuWeather, and The Weather Channel.
- **Health research-** Major websites like PubMed, WebMD, and Mayo Clinic offer a wealth of information to help you better understand your health and make informed decisions related to your well-being.
- **Travel planning-** Travel planning has never been easier with the use of online services like Google Travel, TripAdvisor, and Expedia. These websites make searching for flights, hotels, and activities simple so that you can plan the perfect getaway.
- **Find business info-** Business information can be found through search engines, such as Google, Yahoo, and Bing, which allow you to quickly find contacts and reviews for any business. Additionally, specialized websites such as Yelp and TripAdvisor are excellent sources for finding detailed reviews, ratings, and other helpful information.

- **Artificial intelligence-** Artificial intelligence can be used to quickly find answers to questions and problems. Try ChatGPT, Chatsonic, and YouChat. AI can give you analytical intelligent answers with the power of the collective internet knowledge behind it. It's like having the smartest person in the world as a personal friend. You can ask them anything and they won't judge you!
- **Translate-** Translation services are a terrific way to communicate in multiple languages. Google Translate is one of the most commonly used websites for translation services, and it offers comprehensive translations in over 100 languages. Translate images taken from foreign menus or speech in real-time.

Learning

- **Online courses-** An outstanding way to learn new skills and gain knowledge quickly and conveniently. There are many popular websites that offer courses in a variety of topics, such as Coursera, edX, and Udemy.
- **YouTube videos-** An interesting and creative way to learn. You can find tutorials, lectures, and educational content from various sources on topics like history, math, art, and even cooking. For example, you could watch a video about the history of World War II, or learn how to make a delicious lasagna.
- **Workshops-** A fabulous way to learn a new skill in an interactive setting. For example, you can attend a workshop on coding to learn the basics of programming or a photography workshop to learn the basics of camera operation and composition.
- **Language-** Learning a new language with a computer can be an exciting adventure. Many popular language-learning apps and websites, such as Rosetta Stone, Duolingo, and Babbel, make it easy and fun to learn a new language from the comfort of your home.

- **Music-** Learning to play music with the help of a computer can open up endless possibilities, allowing students to access resources such as virtual instruments, online tutorials, and even virtual music lessons from popular websites such as YouTube, Coursera, and Udemy.
- **Cyber security-** An essential skill to learn, no matter the age. It helps protect your vital information and data from malicious attacks. Several free online courses are available to learn the basics of cyber security, including those offered on sites such as Coursera, edX, and Udemy, which can help you gain the skills and knowledge needed to stay safe online.
- **History-** Learning history is a great way to gain insight into the past and understand why and how the world has changed over time. Popular websites for learning history include Khan Academy, National Geographic, and Smithsonian Learning Lab.
- **Skills and hobbies-** Learning new skills and hobbies has never been easier with the help of online resources! From the comfort of your own home, you can pick up a new hobby or skill with websites like Coursera, Udemy, and Skillshare, offering thousands of courses in many different subjects.
- **DIY fixes-** Learning how to fix things yourself can be a great way to save money and time. Popular websites for DIY fixes include YouTube, Instructables, and DIY Network, which offer easy-to-follow instructions and tutorials on repairing and constructing various items.

Shopping and Hiring

- **Online stores-** Online stores have revolutionized how we shop, allowing us to purchase almost anything from our homes. Popular online stores include Amazon, eBay, and Etsy.
- **Order food-** Gone are the days of pizza being the only delivery option. Now, you can get food delivered from

almost any nearby restaurant. Popular websites like Grubhub and DoorDash make it easy to find restaurants and order delicious food with just a few clicks.

- **Hire a driver-** Driving yourself to your destination can be a hassle and a waste of time. Hire a driver and let someone else do the work for you. Popular websites for hiring a driver include Uber, Lyft, and Gett.
- **Get groceries delivered-** Popular websites like Instacart and Amazon Prime allow you to conveniently select your groceries online and have them delivered right to your door, sometimes within hours. For even more time-saving convenience, you can save a group of regularly bought items such as milk, eggs, and juice, and with one click, reorder them all. Prices are comparable to local stores, so ordering groceries is a no-brainer.
- **Hire independent entertainers-** You can easily hire entertainers for your next event or party with websites like Fiverr or GigSalad. You can browse through thousands of talented performers from comedians to magicians to singers and more. They make it easy to find the perfect act for your special occasion.
- **Hire people for digital projects-** You can find talented people to help with digital projects quickly and easily at websites like Upwork and Fiverr. These websites allow you to search for freelancers and hire them for one-off projects or ongoing collaborations.
- **Hire people for home services-** Online services like TaskRabbit and Thumbtack make it easy to hire reliable independent people for various home services, from cleaning and plumbing to carpentry and landscaping. These services give you access to reliable workers to get your projects done quickly, professionally, and lower cost than hiring big businesses.
- **Meal kit delivery-** Meal kit delivery is an increasingly popular way to enjoy restaurant-quality meals without leaving home. Popular sites like HelloFresh, Blue Apron, and Sun Basket provide pre-measured ingredients and

recipes right to your door so that you can whip up delicious meals in a snap.

- **Home massages-** Getting a home massage is a great way to relax and unwind without ever having to leave your house. Popular websites such as Zeel and Soothe offer certified massage therapists that come to you to provide the massage of your choice.

Productivity

- **Banking-** Online banking is the ultimate convenience. You can do everything from check your balance, make check deposits, and transfer money, all in a matter of seconds. Plus, you can do everything from anywhere, anytime, making your banking experience hassle-free.
- **Bill paying-** A great way to streamline your finances. It's secure, convenient, and saves time by eliminating the need to write checks, buy stamps, and mail payments. Plus, you can set up automatic payments, so you don't have to worry about being late.
- **Investing-** An incredibly convenient way to manage and grow your finances. With access to real-time stock market information, the ability to buy and sell stocks with the click of a button, and the ability to monitor investments and make decisions on the fly, it's easy to see why so many people have embraced this form of investing.
- **Stay organized-** With the use of a computer, staying organized has never been easier. From to-do lists and reminders to calendar events and email alerts, you can manage your tasks with efficient and intuitive tools, allowing you to focus on the things that matter most.
- **Create documents and spreadsheets-** Creating documents and spreadsheets is a great way to stay organized and manage finances. For example, retirees can use a spreadsheet to track their monthly expenses or create a document to store important contact information.

- **Use online storage for backing up important digital files-** An essential task for protecting your important documents and memories. This could mean keeping digital copies of tax documents, photos, or other important records in a secure, off-site location for easy access in the event of a computer crash or emergency.
- **Track possessions-** Trackers, such as Apple AirTags, are a great way to keep track of your possessions. With a simple tap from your phone or computer, you can determine the location of your keys, wallet, laptop, or anything else you might misplace. You can even share the location of your possessions with family or friends, giving you the peace of mind that your valuables are safe.
- **File taxes-** Filing taxes online is a convenient and efficient way to get your taxes done quickly. Popular websites like TurboTax, H&R Block, and TaxAct make it easy to securely file your taxes online and even receive personalized tax advice.

Stay Fit

- **Workout videos-** Exercising is an important part of living a healthy lifestyle, and with the help of the internet, there's no shortage of exercise videos available. Popular websites like YouTube, Instagram, and Fitnessblender are all excellent sources of free exercise videos.
- **Online exercise classes-** Offering the ultimate convenience of staying fit from the comfort of your own home. Popular websites such as Peloton and Nike Training Club provide streaming classes and personalized plans to help you achieve your fitness goals.
- **Fitness tracking and monitoring with wearable technology-** Revolutionizing how we stay on top of our health goals. Popular tracking apps like Fitbit, Apple Health, and Strava allow us to monitor and analyze our physical activity and health, giving us a comprehensive view of our fitness goals.

- **Customized nutrition and meal planning-** An excellent way to keep your diet on track and ensure you get the proper nutrition. Popular websites such as MyFitnessPal, Dietician.com, and CalorieKing allow you to personalize your meal planning and track your progress.
- **Online personal training and coaching services-** These offer a convenient way to get fit and healthy. Popular websites include Trainerize, FitPlan, and MyFitnessPal, which provide personalized coaching and diet plans to help you reach your fitness goals.
- **Virtual reality environment for running or cycling-** An immersive and realistic way to experience the outdoors indoors. Popular sites such as Zwift and Peloton offer virtual routes to explore and race against other riders from all over the world.

Make Money

- **Freelancing-** A great way to earn money online, allowing you to work on your own terms and on your own schedule. Popular websites such as Upwork, Fiverr, and Freelancer offer a wide range of opportunities, from content writing and web design to copywriting and graphic design.
- **Online tutoring-** Popular websites like Chegg and Tutor.com allow you to tutor students in various subjects, such as Math, Science, and English, and pay you an hourly wage for your services.
- **Teach English online-** Teaching English online is a great way to share your knowledge and expertise with students from around the world. Platforms such as Verbling, Cambly, and Preply offer an easy and convenient way to get started.
- **Selling products on e-commerce platforms-** Popular websites like Amazon, eBay, and Etsy offer a wide variety of options for individuals to create an online store and start selling their arts and crafts or other products to customers worldwide.

- **Dropshipping-** Selling products without holding any physical inventory is an advantageous way to make money online, as it requires no inventory, shipping, or overhead. With platforms like Shopify, Oberlo, and AliExpress, you can quickly start dropshipping and make money with minimal effort.
- **Consultation services-** Put your knowledge and skills to good use. Popular sites for offering consultation services include Upwork, Fiverr, and Guru.
- **Affiliate marketing-** Popular websites include Amazon Associates, Clickbank, and CJ Affiliate, allowing you to promote products and services to your audience and receive a commission for every successful sale.
- **Investing-** Revolutionizing how people make money, offering convenience, flexibility, and the potential for substantial gains. Many popular websites such as E-Trade, Robinhood, and Coinbase facilitate investing in stocks, real estate, and cryptocurrency, allowing users to easily make low-cost investments.
- **Write and publish books-** This can be a fantastic way to make money by leveraging the power of the internet. Popular websites for writing and publishing books include Amazon Kindle, Apple iBooks, and Google Play Books.
- **Create a blog and monetize it-** Creating a website and blog and monetizing it with ads, affiliate links, and sponsorships is easy with platforms like WordPress, Wix, and Blogger.
- **Create online courses-** An exceptional way to utilize your knowledge, experience, and skills. Popular websites include Udemy, Skillshare, and Teachable, allowing you to create and share your expertise to earn a passive income.

Create

- **Graphic design-** Using software such as Adobe Photoshop or Illustrator to create digital images, logos, and designs.

- **Web design-** Build and design websites using tools like HTML, CSS, and WordPress.
- **Video editing-** Combine and edit video footage using software like Adobe Premiere Pro or Final Cut Pro.
- **3D modeling-** Create 3D objects and animations using software such as Blender or Autodesk 3ds Max.
- **Music production-** Compose and produce music with digital audio workstations like FL Studio or Ableton Live.
- **Game development-** Design and build games using game engines like Unity or Unreal Engine.
- **Writing-** Compose text for articles, blog posts, books, and more using word processors like Microsoft Word or Google Docs.
- **Photography editing-** Enhance and retouch photos using software such as Adobe Lightroom or Photoshop.
- **Digital art-** Create art using software such as Procreate or Krita.
- **Infographics-** Use tools like Canva or Adobe Illustrator to create visually appealing data presentations.
- **YouTube videos-** Script, video, edit, and upload to YouTube to help or entertain others.

Resources

1. Internet basics: A complete guide for older adults link
2. How Older Adults Can Improve Their Personal Cyber Security link
3. US Census- Computer and Internet Use in the United States link

Products

1. MacBook Air Laptop link
2. iPad Air link
3. Portable 5TB External Hard Drive USB 3.0 for PC and Mac link

Books

1. Macbook For Seniors: The Ultimate step-by-step guide to mastering your MacBook Air and Pro. Discover all the features and become an expert in less time. Tips and tricks included. by Henry Richard link
2. Seniors Guide to Windows 11: The Most Comprehensive & User-Friendly Guide on Learning How to Use Windows Step-by-Step with Pictures, Simple Explanations, and the Best Tips and Tricks by Richard Reed link
3. Computers for Seniors: Email, Internet, Photos, and More in 14 Easy Lessons by Chris Ewin link
4. iPad Seniors Guide: A Step-by-Step Manual for Non-Tech-Savvy to Master Your iPad in No Time by John Halbert link

Pairs well with: 3D printers, travel planning, online business

You might also like: Smart homes, cool gadgets, artificial intelligence

Chapter 8

Get Crafty

We can't constantly be stomping around the world checking off bucket lists. Sometimes we need a little downtime at home. Craft hobbies can be an enjoyable way to spend leisure time. With a world of craft possibilities, there is something everyone will love creating. Don't be intimidated by trying to learn any of these crafts. As obscure as some of them might seem, there are "how to" books with photos and videos online that will walk you through everything you'll need and provide step-by-step instructions on making them. If you can follow a recipe, you can learn how to make any of these fun crafts.

Before diving into finding your next crafty obsession in this chapter, let's examine why people enjoy this hobby.

10 Reasons to Love Craft Making

1. **Creativity-** Arts and crafts allow people to express themselves creatively and explore their artistic side.
2. **Relaxation-** Many people find that working on arts and crafts projects is relaxing and helps to reduce stress.

3. **Sense of Accomplishment-** Finishing a project can give a sense of accomplishment and pride.
4. **Socialization-** Many arts and crafts hobbies can be enjoyed with friends or in groups, which can be a great way to socialize and make new friends.
5. **Mental stimulation-** Arts and crafts can help keep the mind active and engaged, which can benefit cognitive health.
6. **Physical activity-** Some crafts like knitting, crocheting, pottery, and woodworking can also be a form of physical activity enjoyed by seniors or people with disabilities.
7. **Cost-effective-** Many arts and crafts can be done with materials that are inexpensive, easily accessible, and can be found around the house.
8. **Personalization-** Arts and crafts allow people to personalize their living space and make unique gifts for others.
9. **Learning-** Some crafts like calligraphy, beading, or woodworking can also be a fun way to learn a new skill.
10. **Make money-** Some people sell their arts and crafts online, at stores, or events.

Chapter 8 Website Links

* * *

Explore Your Creative Side

Unleash your imagination

Creativity is a chance to paint a masterpiece of colors with the brush of imagination. To pour life into the canvas of dreams and fashion beauty from within. It's the courage to dream, to see beyond what is, and to believe in what can be. It's not only about the end result but about the journey of self-expression and exploring the boundless potential of the mind. To be creative is to ignite the spark within, live life with passion, and add a touch of wonder to the world around us.

28 Creative Pursuits at Home

1. **Learn to draw-** Unleash the artist within and let your imagination flow onto the paper as you bring your thoughts to life with every stroke of the pen.
2. **Paint-** From watercolors to numbered paintings, let your brush become an extension of your soul as you splash vibrant colors onto the canvas and create a masterpiece.
3. **Read and write poetry-** Get lost in the rhythm and rhyme as you delve into the depths of your own emotions and express them through the timeless art form of poetry.
4. **Record a song-** Sing your heart out and let your voice soar as you lay down a track that captures the essence of who you are and what you want to say to the world.
5. **Sketch a self-portrait-** Take a step back and examine the person you are and the person you want to become as you put pencil to paper and create a visual representation of yourself.
6. **Write a children's book-** Bringing your imagination to life on paper and captivating young minds, writing a children's book is a playful and delightful creative pursuit. Let the adventures unfold as you pen down tales that inspire and instill joy in the hearts of children.

7. **Create puzzles-** Put your problem-solving skills to the test and challenge your loved ones with the puzzles you create. Designing crossword, trivia, or jigsaw puzzles is a fascinating and entertaining way to keep your mind sharp and engage with others.
8. **Invent a game-** Inventing a game is a fun and imaginative way to spend time with loved ones. Get your creative juices flowing as you dream up new rules, objectives, and strategies, and share the excitement of victory and defeat with your friends.
9. **Sculpt sandcastles-** With just sand, water, and your imagination, sculpting sandcastles is a mesmerizing and delightful creative pursuit. Let your hands work their magic and bring stunning structures of sand to life, fit for a king or queen.
10. **Landscape painting-** Bring a touch of nature to your home or canvas with the art of landscape painting. Let your brush strokes and color choices tell a story as you create breathtaking scenes of rolling hills, serene rivers, and vibrant forests.
11. **Start a YouTube channel or podcast-** Starting a YouTube channel or podcast is an exciting opportunity to share your passions, creativity, and talent with the world. Unleash your creativity and let the world see the real you!
12. **Ice sculpting-** Ice sculpting is a cool and refreshing way to unleash your creativity. With just a block of ice, your imagination, and a few tools, you can create a magnificent masterpiece that will last through the cold winter.
13. **Bullet journaling-** A creative and therapeutic way to organize your life, reflect on your thoughts, and bring focus to your goals. With colorful pens, stickers, and a few fun layouts, your bullet journal will be a masterpiece of self-expression.
14. **Adult coloring books-** A fun way to tap into your inner child and unleash your inner artist. With a box of colored pencils and a quiet afternoon, you can lose yourself in a world of colors and patterns.

15. **Colored powder floor art-** A vibrant and playful way to express yourself. With a few puffs of colored powder and a little bit of movement, you can create beautiful and lively artwork that will brighten up your day.
16. **Art journaling-** Art journaling allows you to express your emotions and thoughts colorfully and artistically, creating a visual diary of your life's journey.
17. **Mural art-** Mural art transforms any blank wall into a captivating masterpiece, blending creativity, imagination, and color to bring your vision to life.
18. **Drawing Zentangles-** A meditative form of art therapy where simple repetitive patterns are used to create stunning abstract works of art, providing a sense of calm and relaxation.
19. **Designing unique face masks-** A playful way to bring a pop of personality to your everyday life and show your creativity to the world.
20. **Nature writing-** Nature writing brings the beauty of the outdoors to life through words, capturing the essence of the environment and inspiring others to appreciate nature.
21. **Gingerbread house making-** A delightful treat for the senses, combining the love of baking with creativity and imagination, creating a unique and sweet work of art.
22. **Calligraphy-** Put pen to paper and unleash your inner artist with calligraphy. This beautiful and timeless form of handwriting allows you to create stunning works of art with just a few strokes. It's a perfect opportunity to relax, unwind, and explore your creative side.
23. **Upcycling-** Transform discarded items into works of art or functional objects with imagination and creativity. Upcycling is a wonderful way to give new life to forgotten treasures and express your individuality.
24. **Cooking-** Cooking is an art form that allows one to unleash their culinary creativity, combining ingredients to create delicious dishes that tantalize the taste buds. With endless recipes to choose from, cooking is a wonderful way

for a retired person to enjoy their time and showcase their culinary skills.

25. **Pottery-** A timeless craft that offers a chance to mold and shape clay into beautiful pieces of art. From bowls and vases to sculptures, pottery provides an opportunity to express creativity and bring a personal touch to everyday objects.
26. **Crafting-** A rewarding hobby that lets one bring their imagination to life. Whether knitting, crocheting, or cross-stitching, crafting provides a chance to slow down and enjoy the creative process, resulting in one-of-a-kind, practical, and beautiful pieces.
27. **Woodworking-** A hands-on hobby that allows one to bring their woodworking dreams to life. From simple shelves and birdhouses to intricate furniture, woodworking is a wonderful way to create functional pieces while honing one's skills and expressing creativity.
28. **Gardening-** A fulfilling hobby that brings one close to nature and allows one to enjoy the beauty and tranquility of the outdoors. From planting and nurturing flowers and vegetables to designing beautiful outdoor spaces, gardening is a fantastic way to enjoy the outdoors, get exercise, and unleash one's creativity.

Resources

1. 69 Creative Hobbies for a Better You link
2. 150 Creative Hobbies to Start or Revisit link
3. 101 Creative Hobbies to Promote a Balanced Life link

* * *

Make Crafts for Others

Turn your hobby into a side hustle

If you enjoy crafting, consider selling some to add an extra dimension of fun to your hobby. Below are examples of smaller crafts that you might enjoy making but only need to keep a few of them to yourself, such as dreamcatchers. These crafts are things that might make good products to sell at a craft market, such as Christmas ornaments.

17 Crafts You Could Sell

1. **Candle making-** Create waxy decorative works of art in an infinite variety of shapes, sizes, colors and fragrances.
2. **Jewelry making-** Use your creativity and self-expression to create decorative pieces, such as necklaces, earrings, bracelets, and rings, using materials such as precious metals, gemstones, beads, and glass. Jewelry can be made by hand using traditional techniques such as soldering, hammering, and setting stones or using modern tools like pliers and wire cutters. There are many styles and techniques in jewelry making, such as beading, wire wrapping, and metalsmithing. Some jewelry makers specialize in creating one-of-a-kind pieces, while others mass-produce their designs. Craft stores often have classes to learn these skills.
3. **Soap making-** Create uniquely colorful soap with wonderful fragrances that leave you feeling clean, moisturized, and refreshed.
4. **Bath bomb making-** Create relaxingly fragrant bath bombs that hydrate, fizz up, and look yummy enough to want to eat.
5. **Mobile making-** Mobiles are free-moving, hanging objects you'd typically see entertaining a baby above their crib.
6. **Gourd craft and ornament making-** Create a range of decorative ornaments, boxes, and birdhouses from this versatile vegetable. Gourds grow in a variety of shapes and sizes, so pluck one up from the garden and get creative.
7. **Leather crafting-** Learn the skills of forming, molding, stitching, lacing, braiding, and embossing leather to make

beautiful belts, wallets, purses, holsters, cases, jewelry, and home accessories.

8. **Carving wooden gnomes-** In folklore, gnomes are believed to protect homes, gardens, and nature from thieves and pests. You either love or hate them, so carve an army of protectors for your yard or set them free for the magical benefit of others' lawns.
9. **Dreamcatcher making-** A dream catcher is a traditional Native American craft believed to filter out bad dreams and only allow good dreams to pass through to the sleeper. The dream catcher is usually made of a willow hoop, with a web of sinew or cord stretched across it, decorated with feathers and beads. It is often hung above the bed or in a window. It is considered to be a spiritual object and symbol of protection.
10. **Glass bead making-** Fire up the torch and sprinkle on the colors. Making beautiful glass beads of art for jewelry might be your next passion.
11. **Christmas ornament making-** The options for creativity are endless.
12. **Decorative wooden boxes-** Hone your woodworking skills of cutting, sanding, staining, assembling, and decorating to craft some fancy little boxes.
13. **Stained glass boxes-** One of the most popular glassworking projects, your little stained glass boxes could be someone's next treasure.
14. **Amigurumi stuffed toys-** Crochet cute stuffed toys with this popular Japanese craft.
15. **Picture frame making-** Learn the art of creating beautiful wooden picture frames for your walls and others.
16. **Resin crafts-** A delightful and creative way to make unique and eye-catching pieces of art or jewelry using a type of synthetic polymer material called resin. It can be mixed with other materials such as pigments, glitter, or small objects like flowers, shells, or beads, to create a wide range of unique and customized objects. The mixture is then poured into a mold, where it hardens and takes on the

desired shape. Some common resin craft projects include jewelry, coasters, keychains, and home decor items.

17. **Custom sticker designs-** Create stickers with witty sayings using a Cricut machine. It's a fun and creative way to add a humorous touch to bumpers or belongings.

Go for it! Simple start steps:

1. Purchase a how-to book, or watch instructional videos online to learn the craft.
2. Purchase the tools and supplies.
3. Begin your crafty project.

Books

1. Art Of Candle Making Business Startup: How to Start, Run & Grow a Million Dollar Success From Home! By Suzanne Carpenter link
2. The Natural Soap Making Book for Beginners: Do-It-Yourself Soaps Using All-Natural Herbs, Spices, and Essential Oils by Kelly Cable link
3. Making Mobiles: Create beautiful Polish pajaki from natural materials by Karolina Merska link
4. 50 Beaded Bracelets: Step-by-Step Techniques for Beautiful Beadwork Designs by Tammy Honaman link
5. Get Started in Leather Crafting: Step-by-Step Techniques and Tips for Crafting Success (Design Originals) Beginner-Friendly Projects, Basics of Leather Preparation, Tools, Stamps, Embossing, & More by Tony Laier link
6. How to Make Bath Bombs: A Beginner's Guide to Making Homemade Bath Bombs Step-By-Step by Rebecca Wellner link
7. Carve a World of Gnomes: Step-By-Step Techniques for 7 Simple Projects (Fox Chapel Publishing) Full-Size Patterns,

Step-by-Step Instructions, Painting and Finishing Tips, Gnome Backstories, and More by Nikki Reese link

8. Dream Catchers: Homemade Mobiles, Wall Hangings, and Jewelry by Charline Fabregues link
9. The Complete Book of Glass Beadmaking by Kimberley Adams link
10. Carving & Painting Christmas Ornaments: Easy Techniques for 23 Patterns in Wood (Fox Chapel Publishing) Step-by-Step Projects for Beginner, Intermediate, and Advanced Carvers, plus Original Designs by Betty Padden link
11. Making Gourd Ornaments For Holiday Decorating by Angela Mohr link
12. Tauntons Complete Illustrated Guide to Box Making by Doug Stowe link
13. Easy-to-Make Stained Glass Boxes: With Full-Size Templates by Ed Sibbett Jr. link
14. Crochet Cute Critters: 26 Easy Amigurumi Patterns by Sarah Zimmerman link
15. How to Make Picture Frames: 12 Simple to Stylish Projects from the Experts at American Woodworker (Fox Chapel Publishing) Matting, Mounting, Router Moldings, Table Saw Frames without Jigs, and More by Editors of American Woodworker link
16. First Time Jewelry Making: The Absolute Beginner's Guide--Learn By Doing Step-by-Step Basics + Projects by Tammy Powley link
17. Sell Your Crafts Online: The Handmaker's Guide to Selling from Etsy, Amazon, Facebook, Instagram, Pinterest, Shopify, Influencers and More by James Dillehay link

* * *

Enjoy the Process

Get caught up in the craft

If you're interested in putting more time and effort in, you'll be able to craft detailed works of art. These longer or larger crafts might not be produced in quantity very quickly, but the result will be a quality craft you'll be proud of.

16 Longer Craft Projects

1. **Mosaic projects-** Piece together eye-catching mosaic tiles for crafts that cover window sills, walls, coffee tables, flower pots, picture frames, trays, and more.
2. **Tapestry crochet-** Unravel the yarn because tapestry crochet has the flexibility and portability of crochet, but the finished pieces look woven in the bags and other fabric pieces.
3. **Tiffany lamp-** Create a handmade heirloom while assembling glass tiles and soldering to make these antique-style lamps.
4. **Polymer clay sculptures-** Enjoy the fun of sculpting figures, animals, and objects with clay that only requires an oven to set.
5. **Wood carving faces-** Master the craft of carving different faces like a cowboy, Santa, wood spirit, witch, ugly faces, and maybe even your face!
6. **Model railway building-** Create a miniature world for your electric train set.
7. **Painting miniatures-** More than simply small paintings, miniature painting requires special techniques to achieve their unique glow and luminosity.
8. **Dollhouse miniatures-** Craft miniature furnishings for dollhouses.
9. **Military diorama making-** Create a miniature war scene with aircraft, tanks, battleships, and soldiers.
10. **Putz houses Christmas village-** Putz houses are miniature stylized buildings blanketed in deep winter snow, often put together with trains and forests to create a Christmas village.

11. **Nativity scenes-** Miniature scenes featuring the birth of Jesus.
12. **Modern quilting-** Quilting combines three or more pieces of fabric by stitching or sewing to make quilts to hang or for beds.
13. **Fairy gardens-** Create a magical miniature fairy garden by designing and planting your enchanting miniature landscapes, complete with pint-sized accessories, diminutive plants, and quaint fairy figures.
14. **Wool applique folk art sewing-** This needlework craft uses wool to create things like appliqué pillows, bed toppers, and table runners.
15. **Whittle small wood objects-** Carve cute little animals and characters.
16. **Yarn mandalas-** Weave colorful wall art composed of geometric patterns and symbols.

Books

1. Beginner's Guide to Making Mosaics: 16 Easy-to-Make Projects for Any Space (Fox Chapel Publishing) Step-by-Step Instructions & Photography for Window Sills, Tables, Flower Pots, Picture Frames, & More by Delphine Lescuyer link
2. More Tapestry Crochet: Digital by Carol Ventura link
3. Making Tiffany Lamps: How to Create Museum-Quality Authentic Reproductions by Hugh V. Archer link
4. Polymer Clay for Beginners: Inspiration, techniques, and simple step-by-step projects for making art with polymer clay by Emily Chen link
5. Carving Faces Workbook: Learn to Carve Facial Expressions with the Legendary Harold Enlow (Fox Chapel Publishing) Detailed Lips, Eyes, Noses, and Hair to Add Expressive Life to Your Wood Carvings by Harold Enlow link
6. Building a Model Railroad Step by Step by David Popp link
7. Painting Miniatures by Pauline Denyer-Baker link

8. Making Dolls' House Miniatures in 1/12th Scale by Julie Warren link
9. A tutorial for making military DIORAMAS and MODELS Vol 4 by Bjorn Jacobsen link
10. Urban Quilting: Quilt Patterns for the Modern-Day Home by Wendy Chow link
11. Fairy Gardening: Creating Your Own Magical Miniature Garden by Julie Bawden-Davis link
12. Wool Appliqué Folk Art: Traditional Projects Inspired by 19th-Century American Life by Rebekah L. Smith link
13. Weekend Whittling Projects: Four Quick and Easy Characters to Carve and Paint (Fox Chapel Publishing) (Woodcarving Illustrated) Patterns and Step-by-Step Instructions for Penguin, Bear, Snail, & More by Sara Barraclough link
14. Yarn Mandalas For Beginners And Beyond: Woven wall hangings for mindful making by Inga Savage link

Chapter 9

Feed Your Soul

Food is about more than just nourishment. It's about taking the time to enjoy the simple things in life, like savoring the smell of a fresh coffee pot and sinking into a steaming cup's warmth. It's about enjoying each sip or bite and appreciating the flavors. It's about slowing down, savoring the moment, and letting it linger a little longer.

Taste can be an experience like no other, and the journey of exploration a delicious one. As the flavors dance and swirl around your mouth, it's hard not to be filled with wonder. Every bite is like a tapestry made of all the different aromas and tastes, blending together to create something truly unique.

Food also has a strong emotional connection. We may not realize it, but food can bring back memories of a childhood filled with love, laughter, and togetherness. A dish can remind us of a place we visited and of the experiences we shared. Memories we thought were long gone can come flooding back, and they can be a comforting reminder of simpler times.

Food and cooking can be a simple pleasure in life that we often overlook. It's not just about combining ingredients and making something edible; it's a creative process, a source of comfort and joy, a way to get creative and gather with friends and family.

When you cook a meal, it's a special kind of magic. You're taking raw materials and transforming them into something delicious and enjoyable. You're taking ingredients, making choices, experimenting, and creating something that's uniquely yours. It's a calming and meditative process, with the bonus of producing something delicious.

Cooking is also a way to bond with people. You can involve friends and family in the process and make it a fun, collaborative experience. There's something about the act of creating something together that brings people closer.

Food is also a way to show love and care. When you cook a meal for someone, it's like a hug you can eat. You're taking the time and effort to make something special, and that says something. You get to see the joy and pleasure your cooking brings to the people around you, which is beautiful.

Food and cooking are more than just sustenance; it's a way to connect with others, explore something new, or give something back. It can be a source of pleasure, comfort, and joy, and it's something we should all enjoy more. So, get creative in the kitchen, bond with your loved ones, and savor the simple pleasure of cooking to feed your soul.

Chapter 9 Website Links

* * *

Savor the Flavor

Find joy in eating

Retirement is a time to slow down, relax, and enjoy life's simple pleasures, and food is one of them.

Retirement's a time to kick up your feet,
And bask in the joys of life's tasty treat,
From juicy burgers to pizza's heat,
Let your appetite soar, it's time to eat!

No more deadlines to race and meet,
No more bosses to please and greet,
Just delicious morsels to taste and eat,
Retirement's the life, let's make it sweet.

Sink your teeth into a juicy steak,
Or a chocolate cake, for heaven's sake,
The flavors will dazzle, your heart will quake,
And your taste buds will dance, make no mistake.

So come on down, let's grab a seat,
And savor the foods that can't be beat,
For in retirement, life is sweet,
And every meal is a tasty feat.
- The Taste of Retirement -

30 Fun Ways to Celebrate Food and Drink

1. **Keep an ice cream sundae bar-** Treat yourself to a sweet indulgence with a fully stocked ice cream sundae bar. Fill it with your favorite toppings and enjoy a delicious, cool treat on a hot summer day.
2. **Learn about food pairings-** Experiment with different food and drink pairings, such as cheese, wine,

chocolate, and coffee. You'll be surprised by the depth of flavor you can discover.

3. **Host an afternoon British-style tea party-** Get together with friends and family for an elegant and refined afternoon tea party. Serve up scones, clotted cream, and an array of dainty sandwiches.
4. **Join a cooking class-** Whether you're a seasoned cook or a beginner, enrolling in a cooking class can be a fun and rewarding way to learn new skills and try new recipes.
5. **Grow herbs and vegetables-** Start a garden and grow your own herbs and vegetables. You'll enjoy the fresh and delicious produce and the sense of pride that comes from growing it yourself.
6. **Create a home bar-** If you enjoy a good drink, why not create your own home bar? Stock it with your favorite spirits, mixers, and garnishes, and enjoy a cocktail or two in the evening.
7. **Visit a farmer's market-** Support local farmers and try new and unique ingredients by visiting your local farmer's market. You'll be amazed at the quality and flavor of seasonal produce.
8. **Make a special dinner-** Plan and prepare a special dinner for a loved one, such as a romantic candlelit dinner for two or a fun family dinner with games and laughter.
9. **Try a new type of food-** Take the opportunity to explore a cuisine or ingredient you've never tried before. Whether it's sushi, pho, or Ethiopian food, embrace the adventure and let your taste buds lead the way.
10. **Discover new local restaurants-** Try a new restaurant in your neighborhood that you've always wanted to visit.
11. **Craft beer sampling-** Learn about all the different craft beer styles, then visit local breweries and sample them.
12. **Foraging-** Go foraging for wild ingredients and use them to create new and exciting dishes.

13. **Michelin-star restaurant experience-** Treat yourself to a Michelin-star restaurant and indulge in a gourmet dining experience.
14. **Wine cellar creation-** Start your wine cellar and learn about the different wine varieties and their flavor profiles.
15. **Baking classes-** Take baking classes and perfect your skills in making cakes, pastries, and bread.
16. **Gourmet food shopping-** Explore specialty food stores and try new and exotic ingredients.
17. **Food festivals-** Attend food festivals and sample dishes from around the world.
18. **Tour a food factory-** Discover how your favorite treats are made and discover new products you may not have known about.
19. **Eat bizarre food-** Whether you're an adventurous eater or not, seeking out and eating bizarre food, whether it's a fried scorpion or an unusual animal, will give you a unique experience and fun memories.
20. **Milk a cow-** Get up close and personal with some dairy cows and practice milking them. You'll get a good workout and have a great story to tell.
21. **Extract honey from a bee hive-** An experience like this will give you a newfound appreciation for the hardworking honeybees.
22. **Wade in a cranberry bog-** Experience cranberries in their natural environment. Make sure to bring rubber boots to keep your feet dry.
23. **Tour a vineyard-** Get an up-close look at how wine is made and sample some of the best vintages.
24. **Cook with a celebrity chef-** Take a class with a celebrity chef and learn how to make some of their signature dishes.
25. **Pick your fruits and vegetables from a farm-** With the help of a farm guide, go out in the field and pick your fruits and vegetables.

26. **Take a food tour-** Take a food tour in a foreign country and explore the local delicacies.
27. **Focus on nutrition-** Take advantage of your newfound free time to focus on healthy eating habits. Plan your meals and shop for fresh, whole foods that will keep you feeling energetic and strong.
28. **Join a dinner club-** Connect with like-minded retirees and discover new flavors together. Share recipes and plan meals to cook as a group.
29. **Host a cooking competition-** Get together with some friends and challenge each other to create the most delicious dish. Award your own prizes and share the creations with everyone.
30. **Become a connoisseur of coffee or tea-** Learn the art of making perfect coffee or tea. Visit coffee roasters and tea shops to sample different blends and find your favorites.

Resources

1. Ultimate Foodie Bucket List link
2. Play With Your Food: 10 Delicious Activity Ideas Foodies Will Love Getting Involved In link
3. Top 9 Activities for the Foodie and Drinkie Couple link

Chapter 10

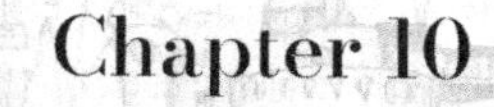

Get Techie

Retirement could be the perfect time to reassess your relationship with technology. Rather than fear it, we can harness its potential to entertain and help us in many ways. Learning something new can seem daunting, especially if you've never had much exposure to it, but it's essential to keep our brains from fading.

An unsurprising thing happens when we stop using a muscle. It shrinks. And like a muscle, if you're not using your brain in any challenging way other than to make easy everyday routine decisions on how to exist (what to eat, dress, watch, shop, etc.), it will get soft and shrink. When we need it again, tapping into our memories is difficult, and solving relatively easy problems becomes unnecessarily confusing. When it's gone, it's difficult and potentially impossible to get back. Unfortunately, the brain workout and stimulation you probably took for granted at your job is now gone. It's a huge mental void that must be actively and consciously filled.

With independence, we don't have to do anything we don't want to. Many retired people choose to relax their bodies and minds, which is fine in moderation, but overdoing it harms their mental and physical health. Make it a point to exercise your brain regularly by challenging it with complex things like learning, problem-solving, planning, creativity, and applying what you've learned.

Reading a book on something new, like history or animals, is good, but it's primarily just for entertainment. It has limited value for your brain because you'll likely never need to tap into your memories to apply your new knowledge to do something or solve a problem. The critical thinking part of applying what you know or have recently learned is vital to staying sharp.

So if technology is challenging for you, it's the perfect place to strengthen your brain and gain the benefits of humankind's significant innovations. Many of the newest gadgets and gizmos are tools that will help us as we grow older.

So before the world is taken over by artificial intelligence and robots, let's learn in this chapter how to harness technology for our good!

Chapter 10 Website Links

* * *

Get a Smart Home Virtual Assistant

Become friends with an artificial intelligence (AI)

Do you remember the revolutionary sci-fi film 2001: A Space Odyssey from 1968, where the Artificial Intelligence HAL 9000 could think and respond to the astronauts, even control the spaceship? Of course, that was before it malfunctioned and tried to kill everyone...but the point is this type of technology is no longer a thing of science fiction. It's here now. And it's priced so low (starting at under $50) it's accessible to just about everyone. Smart speakers and displays from Amazon Alexa and Google Assistant have built-in voice recognition AI that can bring the power of the internet to answer almost any question you might have in seconds. And a whole lot more.

What can it do?

We decided to pick up the Amazon Echo Dot smart speaker when it first came out several years ago and have since upgraded to the Amazon Echo Show Display (Google also makes similar products). Here are a few of the favorite things we use it for.

- **Answer questions-** Voice recognition and AI have developed quickly. It can understand you and answer questions about people, sports, history, news, events, businesses, nature, distances, calculations, translations, health, cooking, fashion, and nearly anything else.
- **Streaming music-** By far our most used feature. We say the song or music genre we want to hear, and it starts playing. Bluetooth speakers allow music to play through the house if we choose. This feature is fantastic—no more shuffling with discs or setting up computer playlists. If we feel like listening to some relaxing Spanish guitar for dinner, it's only a request away. Dance party? It's ready to go. The display will even show the lyrics so we can actually figure out what the artist is singing about.
- **Reminders-** Set timers for cooking, reminders to turn off the water outside (it will say whatever you want, like "turn off the water"), or schedule reminders for recurring events and appointments.
- **Cooking tips-** We sometimes ask how to cook certain things or how long to do something like BBQ vegetable kebabs. The display can even show you recipes and cooking videos.

- **Controlling lights-** With inexpensive smart electrical plugs, you can turn on and off anything with your voice. Other smart lights can change colors and dim whenever we want. We schedule the light to come on automatically as a gentle alarm in the morning. Outdoor Christmas lights automatically adjust to the changing sunset time, come on 30 minutes after dark, and turn off a few hours later.
- **Control other devices-** We set up the coffeemaker to turn on automatically in the morning, so it's ready when needed.
- **Phone or video calls-** Say "call Bob," and it calls Bob. No phone is required. We use this feature more often than not to call our misplaced phone! Video calls can also be made, as well as "drop-ins" where you can listen in to your home or call someone elses' smart speaker.
- **Intercom-** Make announcements in other rooms through smart speakers in those rooms and even use them as an intercom. Dinners ready!
- **Slideshow of photos-** We use the unlimited photo storage benefit from Amazon Prime, allowing it to create an automatic photo slideshow for display.
- **Weather alerts**- Severe weather alerts pop up automatically.
- **Videos-** Watch video clips or even movies on the display.
- **Games-** Trivia games, mostly.
- **Audiobooks and podcasts-** Convenient access to listen to our favorites.
- **News-** Get caught up on the interesting stories of the day.
- **Funny things-** It can tell jokes, sing silly songs, make fart noises, and do other fun things.
- **Everything else-** This is just scratching the surface of what these smart devices can do. It's remarkable, and all without a monthly fee!

Go for it! Simple start steps:

1. Decide if you want to use Amazon Alexa or Google Home devices.
2. Buy one and download the corresponding app to your phone.
3. Use the app to set up the smart speaker or display to your wifi network.

Resources

1. Google Home vs. Alexa: Which Assistant is Best? link
2. What can Alexa Do? link
3. Google Assistant Features link
4. 10 Best Things You Can Do With An Amazon Alexa Device link

Products

1. Amazon Echo Show 8 HD Smart Display link
2. Google Nest Hub link
3. Amazon Echo Dot Smart Speaker link

Pairs well with: Smart home devices (lights, cameras, alarms, sensors, speakers, etc.), kitchens, wearables

* * *

Take an Online Course

Learn just about anything in the easiest way possible

Remember when learning meant showing up for a class or reading a book? Well, the future of education is with online courses. They allow anyone to learn in multiple learning styles from the most competent experts anywhere, anytime, and nearly anything. And we're not just talking about boring hypothetical academic stuff from stuffy college professors who record themselves giving a lecture and upload the video for unfortunate college students to fall asleep watching. Online courses can include casual interest topics like hobbies taught by well-known experts and celebrities, such as learning to cook with Gordon Ramsay or filmmaking from James Cameron.

The learning platforms differ, but most take advantage of a logically thought-out progression of videos, written sections, interactive quizzes or poles, documents, group support areas, and personal support. You'll be able to see your progress through the course, retake sections if wanted, and take learning at your own pace. The sites offering unlimited access memberships have a wealth of knowledge to explore for a relatively small investment, and some courses are free. Become the most interesting and well-rounded person in your social circle!

A Small Sample of Online Course Categories

- **Food-** Cooking all styles, wine appreciation, mixology, gardening, intentional eating, and healthy eating.
- **Design and Style-** Fashion, makeup and beauty, interior design, photography, game design, graphic design, modeling, self-expression, and creativity.
- **Arts and Entertainment-** Screenwriting, filmmaking, acting, directing, comedy, songwriting, playwriting, voice acting, film scoring, magic, effective communication, music, and more.
- **Sports and Gaming-** Tennis, basketball, chess, poker, mindset, coaching, and more.
- **Writing-** Storytelling, poetry, journalism, short stories.
- **Science and Technology-** Space exploration, conservation, mathematics, FBI profiling, and the science of better sleep.
- **Home and Lifestyle-** Dog training, meditation, and design.

- **Community and Government-** Campaign strategy, economics, presidential history, philosophy, activism, leadership, resilience, and diplomacy.
- **Wellness-** Yoga, fitness, wilderness survival, and mental health.

Top Paid Online Course Websites

- **Masterclass** (www.masterclass.com)- Celebrity instructors from Presidents to field experts. Annual membership (currently $180) gives unlimited access to 180+ classes across 11 categories.
- **Skillshare** (www.skillshare.com)- Markets itself as being the ultimate website for learning just about anything imaginable. Learn from over 34,000+ courses, especially creative skills, for a monthly or annual membership (currently as low as $168).
- **LinkedIn Learning** (www.linkedin.com/learning)- A top pick for corporate professional learners. Get unlimited access to 16,000+ expert-led courses with a monthly or annual membership (currently as low as $240).
- **Nas Academy** (https://nasacademy.com)- Aimed at giving content creators skills (photography, videography, editing, publishing, social media, etc.) to grow their following and monetize their activities.
- **Coursera** (https://www.coursera.org)- Collaborating with 275+ leading universities and companies, learn from 7,000+ unlimited career focus courses, and even get online degrees starting at $399/year.
- **Udemy** (www.udemy.com)- An astonishing 213,000+ online video courses with a significant focus on business skills. Pricing varies from $20- $200 per course.
- **TED Courses** (https://courses.ted.com)- A few scheduled courses from the world-rethinking TED Talk speakers.

. . .

Free Online Courses

- **TED Talks** (www.ted.com/talks)- Not exactly an online course, but there are over 4,100 videos from speakers with ideas that will spark your curiosity. Also, search YouTube for @TED to see more videos in different formats.
- **EDx** (www.edx.org)- Online courses from the top universities in the world. Founded by MIT and Harvard, "As a mission-driven organization, we're relentlessly pursuing our vision of a world where every learner can access education to unlock their potential, without the barriers of cost or location."
- **Khan Academy** (www.khanacademy.org)- Aimed primarily at students, there's a lot of refreshing of your high school academics possible on this site.

Go for it! Simple start steps:

1. Look over the course offerings from several companies and decide what you're interested in learning.
2. Sign up for a free trial and test the content from a few learning companies.
3. Enjoy learning.

Resources

1. Best Online Courses and Online Class Sites link
2. Here are The Top 7 Websites For Free Online Education link
3. 48 Free Online Courses to Help You Learn Just About Anything link

You might also like: Music learning apps, creating your own online course, audiobooks

* * *

Use Online Shopping, Delivery, and Rideshare Apps

Let someone else do the driving

You're missing out if you're not taking advantage of the convenience of online shopping, delivery, and rideshare services. They are life-style upgraders. It's like having an affordable personal chauffeur anywhere, anytime, and you don't have to pay them to sit around while you're out and about. You tap on your phone, and they come and take you anywhere. It's that simple. And just as easy is online delivery services like Amazon, and Uber Eats, where you click or tap on something, and it shows up quickly. A word of warning, however, online shopping, rideshare apps, and food delivery apps are all very addicting. Once you try them, you'll understand and likely start using them frequently. You've been warned!

Amazon, the King of Online Shopping in the US

Nearly 70% of Americans have a Prime membership and spend an average of $1,400/year. Amazon (www.amazon.com) sells over half of everything purchased on the internet in the US and is currently the world's 5th largest company currently, with a value of nearly 1 trillion dollars. I don't need to spend much time talking about why this company is fantastic. You probably already know. If you're not taking advantage of online shopping, you're missing out.

- **Selection-** Access to over 12 million products at reasonable prices.
- **Ridiculously fast delivery-** Some locations can deliver within hours, depending on your location.

- **Free delivery on most products-** Spend the minimum (currently $25) or have a Prime membership and get free delivery on most items.
- **Convenience-** Why wander a store's aisles? Go online, compare prices, and have it sent before you can even get to your local store. There's low risk of not liking the products as many offer free returns.
- **Food-** Amazon Fresh delivers groceries the same way you get products delivered. You can schedule the drop-off time and even reorder the same food staples with one click.

Other online retailers with market share as of 2023 are #2 eBay, #3 Apple, #4 Walmart, #5 Home Depot, #6 Best Buy, and #7 Costco.

Rideshare Apps

I had never used a rideshare app until recently because of "stranger danger." Getting into a personal car with someone I didn't know just seemed like a bad idea, even having heard how popular it was becoming. Planning for a trip to South America, I was surprised to read from a State Department Country Report that for transportation safety, they recommended using car-share apps as opposed to hailing taxis on the side of the road. I never thought that getting into a cab was just like getting into a car with a stranger, but it is. If you hail one on the side of the road, no one knows you got inside, and you're at their mercy, hoping they don't take you somewhere you don't want to be.

With rideshare apps, there is a level of oversight. You can usually see how many jobs the driver has done and their rating. Their car and your phone app are being GPS tracked in real time. The app tells the driver how to get there, so as you look at your mapping software built into the rideshare app, you'll know if you're not on the route. There is usually a "get assistance" button ready to be pressed in the app if things seem off. So long story short, we were tired of walking one day, and it started to rain. I downloaded the Uber app and called a driver. It turned out to be half the price of calling a taxi. I didn't need to explain where I wanted to go in a foreign language or haggle about the price. I didn't need any cash, and they took me right where I needed to go without a fuss. From that day on, I was sold and have taken many rideshare rides all over without any issues.

Top RideShare Apps

- **Uber** (www.uber.com)- The most popular ridesharing app with 93+ million users worldwide. You can usually choose the type of vehicle to pick you up, such as luxury, economy, SUV, minivan, or even environmentally friendly.
- **Lyft** (www.lyft.com)- The second most popular RideShare company by volume. Lyft has drivers in 644 US cities.
- **Gett** (www.gett.com/uk)- An Israel-based company with service in 100 cities globally. The majority are in Israel and the UK.

Food Delivery Apps

Pizza isn't the only food delivery option anymore. Sometimes you don't feel like cooking, and driving to a restaurant isn't in the cards for whatever reason. Maybe it's weather concerns, traffic, a broken down vehicle, or you're not feeling great and want to avoid spreading germs; getting your favorite food from nearly any nearby restaurant is no problem with Food Delivery Apps. You'll want to try one of these on a rainy day.

- **DoorDash** (www.doordash.com)- The leader in food delivery services controlling as much as 45% of the market with 390,000 restaurants in 4,000 North American cities.
- **Grubhub** (www.grubhub.com)- 365,000+ restaurants available in 4,000 cities in the US and UK.
- **UberEats** (www.ubereats.com)- The most popular international food delivery service with 81 million users

worldwide. 6,000 cities are serviced in 45 countries with 900,000 partner restaurants.

Resources

1. Amazon Statistics link
2. Amazon Popularity link
3. Best Rideshare Apps link
4. Best food delivery services in 2023: Grubhub vs UberEats vs Doordash link

* * *

Unlock Your Smartphone

Discover the power in your pocket

Remember when a phone had a long, springy, plastic wire, and you had to move your finger around a circular dial to stop at each number? Or when we finally lost the cables and could go outside with our mobile phones, the most exciting thing we could do was send a text message by poking away at the number pad multiple times to select each individual letter and hopefully make a sentence maybe five minutes later? Oh, how times have changed. When the first iPhone came out in 2007, it was a game changer. This was now a tool that could do much more than make calls. It was a smartphone. A little computer in your pocket that's ready to help whenever you need it.

Now, the latest smartphones are more advanced than ever. The cameras use multiple lenses and LIDAR (Light Detection and Ranging) to calculate the distance to objects and blur the background for appealing portraits. They also use "computational photography" by harnessing the phone's processing power to analyze a scene for the best photos and videos that can be almost as good as high-end large cameras. Built-in GPS unlocks a whole world of helpful features for navigating.

The catchy slogan "there's an app for that" is absolutely true. You can find a helpful app for just about anything from banking to virtual reality to knowing where every star in the sky is and where it's heading simply by moving your phone around. Throw in a virtual voice recognition assistant like Siri or Google Assistant, and forget about it. Modern smartphones are a world of possibilities and potential to unlock. It's worth taking a little time to learn how to use it beyond making calls.

Helpful Features and Apps of Smartphones

Voice control: Learn to use your voice to do things without touching your phone. You can make phone calls and send text messages, set reminders and alarms, search the web for information or news, get directions, create a new calendar event or check your schedule, take a note or create a list, play music, and translate a word or phrase.

Accessibility: There are several accessibility features built into new phones, such as:

- Large text and high contrast mode make it easier to read text on the screen.
- Zoom allows users to magnify the entire screen or specific areas.
- Speak Screen reads the text on the screen out loud.
- Fall detection can automatically call for help if the phone detects that the user has fallen.
- Emergency SOS allows the user to quickly call for help in an emergency.
- Magnifying glass feature allows a user to use the phone's camera as a magnifying glass for small text on bottles or other products.

Apps: There is a whole universe of free applications, from banking to games and everything in between. Here are a few helpful ones.

Banking: Your bank has an app that makes banking almost effortless. I love the ability to use facial recognition to auto login without needing to remember my username and password, easily make transfers, and the ability to take a photo of a check and make mobile deposits at home is very helpful.

Navigation:

- Maps- Get turn-by-turn directions to anywhere with real-time traffic rerouting to find the fastest route. Also helpful is the ability to save your parking spot location in Maps so it can guide you back if you forget.
- All Trails- Find popular hiking and biking routes nearby.
- Gas buddy- An app that shows you the current prices of gas and routes you to the cheapest stations wherever you are.

Video Chat: Go face-to-face with the person or group you're talking with. Some popular apps are Facetime, WhatsApp, Google Meet, Zoom, and Skype.

Health & Wellness:

- Mindfulness and meditation apps like Headspace offer guided meditations, sleep sounds, and mindfulness exercises.
- Track your sleep, and exercise with apps like MyFitnessPal, Nike Training Club, 7-minute workout, and Fitbit.
- SmartBP- An app that can help you take your blood pressure.

Social Media: Keep connected with friends and family on popular apps like Facebook and Instagram.

Wireless Payments: Enter your credit card info into your phone and then use your phone to pay wirelessly with Apple Pay or Google Pay.

Entertainment: Watch videos, play games, read news, get weather, read and listen to books.

Other Apps:

- SkyView- Allows you to point your phone at any star and find out what it is, where it will be in the sky at any time, the constellation it's part of, sunrise and sunset locations, and more.
- Altimeter- Know what elevation you're at anywhere.
- Compass- Move your phone just like a compass.
- Street View- See 360-degree tours of roads, trails, famous buildings, museums, inside the ocean, and more.
- Flashlight- Use your phone's flash as a handy flashlight.
- Buy things- Compare prices in stores with the Amazon app and scan the barcode to see if a lower price is online.

Resources

1. 19 Things You Didn't Know Your Smartphone Could Do link
2. Best Phone Apps For Seniors link
3. iPhone user guide link
4. A beginners guide to Android link

Products

1. iPhone 14 link
2. Google Pixel 7 link

Books

1. Seniors Guide to iPhone: The Most Exhaustive and Intuitive Step-by-Step Manual to Master your New iPhone with Tips and Tricks for Senior Beginner Users (Updated and Illustrated Edition) by Richard Reed link
2. Android Phones for Seniors in easy steps by Nick Vandome link
3. iPhone 14 User Guide: An Easy, Step-By-Step Guide On Mastering The Usage Of Your New iPhone 14. Learn The

Best Tips & Tricks, And Discover The Most Useful Secrets To Get The Max Out Of Your Device by Ethan Copson link

You might also like: Tablets, phone photography, creating a YouTube channel

* * *

Discover Cool Gadgets

Let technology serve you

The thing I love about new technology is that it has the power to change our lives for the better. The things we take for granted today, like microwaves, TVs, and dishwashers, were revolutionary at one time. While most new technology won't drastically change our lives, it might be a better way of doing things or simply more fun. Let's look at some new gadgets and see how they can serve us better.

16 Fun Tech Gadgets

1. **Robotic Lawnmower-** Does anyone enjoy cutting grass? Unleash your little robotic helper to do it for you! Or better yet, get artificial turf and just be done with grass maintenance forever.
2. **Smart Toilets-** Seriously, it's a thing. And so popular in Japan. Why settle for a dumb toilet when yours could enlighten you with a nice and cozy warm seat for your bum, self-flush, self-clean, wash your boodie, and even play music to put you in your happy place.
3. **Automatic Pet Water Fountain And Feeder-** Tired of bending over to fill the water and dinner bowl for your furkid? Get an automatic water fountain and pet feeder and spend your new free time just being amazing.

4. **AirTag-** Frequently lose things or want a little recovery piece of mind in case something gets stolen? Inexpensive GPS trackers like Apple AirTags could be for you. Stick or clip a tiny little tile onto something like a keychain, pet collar, luggage, your car for when you forget where you parked, purse or wallet, bike, or even a wandering spouse with dementia, and use the app to locate it.
5. **Wireless Meat Thermometer-** Shove it in your meat and get updates on your phone so you never overcook that beautiful carne.
6. **Electric Kettle-** Never worry about leaving the kettle on and burning down the house with an electric kettle. As a bonus, it's incredibly fast and always cool to pick up and pour.
7. **Tablet-** If you don't have a tablet like an iPad or Amazon Fire, they are worth it. They're the perfect size and weight for reading ebooks, watching videos, using apps, and staying connected with loved ones while relaxing comfortably at home on the couch.
8. **Automatic Medicine Dispenser-** Effortlessly keeps you on schedule with your meds. It can even alert you or your family if you've missed a dose.
9. **Robot Floor Cleaner-** Little circular robots that clean your floor, like Rhoomba, aren't new anymore, but they're smarter than ever. Some models will mop your floor or wake up to automatically clean, dump the trash, and recharge themselves. Get it done, robot!
10. **Smart Locks-** Keys are a pain. Change out your door with a biometric lock, pin lock, or one that can be unlocked with your phone from anywhere.
11. **Smartwatch-** Leave the phone at home and still receive or make calls while on a run or anywhere. Worried about a loved one living alone, falling, and not being able to get help? Give them a smartwatch to wear around the house, and help is always just a watch call away. Smartwatches monitor your health with pulse, oxygen level sensors,

irregular heart rhythm notifications, fall detection, unsteady walking that may signal an upcoming problem, and more.

12. **Automatic Indoor Herb Gardens-** A compact vertical little indoor garden with lights and hydroponic water circulation. Grow just what you want without the outside effort, bending over, or getting dirty.
13. **Automatic Beer Brewing Machines-** Put in the primary ingredients (water, hops, barley, and yeast), and it will take care of the rest. Sure, you'll have to wait about two weeks to enjoy your fresh and fizzy creation, but you will be the envy of all your beer-drinking friends.
14. **Smart Fridge-** Imagine being at the grocery store, unsure if you need to get milk, then pulling out your phone and looking at a live video feed inside your fridge. Necessary? Perhaps not. Super cool? Absolutely.
15. **Digital Electric Smoker and Grill-** Plop your meat in and let it do the rest. You'll get alerts on your phone when it's perfectly smoked or grilled. Easy breezy.
16. **Self-Driving and Electric Cars-** It's here. Cars from many manufacturers use sensors like radar, cameras, lidar, GPS, and more to drive, park, change lanes, avoid collisions (hopefully), and more. Electric cars without emissions are environmentally friendly, fast and silent, and can be free to charge with house solar panels or a nearby mall charging station.

Resources

1. The Best Robotic Lawn Mowers link
2. 20 Surprisingly Practical Uses for AirTags link
3. Best Automated Beer Brewing Systems link
4. The Best Self Driving Cars link
5. Best Electric Cars Now link

Products

1. Robotic Lawn Mower link

2. Smart Toilet link
3. Automatic Pet Feeder link
4. Automatic Pet Water Fountain link
5. Electric Water Kettle link
6. Apple Watch link
7. Hydroponic Indoor Growing System link
8. Electric Smoker link

* * *

Read eBooks and Listen to Audiobooks

Go digital with your books

Paper books are fine and dandy, but they are just one format. There are some advantages to digital ebooks and audiobooks you might want to consider.

9 Ebook Advantages

1. **Convenience-** Easily downloaded and stored on electronic devices, such as smartphones, tablets, and e-readers, allowing easy access and portability.
2. **Cost-** Often less expensive than print books, as they do not require the costs associated with printing and distribution.
3. **Accessibility-** Available in various formats, including large print and audio, making them accessible to a broader audience, including those with visual impairments.
4. **Environmentally friendly-** They're a more sustainable option without paper, ink, and other resources associated with print books.
5. **Searchability and organization-** Find specific information quickly with a search. Organize into digital libraries to keep track of what you've read.

6. **Annotation and note taking-** Take notes, highlight, and make annotations directly on the ebook, making it a more interactive and personalized reading experience.
7. **Hyperlinks-** If an ebook has hyperlinks, you can jump straight to the website for more information.
8. **Space saving-** You can store an entire library of books on a computer or tablet, which is excellent for travel.
9. **Word lookup-** If you see an unfamiliar word, you can select it and get the definition immediately.

6 Audiobook Benefits

1. **Convenience-** Listen while doing other activities, such as exercising, cooking, or commuting.
2. **Accessibility-** An excellent option for people with visual or reading impairments.
3. **Variety of voices-** Narrated by a variety of voices, it can add an extra dimension to the listening experience.
4. **Increased comprehension-** Some research suggests that listening to audiobooks can improve comprehension and retention of the material.
5. **Increased reading-** People who don't have as much time to read can still enjoy the experience of reading.
6. **Language Learning-** An effective tool for language learners to practice listening and comprehension of a target language.

Unlimited Ebooks and Audiobooks

If you're a big reader or audiobook listener, consider getting a membership to Kindle Unlimited or Audible. Currently, for less than $10 per month, Kindle Unlimited allows you to read as much as you want, choosing from over 3 million ebooks, thousands of audiobooks, and electronic magazine subscriptions. Audible has unlimited audiobook listening plans currently for under $10 per month as well. Also, you can download an app and read your ebook or listen to the audiobook on any device, such as an iPad. You don't need an Amazon Kindle tablet.

Another option is to look into your public library. It may have many ebooks and audiobooks to check out for free.

Resources

1. The Advantages of Audiobooks Over Ebooks link
2. Kindle Unlimited Ebook and More Membership link
3. Audible Audiobook Memberships link

Pairs well with: Tablets, smart speakers, drives, travel

* * *

Go Drone Fishing

Search for fish to catch from the sky

If you love to fish and want to boost your luck, drone fishing is for you. Instead of casting into the blue abyss hoping for a bite, drone fishers use their drone's aerial camera to search for fish and drop the bait from the drone exactly where fish are.

What's special about a drone?

- **Easy to fly-** They have GPS that stabilizes the drone in the wind and will stay in one spot (automatically compensating for the wind) when you take your hands off the controls.
- **Never get lost in the air-** A live map on your phone shows where the drone is heading, its location, speed, and climb rate.

- **Comes back automatically-** At the push of a button, the drone will rise to a safe altitude, fly back to you, and land. No skill is needed.
- **Avoids obstacles-** Sensors detect obstacles such as trees and can avoid them automatically.
- **Live camera feed-** The onboard drone camera transmits live video to your mobile phone or immersive headset. The world looks different from above, and with the headset, you can feel right there flying with the birds.
- **Recording-** Take videos and photos of your flight to enjoy later. They can even automatically stitch together multiple images for a wide panorama or a nearly 360-degree photo.
- **Quiet-** The smaller the drone, the quieter it is in the sky. In the past, drones were big, loud, and annoying. Now they are tiny and nearly silent from 50 feet up.
- **Compact-** Drones, such as DJI Mini 2, fold up into the palm of your hand and can easily fit in a small bag.
- **Smart-** They can be programmed to fly complex patterns on their own, recognize objects and track them automatically, and even be controlled by hand signals.
- **Efficient-** Drones can now fly on a tiny battery for 30+ minutes. Swap the rechargeable battery, and you can have hours of fun.
- **Range and height-** Depending on the airspace rules, they can usually be flown up to 400 above the ground and have a radio range of miles. However, FAA laws require drones to stay in sight of the operator at all times.

How much are drones?

Quality GPS drones are as little as $500. One of the best manufacturers that's leading the way in innovation is DJI.

. . .

Use Caution

Check your state and local regulations to ensure there are no restrictions on drone flying or fishing in your area. Download the FAA app "B4UFLY", which shows a map of any airspace restrictions, and keep an eye out for local no-fly signs. Other rules, such as registering your drone with the FAA and how you can fly, can be found on the FAA site or from local regulations.

Resources

1. DJI Drones (One of the best manufacturers) link
2. FAA Drone Registration link
3. Drone Fishing - The Ultimate How To link

Products

1. Great Inexpensive Starter Mini Drone link
2. Expensive Waterproof Fishing Drone link
3. FPV (First Person View) Drone and Goggle Kit link

Pairs well with: Video and photo editing, parks, the ocean

You might also like: Remote controlled boats, photography, spearfishing

* * *

Build a Fighting Robot

Become a master of robot combat

First airing in 2000, the TV show BattleBots is now broadcasted in 150 countries worldwide. Robot combat is the perfect engineering sport. It combines engineering, electronics, CAD, physics, and design disciplines. Contestants design and build robots and then fight it out in the ring to see who will survive. There are local robot fighting competitions to test out your weapon systems and hone your fighting style, so someday, you can apply and be a contestant in the ultimate heavyweight robot fighting competition, Battlebots! They take applications yearly for the next season, which is currently aired on the Discovery Channel.

Get Started in Robotics

Many different STEM robotics kits are available to start building your first robot. The inexpensive and highly versatile Raspberry Pi is a small single-board computer typically used and programmed when building robots.

Go for it! Simple start steps:

1. Watch past episodes of BattleBots to think up your winning design.
2. Go to the #1 resources link below for instructions on how to apply and build your fighting robot.
3. Build it and kick some bot.

Resources

1. How to Get On BattleBots link
2. So You Want To Build Your Own Fighting Robot link
3. Getting Started in Combat Robotics link

Products

1. Robot Building Kit link
2. Solar Robot Kit link
3. Raspberry Pi Robot Kit link

Books

1. Kickin' Bot: An Illustrated Guide to Building Combat Robots (ExtremeTech) by Grant Imahara link

2. RioBotz Combat Robot Tutorial by Marco Antonio Meggiolaro link
3. Robot Wars: Build your own Robot Manual (Haynes Manuals) by James Cooper link

* * *

3D Printing

Start a Tony Stark-like creative workshop

Ever watched the Ironman movie and dreamed of having a home workshop with a machine that can build anything? Unless you're also a billionaire like Tony Stark, that won't happen. But if your dreams are of small plastic things, then you're in luck!

Be a Maker

Creative techies, aka makers, can now print plastic objects at home or order online. For about the same price and size as a desktop color printer, you can have an at-home 3D printer. Create a 3D model with software, or download a file created by someone else and then send it to the 3D printer. The machine uses a spool of colored plastic, melts it through the hot nozzle, and builds an object from the bottom up from tiny plastic squirts.

Make novel stuff (custom chess pieces, cell phone cases, action figures, ornaments), helpful things (phone stands, pencil holders, drink coasters), and print things to sell online or at craft fairs.

There is something very cool about an average person being able to dream up an object, design it reasonably quickly with a computer program, and physically hold it within hours for only a few bucks.

During an overly ambitious creative point in my life, I used a 3D printer with the hopes of inventing something new. My first attempt was to create a "rooster tail" of water shooting up on the back of my surfboard, as you sometimes can see on the back of some jet skis. I made some measurements, designed a low-profile funnel to stick on the bottom back of my board, and printed it. Later that day, I took it out to the lineup, eager to catch a wave and astonish my fellow surfers as I glided by with water spraying up to the heavens. But that didn't happen. After three design tweaks, I gave up. However, I like to think I succeeded in creating a surfboard anchor that, unfortunately, wouldn't allow me to catch a wave!

In the recent past, expensive 3D printers were only accessible to companies looking to do rapid prototyping when designing new products. Now it's accessible to everyone. What will you create?

Did you know?

- 3D printing can be used to print houses! What?
- There is a 3D printer on the international space station.
- You can build your own 3D printer.
- Your design can be printed in many types of plastic and finishes, even metal.
- NASA plans to build 3D-printed colonies on Mars.

No printer? No problem.

Get started today without needing a personal 3D printer! Companies like Sculpteo allow you to send your 3D model file to them over the internet, and they'll print it for you. They have many different material choices, and the quality is usually much better than at-home 3D printers. Pricing is based on the object's size but is generally under $20 and will be delivered to your door in a few days. Also, check with your local libraries because they often have 3D printers available to bring your creation to life for a small fee.

Keep things simple at the start. It's easy to jump into figuring everything out when you're learning a new hobby and get bogged down with analysis paralysis. It's understandable wanting to be prepared, but not necessary for this hobby. The fun part is creating things, so don't overthink it. Download a free 3D design program, make something small, and send it to an online printing company to print. You'll feel accomplished holding something you dreamed up, designed, and brought to life!

Top Online 3D Printing Companies

Just upload your file for an instant quote.

1. Sculpteo (www.sculpteo.com)
2. Shapeways (www.shapeways.com)
3. Hubs (www.hubs.com)

Go for it! Simple start steps:

1. Download. Try a few free 3D modeling software to find the one you like best.
2. Create. Design your object in the software or tweak someone else's object.
3. Print. Upload your 3D model file to an online printing service or print on your machine.

Resources

1. Free 3D design software link
2. Get inspired with objects you can download and print link
3. Free online 3D design website (tinkercad.com) link
4. Free 3D CAD files to download and print (thingiverse.com) link

Products

1. Highly rated starter (under $200) home 3D Printer link

Books

1. 3D Printing Projects link
2. 3D Printing Made Easy for Newbies link
3. Make 3D Printing: The essential guide to 3D printers link

Pairs well with: Robotics design, entrepreneur types, model builders, jewelry designers

You might also like: Model building with a 3D printing pen called 3Doodler.

Chapter 11

Turn Up the Excitement

Here. We. Go. In this final chapter we turn up the excitement to level 11. There are no filters on this chapter. There are things in here that might scare Evel Knievel. Things that most of us mortals will never partake in but are reserved for only the most daring or psychotic. The days of some of these activities may be over, but perhaps not.

Retirement can be a time to take a step back from the hustle and bustle of daily life and enjoy the fruits of one's labor. However, it can also be a time to seek out new experiences, to feel the thrill of adventure, and to embrace new challenges. In this chapter, we will explore the importance of turning up the excitement and finding ways to add a spark to your life in retirement.

Our bodies may slow down as we age, but our minds and spirits can still soar. The joy of discovering new things and pushing our boundaries is a feeling that is timeless. Whether trying a thrilling activity for the first time or stepping outside your comfort zone, there is no better time to turn up the excitement.

So put down the knitting needles, lace up your hiking boots, and join us as we discover the importance of adding excitement to your life in retirement. From skydiving to whitewater rafting, from ziplining to hot air balloon rides, the possibilities are endless.

In this chapter, let's turn up the excitement and start exploring all that life has to offer.

Chapter 11 Website Links

* * *

Step into Adventure

Get your heart pumping

Patrick had always dreamt of experiencing the thrill of skydiving. As he approached retirement, he found himself reflecting on all the things he'd wanted to do but had never gotten around to. He realized he didn't want to miss out on the opportunity to live life to the fullest and make the most of his newfound free time.

One day, he mustered up the courage and finally made the reservation for a skydiving adventure. As he stood on the edge of the airplane, the wind blasting past his face, his heart pounding in his chest, he felt a rush of excitement unlike anything he'd ever experienced. With a deep breath, he took the leap and was immediately consumed by the sensation of falling through the sky.

The view was breathtaking; the world below looked like a painting as he gazed at it from above. He felt an incredible sense of peace and serenity as he glided through the air and an overwhelming feeling of joy and fulfillment as his parachute opened and he slowly descended back to earth.

As Patrick landed, he was beaming from ear to ear. He had finally accomplished something he had always wanted to do, and he felt an immense sense of satisfaction and pride. The experience was not only exhilarating but also helped him realize that it's never too late to pursue your dreams and experience new adventures. He now had a newfound appreciation for life and was inspired to keep pushing himself to try new things and make the most of his golden years.

48 Adventures Await! Inspiration for the most daring adventurers.

1. **Paragliding-** Soar above the earth and feel the wind beneath your wings in this high-flying adventure.
2. **Zip lining-** Zip through the trees, experiencing the thrill of speed while taking in the stunning scenery.
3. **Skydiving-** Free fall through the sky and feel your heart race as you experience one of the ultimate adrenaline rushes.
4. **Whitewater river rafting-** Navigate rapids and experience the rush of adrenaline as you conquer the wild rapids of a river.
5. **Powered paragliding-** Zoom through the sky like a bird, using the power of a motor to enjoy the freedom of flight.
6. **Flyboarding-** Unleash your inner superhero as you soar over water powered by a jet of water.
7. **Hot air balloon ride-** Gently float through the skies, marveling at the stunning scenery below.
8. **Drive a racecar-** Experience the rush of speed and adrenaline as you race around a professional track.
9. **Hang gliding-** Soar above the earth, experiencing flight's pure freedom and beauty.

10. **Bungee jumping-** Take the leap of a lifetime as you experience the thrill of falling.
11. **Shark cage diving-** Get up close and personal with these fascinating creatures in their natural habitat.
12. **Aerobatic biplane ride-** Experience the thrill of high-flying stunts and breathtaking aerial views.
13. **Mountain biking-** Pedal your way through rough terrain, challenging yourself with every turn of the wheel.
14. **Rent an exotic car-** Cruise the streets in style behind the wheel of a sports car of your dreams.
15. **Spelunking-** Explore the hidden wonders of the underground world with a guided tour of a natural cave system.
16. **ATV/UTV driving-** Get off the beaten path, and tackle rugged terrain with the power of an all-terrain vehicle.
17. **Swim with whale sharks-** Get up close and personal with the ocean's gentle giants for a once-in-a-lifetime experience.
18. **Race an F1 car-** Put your driving skills to the test as you race against the clock in a high-speed formula one car.
19. **Motorcycle cross country-** Take a scenic ride across the country on the back of a motorcycle.
20. **High altitude skydive-** Freefall from the edge of space for the ultimate adrenaline-fueled adventure.
21. **Rock climbing-** Scale new heights while testing your physical and mental limits.
22. **Zorb-** Experience the thrill of rolling down a hill inside an inflatable ball.
23. **Build an experimental aircraft-** Live your aviation dreams and create a unique flying machine.
24. **Skywalk on top of a skyscraper-** Marvel at the breathtaking panoramic views from the pinnacle of a towering structure.
25. **Hydro Attack Seabreacher X-** Dive, jump, and roll in a personal sub like a marine mammal.

26. **River surfing-** Ride the waves of a river and experience the rush of an adrenaline-fueled sport.
27. **Water sledging-** Adventurers can enjoy the thrill of speeding across the water while sitting on a floating sled, getting drenched by the river waves.
28. **Luge-** Get ready for an exciting ride down a steep, twisting track on a small one-person sled at high speeds for a rush of adrenaline.
29. **Ice climbing-** Tackle frozen waterfalls and conquer vertical walls of ice with a mixture of strength, technique, and grit.
30. **Kitesurfing-** Combining the power of wind and waves, this extreme sport requires a balance of strength, skill, and courage as you soar across the water propelled by a kite.
31. **Sandboarding-** Sliding down sand dunes on a board is a unique and thrilling experience that tests your balance, speed, and endurance.
32. **Powered foilboarding-** This high-tech water sport involves riding a board with a hydrofoil attached, which lifts the board out of the water and allows riders to soar over waves with ease.
33. **Giant swing-** Located in New Zealand, this thrilling attraction involves being suspended high above the ground and swinging at speeds up to 75 mph.
34. **Jet boat ride-** A heart-pumping, high-speed ride through narrow canyons, past cliffs, and waterfalls in a powerful jet boat is a must-try for any thrill-seeker.
35. **Ice fishing-** Plunge a line through a frozen lake and enjoy a peaceful, tranquil day surrounded by the beauty of winter and the thrill of the catch.
36. **Ski base jumping-** Soar through the sky and enjoy the ultimate rush as you take to the slopes and launch yourself off the edge.
37. **Rappelling-** Climb down a cliff face with just your gear and experience the adrenaline rush as you overcome your fears and immerse yourself in nature.

38. **Boxing-** Step into the ring and test your strength, speed, and agility as you go head-to-head with an opponent and hopefully come out on top.
39. **Tombstoning (cliff jumping)-** Leap from the edge of a cliff and feel the thrill of freefall as you plummet into the water below.
40. **Wingsuit flying-** Soar through the air like a bird in a wingsuit, feeling the thrill of pure freedom as you glide through the skies.
41. **Go-kart racing-** Rev up the engine and race your friends on an indoor go-kart track, feeling the rush of adrenaline as you speed down the straightaways.
42. **Mountaineering-** Climb to new heights and challenge yourself with a mountaineering excursion, taking in breathtaking views and feeling a sense of accomplishment as you reach the summit.
43. **Kite landboarding-** Ride the winds with a kite landboarding experience, feeling the rush of speed as you carve turns on a board and soar with the air.
44. **Dinner hanging from a crane-** Dine in the clouds with an unforgettable dining experience suspended high above the city, feeling the thrill of being suspended in mid-air while enjoying a delicious meal.
45. **Rock climbing-** Tackle a towering rock face with just your hands and feet, feeling the rush of adrenaline as you push yourself to the limit.
46. **Martial art-** Master a discipline that blends self-defense, physical fitness, and mental fortitude into one comprehensive workout.
47. **Downhill snow mountain biking-** Hurtle down snowy slopes on a specially designed bike, feeling the rush of wind and snow as you navigate each turn.
48. **Spearfishing-** Become a modern-day hunter, using your skills and stealth to catch fresh fish from the ocean with nothing but a spear.

* * *

Learn to Scuba Dive

Breathe and explore underwater

There is nothing quite like going into the realm of fish and exploring their world. Imagine being suspended, weightless, in the middle of a massive school of fish, or coming face to face with a playful seal, dolphin, or even whale! There is a world of adventure awaiting just below the surface, and you don't have to be young and in the best physical condition to enjoy it. Underwater divers typically move slow and relaxed, letting the fish come to them. Enjoy the thrill and freedom of breathing underwater when you learn to scuba dive. You might find yourself planning vacations to exotic destinations with your new adventurous activity.

Once you learn to scuba dive, you'll be able to do it anywhere you go. I was 18 when a buddy and I became certified in Southern California. Despite the cold water and low visibility, we enjoyed exploring the fish and seals around the kelp forests of La Jolla. Years later, while traveling, being certified allowed me to unlock some tremendous underwater experiences in warmer waters. Diving through lava tubes and around a WWII sunken fighter plane in Hawaii, seeing sharks in Thailand, wall diving in Mexico, and around colorful fish in the Great Barrier Reef were highlights that became possible because I was certified years earlier.

What is Scuba Diving?

Scuba stands for Self-Contained Underwater Breathing Apparatus. It's an underwater swimming activity that includes an oxygen tank, buoyancy compensation device (BCD) vest, weight belt, oxygen regulator, standard snorkel stuff like a mask, and fins. Once certified, people can buy or rent equipment to dive wherever they choose. They can also join a dive group and let a dive master guide them to the highlights of a new underwater location.

. . .

How to learn to scuba dive?

You'll want to find a nearby dive center or one at your vacation destination and take training such as the PADI Open Water Diver course. There are three components to getting this certification.

1. **Knowledge development.** You'll learn from a manual or through an online learning course.
2. **Pool/confined water dives.** You'll develop and practice skills like clearing a mask, buoyancy control, and using your gear.
3. **Open water dives.** You'll head to the ocean and make four dives with an instructor, usually over two days.

You can complete the pool and open water training in as little as three or four days. Depending on the location, the average cost in the US is about $550-$650 for the learning and diving portions of the certification. You'll need to also purchase your mask, fins, snorkel, boots, and gloves in most cases.

Make it what you want.

Once you become certified to scuba dive, you may choose to keep things simple and enjoy the underwater plant and animal life close to the surface, or you can get into other specialties like night diving, wreck diving, photography, videography, hunting, deep diving, wall diving or more.

Go for it! Simple start steps:

1. Search for nearby dive centers to get certified.
2. Visit a few, see their facility, and learn about their training.
3. Purchase your course and buy your dive gear.

Resources

1. PADI dive certifications link
2. 10 Best Dive Sites in the World link
3. Worlds Best Dive Sites Ranked by Activity link

Products

1. Waterproof Duffle Bag link
2. Mask Defog link
3. GoPro Hero11 link

Books

1. 100 Dives of a Lifetime by National Geographic link
2. Dive Atlas of the World link
3. A Divers Guide to the World by National Geographic link

Pairs well with: Travel, boating, kayaking

You might also like: Longboard surfing, skydiving, spearfishing

* * *

Go Electric Hydrofoil Boarding

Levitate over water on an electric hovering surfboard

For those adventurous souls who do not want to slow down, electric hydrofoil boarding (efoiling) could be just the rush you're looking for. It's an electric-powered surfboard with a hydrofoil mast (similar to hydrofoil boats) at the bottom that contains a propeller. The standing rider squeezes a handheld wireless throttle that raises the board out of the water's choppiness a few feet, creating the sensation of smoothly levitating over water. Lakes, rivers, and oceans can be explored while zipping around on the magic carpet ride. What a thrill!

Efoiling is a relatively new sport, so equipment is still a little pricey, in the $10,000+ range. Still, it has some benefits compared to other personal watercraft, such as a jet ski.

. . .

Efoil Compared to Jet Ski

1. **Compact and portable-** No need for a trailer and tow. Just pop the board onto the roof of your car like a surfboard because the hydrofoil detaches. Stores easily at home.
2. **Rechargeable-** No gas, just clean electric power.
3. **Quiet-** Not completely silent, but the electric motor is much quieter than gas.
4. **Smooth-** The hydrofoil lifts the board out of the water, creating that morning glass feel waterskiers love.
5. **Less expensive-** The components are basic compared to a jetski, so it's less costly.
6. **Head turner-** The first time you see someone gliding over flatwater on a levitating surfboard, you'll take notice.

Did you know?

- Efoiling is often called "the future of watersports."
- Speeds of up to 20-28 mph can be reached.
- The electric propeller can run for up to an hour.
- Learning can be challenging.
- Efoiling is very different from other board sports like surfing and snowboarding, so it's optional to have previous experience in these sports to learn.
- Facebook's Mark Zuckerberg rides an efoil around the coast of his Kauai, Hawaii home.

Go for it! Simple start steps:

1. Search for an efoil rental location near you and take a lesson.

2. Research efoil brands and buy one.
3. Have fun exploring different waterways around you while traveling.

Resources

1. How Efoils Work link
2. How to Efoil a 20-minute online video course link
3. Efoil Buyers Guide link

Products

1. O'Neill Life Vest link
2. Long Sleeve Rashguard link
3. Waterproof Floating Waist Bag link

You might also like: Electric stand up paddle boarding (SUP), kayaking, longboard surfing

* * *

When Money Is No Object

Sky's the limit

We can't take it with us when we go, so we might as well have a little extravagant fun before we sign off. If you're one of the lucky few with more money than you know what to do with, this section is for you. For the rest of us, we'll just have to keep guessing numbers, and maybe someday, if we hit the jackpot, we'll refer back to this section. There are many other fun things to do in this book that are free or low-cost, so we're not missing out on much. This just wouldn't be the ultimate book of things to do in retirement if we left out the 1%. So when money is no object, the sky's the limit if you have the imagination. Let the dreams begin!

From exploring the depths of the ocean in a personal submarine to flying high above the earth in a private spaceplane, the ultra-rich have access to experiences that are truly beyond our wildest dreams. So sit back, close your eyes, and let your imagination take you on the ultimate extravagant adventure.

44 Extravagant Adventures

1. **Private space flight-** Imagine being among the few people ever to experience weightlessness and the breathtaking view of our planet from space.
2. **Deep-sea dive in a custom-built submersible-** This is an opportunity to discover hidden wonders of the ocean and witness some of the world's most exotic and mysterious creatures.
3. **Yacht race around the world-** A once-in-a-lifetime experience to sail the world's most beautiful seas and visit the world's most exclusive ports.
4. **Hot air balloon trip over the Serengeti-** Enjoy the breathtaking beauty of the African Savanna from above, surrounded by the roar of lions and the call of the wild.
5. **Trip to the North Pole on a private icebreaker-** This is the chance to stand at the top of the world, surrounded by frozen landscapes, incredible wildlife, and share some hot cocoa with Santa.
6. **Personal jetpack-** Soaring through the sky with the freedom of a bird, the personal jetpack is a tantalizing experience only the ultra-rich can afford.
7. **Robot butler-** With a touch of a button, the robot butler serves, cleans, and caters to your every need, elevating your luxury lifestyle to new heights.
8. **Around the world cruise-** Setting sail on a journey that spans the globe, with stops at the world's most exotic destinations, this cruise is a lavish adventure of a lifetime.
9. **Antarctica tour-** Brave the icy wilderness and behold the breathtaking beauty of the elusive 7th continent with an Antarctica tour, a journey for the bold and the wealthy.

10. **Everest skydive-** Plunging from the top of the world, an Everest skydive is an extreme adventure reserved for the fearless and the flush.
11. **Galapagos Islands cruise-** Embark on an exclusive journey to the Galapagos Islands and immerse yourself in the unique wildlife and natural beauty, a luxury experience for the privileged few.
12. **Fighter jet dogfight-** Soar to new heights as you experience the thrill of engaging in a simulated air battle.
13. **Go heli-skiing/snowboarding-** Access untouched powder in some of the world's most beautiful mountain ranges.
14. **Hire or buy a private yacht-** Set sail on the ultimate luxury adventure with a vessel that caters solely to your desires.
15. **Polo-** Ride horseback and display your skills in the sport of kings, where accuracy, speed, and grace are essential.
16. **Racecar driving-** Push the limits of speed and precision on the track as you get behind the wheel of a high-performance racecar.
17. **Collecting antiques-** Become the curator of a personal museum of priceless artifacts from centuries past.
18. **Buy a cruise ship room-** The Silver Cloud Ship offers an ultimate luxury experience, with private rooms for the very rich.
19. **Horse racing-** Be a part of the excitement at the race track as you watch your thoroughbreds compete for the win.
20. **Mountain climbing-** Scale the peak of Mount Everest and bask in the glory of standing atop the world's highest mountain. The oldest summiter was 80. All you'll need is a small fortune.
21. **Art collecting-** Create your museum-quality art collection, displaying masterpieces from around the world.
22. **Winemaking-** Buy a vineyard and indulge in the art and science of winemaking, crafting your unique blends.

23. **Collecting vintage cars-** Rev up your passion with a collection of timeless and classic cars.
24. **Cigarette boat racing-** Join the thrill of high-speed boating with the sleek and powerful cigarette boats.
25. **Necker Island stay-** Experience Sir Richard Branson's private island paradise in the British Virgin Islands, a stunning and unspoiled area of the Caribbean.
26. **Sky Villa-** Soar above the city with a stay in the luxurious Palms Casino Resort's Sky Villa in Las Vegas, priced at an eye-watering $141,000 per night.
27. **Volcanic dining-** Savor an unforgettable feast surrounded by the fiery beauty of an active volcano in Iceland.
28. **Superyacht cruise-** Embark on a journey of lavish excess with a week-long cruise aboard the magnificent Queen Miri superyacht, starting at 2.8 million dollars.
29. **Dine at SubliMotion in Ibiza, Spain-** Indulge in a multi-sensory dining experience at the world's most expensive restaurant.
30. **Rent celebrities-** Surround yourself with stardom by hiring a celebrity for your special event.
31. **Pure gold toilet-** Pamper yourself in luxury with a solid gold toilet. I wouldn't know, but I suppose it could be a fun thing to doo-doo in.
32. **Luxurious glamping and heli-hiking-** Elevate your outdoor adventure with a fusion of glamor and rugged nature.
33. **Island ownership-** A tropical paradise awaits the owner of a secluded and exclusive island.
34. **Gold-plated facial-** Radiate glamor and extravagance with a pampering session that features a gold-plated facial.
35. **Underwater Hotel Muraka-** A sea of dreams awaits as you sink into the crystal-clear waters of the Maldives and stay at the one-of-a-kind Underwater Hotel Muraka.

36. **Visit the actual Titanic-** Relive history and dive deep into the depths of the ocean to get up close and personal with the iconic Titanic.
37. **Private suite on an airplane-** Soar to new heights of luxury as you take flight in the plush private suite on an Airbus A380.
38. **Try the world's most expensive cocktail-** Sip on a drink unlike any other, "Diamonds are Forever" at the Ritz Carlton in Tokyo, worth a sparkling $25,000.
39. **Take the world's most expensive train-** Embark on an opulent journey aboard the Maharaja Express, with a presidential suite priced at a whopping $4,500.
40. **Record a Bollywood dance with you as the star in India-** Immerse yourself in the world of Indian cinema and make memories to last a lifetime with a star-studded Bollywood dance recording.
41. **Have a different home for each season-** Live like a true jet setter and own multiple homes in different destinations to match your mood and preferences for every season.
42. **Spend a year in Singapore-** Experience the bustling and vibrant English-speaking city-state of Singapore, rich with diverse cultures, fantastic food, and beautiful sights, for an entire year while jet-setting throughout South East Asia for weekend getaways.
43. **Get help with everything-** Indulge in a lifestyle of ultimate luxury and comfort with a personal team of expert chefs, cleaners, masseuses, and health coaches at your disposal.
44. **Help a lot of less fortunate people-** Make a difference in the world by using your wealth and resources to make a significant impact in the lives of those less fortunate.

While having unlimited financial resources can certainly provide opportunities and open doors that may not be available to others, it's important to remember that money can't buy everything, such as happiness, love, or health. Ultimately, it's up to each individual to determine what they truly value in life and how they want to use their resources to pursue their goals and dreams.

Resources

1. 11 Around-The-World Cruises for the Trip of a Lifetime link
2. The Ultimate World Cruise link
3. Travel like a billionaire with this fantasy bucket list link
4. 50 of the world's most lavish travel experiences link
5. Top 15 Most Expensive Experiences That Money Can Buy link

* * *

Running of the Bulls

Celebrate the fine line between bravery and stupidity

Touted as one of the greatest fiestas in the world, The Festival of San Fermin, sometimes called The Running Of The Bulls, became famous worldwide because of Hemingways 1926 book "The Sun Also Rises." He was fascinated when he first visited in 1923 and returned many times until just before his death in 1959. Each July 6th-13th since 1592, the people of Pamplona, Spain, hold a celebration that swells to over a million spectators in honor of the city's first bishop and patron saint, Saint Fermin.

This internationally renowned festival is a mix of respectful religious tradition, cultural eye-openers, and at times rowdy street parties. It feels like a celebration of life and death at times. Spectators dress in the traditional attire of white pants and shirt along with a red scarf and waistband. The week-long fiesta is packed with one-time and repeated daily events.

Perhaps most famous is the morning running of the bulls, or encierro, where hundreds of people run in front of six bulls and six steers for half a mile down a narrow enclosed road to a bullring in preparation for the afternoon bullfight. It's a brush with death for some and actual death for 16 runners of the event since 1910. Once in the bullring, a calf with capped horns is set loose to rampage among a large crowd of young lunatics who allow the bull to jump over them and attempt to dive over the massive animal themselves. It's a chaotic spectacle of terror and humor for the seated crowd's amusement. The afternoon bullfight is electric. The 20,000-person stadium is packed with enthusiastic fans cheering on the skillful bullfighters and horse-riding bullfighters. The event is bloody and can be hard to watch at times for those of us who did not grow up with these bullfights as part of our culture, but afterward, like other cattle, the bull is slaughtered and sold to merchants. Every evening there is a fireworks spectacle.

What I loved about San Fermin was how culturally different it was from what I was used to and the euphoric energy of the celebrations. At the opening Txupinazo ceremony, where hundreds of people all wearing traditional clothes pack into the town square, passion and intensity grow in anticipation with chanting, singing, and jumping wildly for the mayor to announce the beginning of the event. A rocket is launched, and the crowd erupts with cheer and jubilation, soaking themselves in jets of spraying champagne. People dance, drink, and celebrate with friends and strangers around them at a party that can feel like an atmosphere of collective madness. It's impossible not to get swept up in the exuberance of the party. This 8-day medieval spectacle seems to draw the "you only live once" crowd of all ages from around the world. Join the fun and celebrate life!

Tips to (hopefully) survive the bull run

If running for your life in front of 12,000+ pounds of ferocious giant wild animals is on your bucket list, here are a few tips from my experience. First, have an escape plan. Bulls can run up to 35 mph, and the fastest Olympic sprinters can run up to 23 mph for 10 seconds. You're not going to outrun 12 charging beasts for half a mile if they decide to kick it into top gear. When you're waiting anxiously for possibly the final seconds of your life on the enclosed narrow street, decide how far you're going to run before you get out of the way. Some people squish into the corners and hope the bulls stay in the middle, but I wanted a little more peace of mind. I found a temporary fence with slats that were big enough to fit through or climb if I needed to hurl myself to safety. I recommend scouting out a second or third spot further down, in case you get swept up in the crowd and need a plan B or C.

As a youngster, I chose the Santo Domingo area of the run, which is at the very beginning and has the best viewing area for the crowd. I had not done any research on what to expect. At 8 am, I thought the bulls would come rushing up the hill from the corrals hidden at the bottom of the street, but they didn't. A rocket was set off, and everyone excitedly started running a little, but the bulls never came. After some time, we all reset to our original starting spot. Apparently, 8 am is when the coral doors are open, but they get to decide when to leave. After five anxious minutes of waiting, the bulls finally came charging up. There were so many people crowded everywhere that I couldn't see the bulls coming. I could only hear the crowd start to cheer and see the balcony photographers leaning out.

People began to run and scatter like cockroaches. I ran just far enough to get to my escape fence and got out of the way. A few moments later, the bulls charged by. I thought it was over, but a straggler cow came running past us a few seconds later and took everyone by surprise. In the papers the following day, there were photos of someone who got stepped on maybe 30 feet from my starting spot when he slipped while running. I also found myself in the local newspaper running for my life! Good times. ☺

7 Additional Survival Tips

1. Don't end up on the outside corners when the bulls come. They sometimes fall on the turn and can smash into you if you're there.
2. Know that it can be slippery, or you can trip on other people. If you fall, roll out of the way. People getting up can sometimes get a whole lot of bull when they finally stand.

3. Learn where the dangerous sections are and don't end up there. There are sections with sharp corners and no escape routes possible.
4. Be careful of straggler bulls and cows that come after the leading herd.
5. Don't attempt to take photos. You need to focus on dodging obstacles and people without distractions. You want to survive the experience!
6. Consider bringing a little rolled-up newspaper to look like an experienced runner. The local regular runners use the newspaper to whack people in front of them as a warning to get moving or get out of the way!
7. Pick up all the local newspapers the next day. You might find yourself in a few photos from the previous day's run.

Go for it! Simple start steps:

1. Plan your visit very early. Many people go yearly, and hotels book up fast.
2. Consider adding San Sebastian (1-hour drive north) or Barcelona (5 hours southeast).
3. Buy your traditional red and white outfit at the event and tickets to the evening bullfight in advance.
4. Be prepared to have a cultural experience and join in on the party fun.

Resources

1. What is San Fermin link
2. Pamplona is San Fermin link
3. Travelers Guide To The Bull Run Of San Fermin

Books

1. The Sun Also Rises by Ernest Hemingway link

2. Bulls Before Breakfast: Running With The Bulls And Celebrating San Fermin by Peter Milligan link
3. Pamplona: Running Of The Bulls by Ray Mouton link

Pairs well with: Tapas, jamon, calimocho (official drink of red wine, and cola)

You might also like: La Tomatina (Spain Tomato festival), Mardi Gras (New Orleans), Burning Man festival

* * *

Skydive

Overcome fear and experience the rush

While it might seem like pure stupidity, willingly stepping out of a plane thousands of feet in the sky, freefalling towards the earth rushing up at 120 mph, perhaps moments away from a final breath, there's something more to it than simply a death wish. Yes, there is undoubtedly a risk of death. Ten people lost their lives in 2021 out of the estimated 3.5 million jumps. However, more people died from going outside their houses and getting struck by lightning (11) in the same year.

For many, achieving a bucket list life experience is worth the calculated risk. To feel the exhilaration and rush of life by getting close to death. The freedom that comes from knowing they were able to overcome their limiting fears. The simple act strengthens their mind and soul, proves their bravery, creates confidence, and leaves a lasting euphoric feeling. They're empowered to take on their next challenge knowing they are following their true self despite the risks.

Regret

Life is not without risks, but in the end, we'll most likely regret the things we didn't do rather than the things we did. We'll look back and wish we didn't let our fears make us play it safe and miss out on experiencing all that we could have. We'll realize that the things we worried about would have most likely never happened. We'll wish we had been more bold and taken more chances. We'll wonder what could have been if we hadn't let our fears rationalize playing life safe.

What happens on a typical tandem skydive?

Typically when you arrive at a skydiving center, there will be a video, briefing, or paperwork informing you of the risks and what you can expect. You'll wear a jumpsuit, harness, helmet, and clear goggles. Before getting on the plane, you meet your tandem partner, who will go over what to expect and what you'll need to do. You'll then get on a small propeller plane with no seats and possibly no door, and the pilot will climb to between 10,000 and 14,000 feet. You'll be connected to the front of your tandem partner, scoot your way to the open door, and he'll say 3,2,1 jump!

Your heart will beat like crazy, and you'll be freaking out, wondering why you listened to a stupid author. You'll feel weightless and flip over, viewing the bottom of your tiny aircraft flying away. The most powerful wind you've ever felt will rush at you. Your cheeks will flap around, and if you open your mouth, it will puff open your cheeks. The wind is thunderous, and the ground seems so far away. You stabilize and take in the most thrilling 60 seconds of your life. In freefall, you're surprised that you're no longer terrified. Your biggest fear was just before the decision to step out, and now there's nothing that can be done except enjoy the rush and the view. Your tandem partner looks at his altimeter watch and pulls the cord.

A parachute explodes out behind you, and you quickly stop falling. Relief is your overwhelming emotion, followed by more exhilaration. For the next 5 minutes, you dangle your feet, hanging from your partner as he glides you down to the landing zone. You'll raise your feet and slide into mother earth a changed person. The excitement and pride in your accomplishment will last for a long time. You've had a brush with death and now feel completely alive. You go online and write a glowing review of the book that motivated you to do what you had always dreamed of. (I couldn't resist! No, but seriously I read every Amazon review and would love to hear about your skydiving experience or any other positive experience you've had after reading, for that matter. I'm thrilled when I hear about people living their best life in retirement).

Too old to jump?

- Former President George HW Bush marked every 5th birthday after his retirement with a skydive.
- The President celebrated his 75th birthday with a solo parachute near his presidential library in Texas.
- At 90, President Bush took his last jump despite being confined to a wheelchair.

Tip: Popping in a strong mint lozenge like "Fisherman's Friend" before hopping on the skydive plane can help ease a queasy, nervous stomach.

Note: Skydiving isn't for everyone. You should be relatively healthy and in reasonably good shape. Check with your doctor and skydive center about your particular health situation.

Funny Skydiving Shirts

- If your parachute doesn't deploy... Don't worry, you'll have the rest of your life to fix it!
- I jump out of perfectly good airplanes.
- If at first you don't succeed, skydiving is not for you.
- Bucket list: ✓ Skydiving
- The sky is not my limit. It's my playground.
- Oh chute!
- Skydiving. Because other sports only require one ball.

Go for it! Simple start steps:

1. Search online for nearby skydiving centers.
2. Search for a discount on sites like Groupon and LivingSocial (there usually are).
3. Book the earliest date possible, so you don't have time to change your mind.
4. Have an experience of a lifetime.

Resources

1. How Safe Is Skydiving? Link
2. Can You Be Too Old To Skydive link
3. 6 Tandem Skydiving Tips For First-Time Skydivers link

Pairs well with: Red Bull drink, a legal will, another crazy friend

You might also like: Powered paragliding, off-roading, traveling the world

A Final Word

As you come to the end of this book, I hope you feel inspired and ready to embark on a new chapter in your life. Retirement is a time of immense possibility and opportunity, and I'm thrilled that you've taken the time to explore some of the fun things you can do during this exciting new adventure.

I hope you've discovered countless ideas that have sparked your imagination and ignited your passions. Perhaps you've even found some new hobbies, travel destinations, relationship ideas, or volunteering opportunities that have piqued your interest. Whatever it may be, I hope this book has given you the confidence to pursue your dreams and follow your passions.

Remember, retirement is a time to live life on your own terms, to do the things you've always wanted to do, and to fulfill your wildest dreams. It's a time to focus on what truly makes you happy and fulfilled, and to prioritize your mental, physical, and spiritual well-being.

As you move forward, keep in mind the practical advice and best practices outlined in this book. Take the time to recalibrate your mindset and focus on what a fulfilling retirement will look like for you. Build new healthy habits, stay physically and mentally fit, and prioritize the things that will bring you the most joy and fulfillment.

And if you're hungry for more ideas, be sure to pick up Volume 2 of this book, where we delve even deeper into hundreds more exciting possibilities for a happy and fulfilling retirement.

Finally, if you found this book helpful, please consider sharing it with someone else who could benefit from these ideas. And if you have a moment, please leave a review on Amazon to help spread the word. The review link on the next page takes you directly to where you can leave a review. As a small independent author that spent months researching and creating this book, your review is invaluable to me because it signals Amazon to display the book to new readers. Your kindness is greatly appreciated!

Congratulations on your retirement. May it be filled with joy, passion, and endless possibilities.

Oh, seize the day, my dear retiree,
This time is yours, just wait and see!
No more nine-to-fives, no more workday strife,
It's time to live and enjoy your life!

You've earned this rest, this time to play,
To do the things you love all day!
Explore new hobbies, try something new,
The world is your oyster, it's all up to you!

Take a trip, see new sights,
Travel the world, enjoy the flights!
Or stay at home, in your cozy space,
Relax and unwind at your own pace.

Catch up with friends, make new ones too,
There's so much to do, so much to pursue!
Volunteer, give back to the community,
Help others and spread some unity.

So don't waste a moment, don't delay,
Seize the day, in your own way!
Retirement is a chance to live your dream,
So go ahead, let out a scream!

Enjoy your freedom, your time to play,
And make the most of every single day!
- The Time of Our Lives -

* * *

Please take a moment to leave an Amazon review at the QR link below.

Scan the QR to leave a review

A quick review or rating at **Goodreads** is also greatly appreciated at the link below.

For Goodreads Review

Thank you for your support.

Get the free bonus pdf download, Travel Planning Simplified, at https://www.funretirementbooks.com/bonus

Alternatively, scan the QR for "Travel Planning Simplified"

Bibliography

1. Carroll, L. (1865). Alice's adventures in Wonderland. Macmillan Publishers.
2. Covey, S. R. (1989). The 7 habits of highly effective people: Restoring the character ethic. Free Press.
3. Roese, N. J., & Summerville, A. (2005). What we regret most... and why. Personality and Social Psychology Bulletin, 31(9), 1273-1285. https://doi.org/10.1177/0146167205274693
4. Zeelenberg, M., & Pieters, R. (2004). Consequences of regret aversion in real life: The case of the Dutch postcode lottery. Organizational Behavior and Human Decision Processes, 93(2), 155-168. https://doi.org/10.1016/j.obhdp.2003.09.001
5. American Psychological Association. (2013). Stress in America: Missing the health care connection. https://www.apa.org/news/press/releases/stress/2012/impact.aspx
6. Ware, B. (2012). The top five regrets of the dying: A life transformed by the dearly departing. Hay House.
7. Segerstrom, S. C., & Miller, G. E. (2004). Psychological stress and the human immune system: A meta-analytic study of 30 years of inquiry. Psychological Bulletin, 130(4), 601–630.
8. Bowler, D. E., Buyung-Ali, L. M., Knight, T. M., & Pullin, A. S. (2010). A systematic review of evidence for the added benefits to health of exposure to natural environments. BMC Public Health, 10, 456.
9. Bennett, M. P., & Lengacher, C. A. (2008). Humor and laughter may influence health: III. Laughter and health outcomes. Evidence-Based Complementary and Alternative Medicine, 5(1), 37-40.
10. Puetz, T. W. (2006). Physical activity and feelings of energy and fatigue: epidemiological evidence. Sports Medicine, 36(9), 767-780.
11. Lidderdale, T. A., & Stavros, C. R. (2019). Global Cruise Industry: Growth, Trends and Forecast (2019-2024). Mordor Intelligence.
12. Often attributed to Mark Twain, a famous American writer and humorist. However, there is no conclusive evidence that he actually said or wrote this quote.

13. Powers, A. (2022, February 21). What are Michelin stars? A beginner's guide to the ultimate culinary accolade. CNN.
14. Thompson, W. F., Schellenberg, E. G., & Husain, G. (2001). Arousal, mood, and the Mozart effect. Psychological Science, 12(3), 248-251.
15. Gramophone. (2019, October 7). The 50 Greatest Symphonies of All Time.
16. HomeAdvisor. (n.d.). Most common home improvement projects. Angi. https://www.angi.com/articles/top-home-improvement-project-trends.htm
17. Wallethub. (2022). 2022's Best & Worst Places to Retire. https://wallethub.com/edu/best-places-to-retire/6165/
18. Greenback Expat Tax Services. (n.d.). Tax-Free Incentives for Retiring to These Countries. Greenback Tax Services. https://www.greenbacktaxservices.com/knowledge-center/tax-free-incentives-retirement-countries/

List Index

Also by S.C. Francis

The Ultimate Book of Fun Things to Do in Retirement: Volume 2

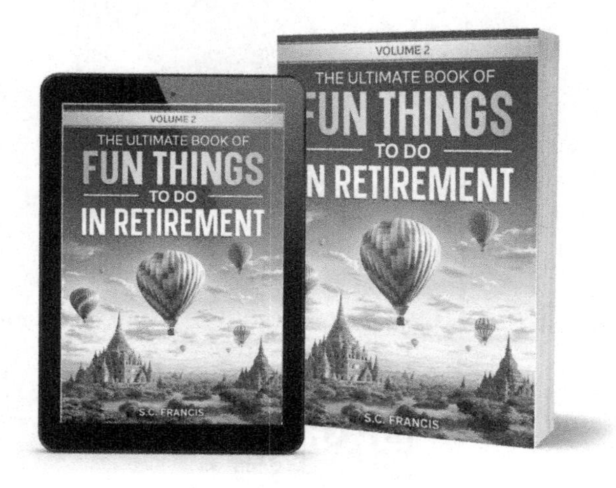

Available in ebook, paperback, hardcover, and audiobook. Grab your copy here.

Volume 2 on Amazon

Cats Wearing Clothes: *A Photo Journey Through the Ages*

Available in ebook and paperback. Grab your copy here.

Cats Wearing Clothes on Amazon

Made in the USA
Las Vegas, NV
28 November 2023